ANCESTRAL VOICES

THE AUTHOR

ANCESTRAL VOICES

JAMES LEES-MILNE

CHARLES SCRIBNER'S SONS

NEW YORK

Copyright © James Lees-Milne 1975

Copyright under the Berne Convention

1 3 5 7 9 11 13 15 17 19 I/C 20 18 16 14 12 10 8 6 4 2

Printed in Great Britain
Library of Congress Catalog Card Number 77-92997
ISBN 0-684-15647-4

CONTENTS

Endpapers

West Wycombe Park   (front)
The property of the National Trust

Blickling Hall   (back)
The property of the National Trust

INTRODUCTION

A distinguished friend (so distinguished that reluctantly I withhold his name) recently suggested that I should record some past encounters with the owners and donors of historic houses during the course of my work with the National Trust. My immediate response was No. A string of disconnected anecdotes and names would not be edifying or entertaining. Pressed once more by my friend I thought again. Well! there were those dusty packets of day-to-day diaries stowed away upstairs. Could I bring myself to re-peruse the adolescent, opinionative, supercilious jottings? I did so, with the partial result here presented. Inevitably I have misgivings, because the priggish young man who wrote them is someone whom I had long forgotten, and someone with whom, upon re-acquaintance, I am not wholeheartedly pleased. Moreover, I no longer share many of his too glibly expressed views.

An introductory word or two seem necessary. In March 1936 I joined the staff of the National Trust. In September 1939 I left it for war service. After a short and inglorious career in the army I was discharged in 1941 for health reasons, and towards the end of that year I rejoined the National Trust staff. When the diaries opened in January 1942 the National Trust office was installed in West Wycombe Park, Buckinghamshire, whither it had been 'evacuated' in the first months of war. Some of the staff, including myself, lodged in the house. The office remained at West Wycombe until January 1943, when the Executive Committee deemed it safe and suitable for the files (and the staff) to return to their old premises in Buckingham Palace Gardens, S.W.1. I then moved into a small house, No. 104 Cheyne Walk, Chelsea, and lived there until the end of the war.

At that period of its history the National Trust, already forty-seven years old, had a membership of only 6,000. It owned 75,000 acres and about half a dozen historic houses open to the public. Today it has a membership of 480,000. It owns 370,000 acres and 230 historic houses open to the public. In 1942 its male staff consisted of the Secretary (D. M. Matheson), a resident representative in the Lake District (Bruce Thompson), an unqualified land agent (Eardley Knollys) and an unqualified historic buildings secretary (myself). The female staff consisted of my

A*

two old friends Florence Paterson and Winifred Ballachey, a typist and a 'junior'. That was the full complement.

I am well aware that the war diaries of civilians sometimes strike readers as reprehensibly frivolous. 'How shocking', they exclaim, 'that while Rome was burning these people were perpetually fiddling!' Yet these civilians may in their small way have been working flat out for ten, sometimes twelve hours of the twenty-four; and may not have felt inspired to record the doleful hours of their mechanical industries, preferring to dwell upon the fleeting interludes of relaxation and sunshine which were, it is undeniable, often spent in the pursuit of trivialities. Nevertheless I must admit that working for the National Trust was in those comparatively distant war days a combination of hard labour and sheer fun. Distinction between one and the other was seldom absolute.

Apart from some necessary corrections of style and several excisions the ensuing pages appear as they were dashed off in long and shorthand, or typed. And here I wish most gratefully to thank Ian Parsons of Chatto and Windus for tirelessly reading through the text and giving me much wise advice on what to leave out. Actually I have pruned the diaries by about a third of their original length. The rejected passages consist chiefly of architectural descriptions of buildings visited, tedious entries about the diarist's ill-health, and accounts of his and his friends' indiscretions. The last are the only excisions I slightly regret. But even the age of permissiveness has its limits. Truth may be beauty; it certainly is not always wisdom. Besides I do not want to lose the friendship of those, alas, too few persons mentioned in the diaries who have had the grace to remain alive.

J. L.-M.
Alderley Grange,
Wotton-under-Edge,
Gloucestershire
1974

1942

West Wycombe Park is a singularly beautiful eighteenth-century house with one shortcoming. Its principal living-rooms face due north. The south front is overshadowed by a long, double colonnade which induces a total eclipse of the sun from January to December. Consequently we are very cold in the winter, for the radiators work fitfully these days. Our offices are in the Brown Drawing Room and Johnny Dashwood's[1] small study beyond it. Matheson, the Secretary, Miss Paterson, Eardley Knollys and I work in the latter room; Miss Ballachey, a typist and the 'junior' (aged 15) in the bigger room with all the filing cabinets. Matheson, Eardley and I are seldom in the office together. Nearly always one and often two of us are away visiting properties.

Monday, 5th January

Early this morning I set out on a short tour in the very old National Trust Austin, which belonged to Hilda Matheson until her recent death. Before I reached Princes Risborough the car practically stopped, and a rather delicious smell of rice pudding, accompanied by a curious knocking sound, came from its inside. I drew up at a garage and asked what could possibly be the matter. The garage man at once, and without any explanations from me, said, 'You've got no water in the radiator.' I was humiliated. I am constantly being humiliated.

I arrived at Althorp [Northamptonshire] more than half an hour late. Lord Spencer was huffy at first because of my lateness, and because of the depreciation of Althorp by the agent whom the Trust had employed to make a report on his property. He understandably associated the Trust with the agent's ignorance and lack of taste. In the end I liked Lord Spencer for not being crosser than he was. He said I was the first National Trust person who had talked sense. Since he is not liberal in compliments I was flattered. Certainly I appreciated Althorp. But the difficulties will be infinite before we get it.

I stayed to luncheon — poached eggs with maize and cabbage — which

---

[1] Sir John Dashwood, 10th Bart. (1896–1966), the owner of West Wycombe house and park, created by Sir Francis Dashwood, 2nd Bart. (1708–81).

we ate in a little panelled room to the right of the Wootton Hall. Lady Spencer, like a goddess, distilled charm and gentleness around her.

I continued to Haselbech for the night, where I found Aunt Con [Ismay] in her new cottage, which is too technological for words, being fitted from top to bottom with electrical gadgets. You press one button beside the bed, and a metal arm offers you a cigarette in a cardboard holder; another, and tea spouts from a tap into a cup; yet another and the mattress becomes as hot as St. Lawrence's gridiron. There was an armchair in my bedroom which, had I been able to find the lever, would have tossed me into the air like a pancake for the good of my liver. The whole room was a tangle of wires inadequately insulated. I was in terror of being electrocuted.

Tuesday, 6th January

After breakfast I left Aunt Con's loaded with provisions, and motored with the sun in my eyes straight to Finedon Hall. The windscreen was so splashed with thawing slush that I could barely see. At intervals I was obliged to stop and wipe the glass with a rag and spit.

Major Greaves lives alone in a cottage which he thinks wonderfully antique. It was built in 1850. He has two tusks, which I knew to be false because they moved up and down as he spoke, and no other teeth, which is very strange. He is mad about ecclesiology and has photographs of smiling choirboys about the house. He patted little boys on the head in the village. He would not get down to business—with me—in spite of my prompting. Finally I persuaded him to show me round the big house. It is interesting in being the childhood home of Digby Dolben, the poet school-friend of Robert Bridges. Dolben suffered from religious mania, walked about Eton in a monk's habit with a cord round his waist, robbed his schoolfellows of their breakfast rolls in order that they might go to Chapel fasting, and played truant to the Eton and Harrow cricket match by spending his long leave at a nunnery.

The colour of the ironstone of which Finedon Hall is built is the most beautiful imaginable, being a deep orange, sprinkled with a powdery grey film of lichen. The Hall, once Elizabethan, was dreadfully altered about 1850 and is not suitable for the Trust. It is unfurnished and at present houses Free French troops. They were most offhand and rude to the poor Major, who I could see was a great tribulation to them, constantly prowling around and extolling his own property. They kept crabbing it in front of him. In the dining-room was a central stove, gothicky and of the period, connected with a flue under the floor. The grounds sad, the elm avenue disordered. The place neglected and pitiable, like the Major. I was not sorry to leave.

Went on at great speed to Bedford and branched off to look at Willington dovecote, a worth-while property. We must try and acquire the barn opposite, built at the same period as the dovecote, namely, Henry VIII, and also corbie-stepped. Bunyan's name is carved somewhere, but I failed to find it. Continued to Potters Bar and Morven Park. Taken round by old Sanderson the donor. A terrible, Victorian, yellow brick villa, and the property unworthy of us. We should never have accepted it.

Wednesday, 7th January

It is freezing hard. Filled the radiator with boiling water from a kettle. The car started at once. Motored straight to Hatfield. Stopped to look at the monument by Maximilian Colt of the 1st Lord Salisbury, James I's Lord Treasurer, holding his wand of office, and lying in full regalia on a cold marble slab upheld by four kneeling figures. Mrs. Esdaile[1] says the staff is the actual one he carried in life. Continued to Brocket and stopped opposite the iron gates erected by the present Lord Brocket[2] in memory of his father. Got out and walked across a style and down a footpath to the James Paine bridge, which the Canadian troops have disfigured by cutting their names, with addresses in Canada, and personal numbers, all complete and inches deep—the vandals. Yet I thought what an interesting memorial this will be thought in years to come and quite traditional, like the German mercenaries' names scrawled in 1530 on the Palazzo Ducale in Urbino, and Byron's name on the temple at Sunium. Looked at Hudnall Common and Ivinghoe in dense fog, and saw nothing at all of Mr. Paradine's land that we contemplate purchasing. I might just as well have been blindfolded. Lunched at Tring off sandwiches and beer. Back at West Wycombe I found troops occupying the village and manœuvres in progress. My bedroom commandeered for a brigadier. The Irish Guards are among the armoured brigade, for Kennedy, once

[1] Katharine Esdaile (1881–1950), leading authority on English post-Reformation sculpture and author of several books on the subject.

[2] 2nd Lord Brocket (1904–67).

5

my servant at Dover, saw me cross the road in the village and asked the estate office to ring me up. I went and talked to him and gave him 10/-. Was pleased he should wish to see me.

I forgot to write that yesterday after passing through Hitchin I noticed a little church dominating a hill on my left, and recollected St. Ippolitt's. I turned the car up the hill and got out to search for George Lloyd's[1] grave. On his deathbed he asked to be buried here. I found his grave huddled amongst ordinary parishioners', which I don't suppose he would have liked. There is no stone yet, but the grave is a double one, waiting presumably for Blanche. Grass was already growing on it. I knew it to be his from a card tied to some Christmas holly with 'To George from Gwen'—his sister—written in fading violet ink. I stood over the grave thinking of him for a quick moment, and left in a hurry, because it was bitter cold. He would have done just the same in my place. Then I turned back for a second and thought, how odd that that body which I had known so well in its dapper Savile Row suits, that familiar body always well groomed, was within a few yards of me and rotting below, in this intense northern cold which he hated. Robert Byron[2] used to say he never thought of his dead friends in connection with their decomposing bodies, but I cannot help it. I suppose this signifies that I have too little faith in the immortality of the spirit.

Saturday, 10th January

Although I had no prearranged plans I went to London this morning, reaching Brooks's in time to lunch by myself. Keith Miller-Jones had Claud Berkeley, a secretary in the War Cabinet, lunching with him. He told Keith that whereas Chamberlain had been a brilliant chairman at Cabinet meetings, Churchill was a bad one. His Cabinets were a muddle; solutions to problems were arrived at not through logical discussions but haphazard, intuitive guesses by Churchill himself. I can imagine the dissatisfaction of his colleagues.

Sunday, 11th January

I am enjoying *Aurora Leigh* as a reflection of mid-Victorian life and

[1] 1st Lord Lloyd of Dolobran (1879–1941), Governor of Bombay, High Commissioner in Egypt and Secretary of State for the Colonies 1940–1. J. L.-M. was his private secretary, 1931–5.
[2] Robert Byron (1905–41), traveller, art critic and writer.

manners, just as *Don Juan* quite apart from Byron's poetry and wit, is a reflection of Regency manners. I think I may read several long poems as I would novels.

Found Eddy[1] at tea and Lady Colefax[2] who is staying. Lady Colefax dressed in thick blue tweed. She must have been pretty once. Her face is now like an intelligent pug's, or a dolphin's. I felt she might snub me if I said something ingenuous, whereas she would not snub Eddy, whatever he might say.

After dinner Lady Colefax talked of Uppark [Sussex] and the wonderful Queen Anne dolls' house there, fitted with every detail. Eddy said that if sold it would fetch as much as £30,000. Lady Colefax explained how Lady Meade-Fetherstonhaugh repairs all the original curtains and hangings, bed covers, etc. at Uppark by a device of her own. She has a huge rack the size of a billiard table upon which each damask thread is picked off and put on to a new backing. Then she washes the old fabrics in a concoction made from the herb *saponaria*, which grows in the park. It gives renewed life to the fabrics.

Monday, 12th January

It is freezing hard and the park is covered with rime. Helen[3] elects to come to London for the free lift, and plumps herself in the front seat by me so that poor Miss Paterson is obliged to sit in the back seat in the cold. All goes well and the two committees, though dull, pass uneventfully. Lord Zetland,[4] the Trust's chairman, is wry, starchy and pedagogic as usual: Lord Esher,[5] like a dormouse, small, hunched, quizzical, sharp and cynical: Ronnie Norman,[6] the eternal handsome schoolboy, noisily loquacious until he finds the conclusion to an argument, when he stops like an unwound clock: Nigel Bond,[7] dry,

[1] Hon. Edward Sackville-West, later 5th Lord Sackville (1901–65), novelist, critic, and musician.

[2] Sibyl, widow of Sir Arthur Colefax, political and literary hostess.

[3] Helen, wife of Sir John Dashwood.

[4] 2nd Marquess of Zetland (1876–1961), Secretary of State for India, 1935–40. Chairman of National Trust's Executive Committee, 1931–45.

[5] Oliver, 3rd Viscount Esher (1881–1963), Chairman of National Trust's Finance and Country Houses Committees; and Chairman of the Society for the Protection of Ancient Buildings.

[6] R. C. Norman (1873–1963), Vice-Chairman of National Trust, 1924–48. Chairman of L.C.C. 1918–19.

[7] Nigel Bond (1877–1945), Secretary of National Trust, 1901–11.

earthy, sound, unimaginative: Sir Edgar Bonham-Carter,[1] twisted by arthritis, fair, impartial, but too subdued to be heeded by the others: Mr. Horne, the old, sweet-sour yet genial solicitor, who has sat in attendance these forty-odd years ever since, as an articled clerk, he helped draft the constitution of the National Trust in 1895. But now he is a little beyond his prime, and he havers.

Thursday, 15th January

Eardley said that at dinner the other night in London a mutual friend commented upon Eddy's fondness for Helen. Harold[2] said, 'Yes, but the parasite feels lovingly towards its protector,' or words to that effect. The other replied, 'But the ivy clings rather to the oak than to the holly.'

I go to London after tea in order to start off early on my National Trust expedition the following morning.

At Cheyne Walk Di[3] confides that she may be going to have an infant. Obviously she is pleased by the prospect, and I think it is a very good thing and tell her so, especially now that Patrick is going abroad. She complains that she has not yet felt sick, and lack of this sure sign worries her. She has been looking after old Princess Helena Victoria while Catherine Fordham[4] is having a holiday. Di already loves the old lady. When they go out shopping the princess produces a large gold chain-bag full of sixpences. These she doles out to Di in the taxi and works out the day's expenses as they drive along. She will herself hail taxis while Di is endeavouring to look for one so that frequently they have several bespoken at the same time. She does not like shops to be forewarned, yet does not relish no attentions being paid her.

Friday, 16th January

I set off for East Sheen to walk across Sheen Common. This is a worthwhile property for it rounds off one corner of Richmond Common. Though the ground is fairly deep under snow I pad across it between

[1] Sir Edgar Bonham-Carter (1870–1956), jurist and administrator.
[2] Hon. (later Sir) Harold Nicolson (1886–1968), diplomat, M.P., and well-known author.
[3] Diona (née Stewart-Jones), Mrs. Patrick Murray. J. L.-M. frequently stayed with the Stewart-Jones family in 97 Cheyne Walk, Chelsea.
[4] Married November 1942 Major-General Sir John Kennedy (1893–1970).

birch trees and over heath. I try to find a way into Richmond Park, but the military have commandeered the whole of it, and there is no ingress whatever. So I walk miles round by Mount Clare, which cannot be seen from the road, and across Putney Heath, today quite beautiful and shimmering under the snow. Before Wimbledon I take a bus into Ewell. There I inspect Hatch Furlong, a wretched property, now a cabbage patch on either side of an arterial road, and surrounded by ribbon development. I lunch with Midi[1] at Ashtead House, the Gascoignes', her in-laws. Lady Gascoigne resembles a cow accustomed to all weathers, with the kindly, rough manners of one.

Before dinner I had a drink with David Lloyd[2] at the Turf. He has the fidgety charm of his father whom he resembles more noticeably now that his father is dead. David adores his memory and regards me, I think, as a small fraction of that memory, as someone who enjoyed his father's confidence. He thinks that in some respects I knew his father better than he did and because of this envies me without resentment, for he has a generous nature.

Saturday, 17th January

In the morning to the William Nicholson and Jack Yeats exhibition at the National Gallery. Yeats all purples and yellows, frankly vulgar, but dashing and virile. I cared most for his early pictures in monochrome. William Nicholson is surely a very good English artist, deep-rooted, sure. *The Hundred Jugs* I call a confident, scholarly work.

I lunch alone hurriedly at Brooks's. I have a word with General Pope-Hennessy. From his slowness of speech and the particulars he gives of his last 'turn' I imagine he must have had a stroke.

I arrive by bus at Leckhampstead House which Mrs. Stewart-Jones has just bought on the Berkshire downs. It is tea-time. The household is very cheerful, domestic and welcoming after the cold outside. The dove is cooing, the lamps are bright, the toast is thick and the tea steams.

Reginald Blunt[3] is living here. He is a dear old man, courteous and cultivated. He is 85, very independent, and with all his wits about him. I talked to him about the Carlyles. He even remembers Mrs. Carlyle,

[1] Hon. Mary O'Neill, wife of Derek Gascoigne, a son of General Sir Frederick Gascoigne.

[2] 2nd Lord Lloyd of Dolobran.

[3] Reginald Blunt (1857–1944), Chelsea historian.

who died in 1866. He used to take a jug of milk from the rectory cow to them each day, and in the proper season mulberries from the rectory garden. One morning Mrs. Carlyle received the mulberries from him at the door of 24 Cheyne Row and said, 'Wait! Mr. Carlyle has a present for you.' She shouted up the stairs, 'Thomas! Thomas!' Presently Carlyle descended in his long dressing-gown, with a rosy apple on a plate. Reginald Blunt was terribly disappointed that the apple on the plate was made of china; but he has it to this day. He knew Rossetti, who used to play whist at the rectory. His language was appalling. The following day he would write a letter to the rector, Blunt's father, apologizing for his swear words.

Blunt is in favour of absolutely rebuilding Chelsea Old Church,[1] though not of absolutely rebuilding on principle. I agree with him. So apparently do Raby and Walter Godfrey, judging from a letter to Blunt from the latter.

Sunday, 18th January

In the afternoon I bicycle to look at Woolley Park, now taken over by the Admiralty. A terrible house, allegedly built on the site of a shooting box of King John's, with only a vestige of the eighteenth century in the central stairwell, where there is a trace of Wyattesque or Adamesque treatment, a frieze with rams' skulls. The bronze stair balusters are all right. The rest of the house is 1862, haphazard, bulky, inelegant and of no merit. There is a drawing-room with painted plaster wall and ceiling decoration of this date. The family furniture, stacked in the middle of the room under dust sheets, seems indifferent. The house will not do. The park looks derelict, the trees in need of attention.

It had snowed heavily the previous night and my ride without any wind was still and muffled. I got warm bicycling and enjoyed it.

Monday, 19th January

In the morning I bicycled to Farnborough Rectory to see Mr. Puxley, the father of Michael Wroughton, the owner of Woolley. I told him all I thought I should but purposely left things vague, for the National Trust can do nothing about the house, although the estate of 4,000 acres covers some very splendid downland. Mr. Puxley sold 6,000

[1] Very severely damaged in a blitz.

acres for his son before he came of age. The son inherited Woolley from his maternal uncle. In Chaddleworth church are many memorials to the Wroughtons.

Farnborough Rectory is most attractive with its small central gablet, red brick symmetrical façade and sash windows. I don't know what its date is, but suppose mid-seventeenth century, with mid-eighteenth-century alterations. An enchanting little house.

Saturday, 24th January

Nancy[1] [Mitford], who is now living at West Wycombe, is mad about the Antarctic Expedition and has collected every book about it she can lay her hands on.

I went up to London with Helen this morning for David Lloyd's wedding. Met Midi at her new club, a fantastic institution of which all the members are M.F.H.s and their wives. We at once decided we were too poor to eat there and must go to a pub. Could not find one, but instead found Claridge's. Midi directed me to the 'Causerie' where she said there was lovely hors d'oeuvre with wine, as much as you liked thrown in, all for 4/-. There was chicken on the menu too and since it was thrown in with my Madeira, we ate it too. After all that the bill came to 18/-.

Sunday, 25th January

Went to Mass at Cheyne Row held in the vestry for warmth. Afterwards to Carlyle's house and sat in the kitchen talking to the Strongs. The Strong family have now been caretaking for a longer period than Carlyle lived in the house; and Mr. Strong's mother worked for Carlyle. There is nothing Mrs. Strong does not know about the Carlyle ménage, and anyone writing on the subject could not do better than glean from her. When I arrived she was very pleased to see me, but rushed downstairs to fetch her teeth before she would let me in. I then went to Brooks's. I stood by the fire in the hall talking to Ran Antrim. We overheard Lord Trenchard saying to Lord Mottistone, 'I don't see how the Japanese can hold out much longer now.' Ran Antrim was

[1] Hon. Nancy Mitford (1904–73), married to Hon. Peter Rodd. Novelist and biographer.

appalled, and asked in wonder what could be the mentality of these two old war horses.

After luncheon I bussed to the Brompton Cemetery to look for the grave of Mrs. Duff, a late benefactress of the National Trust. I had discovered that a condition of our receiving a small legacy from her was that we should see her grave was kept in order. It appears that all these years no one of us has ever bothered even to look for it. I could not find it, for the Registry was closed. Returned and read in the club a book of letters edited by Charles Milnes-Gaskell of his great-grandfather while at Eton. The bullying in Dr. Keate's day was horrifying. Also read a short book by Reginald Blunt on the Carlyle household. Eddie Marsh sat reading beside me but did not speak to me. He merely smiled. This is very civilized club behaviour.

Monday, 26th January

Left earlyish for the Brompton Cemetery again. The coldest day I remember being out in. Biting east wind; and I had not got my fur coat on. Was told approximately where the grave was. After a lot of searching I found a double grave to some Duffs which I supposed to be the one, but now doubt if it was the right one. It seemed in fair order, although neighbouring graves had been considerably disturbed by a recent bomb. One mausoleum was totally destroyed, and the doors of others were wrenched off so that the coffins on ledges were exposed. When I see such things I am more and more determined to be cremated. The sour look of these coffins and their rusted handles! I must always peer at them, horribly fascinated.

Then off to Leatherhead, reading on the way Cherry-Garrard's *Worst Journey in the World*. I found Fetcham Holt, the villa which belongs to us and is to be sold after the war. Most of the contents have already been disposed of, but I took away with me a framed water-colour of a Rowlandson sort and one sepia wash landscape in a maple frame to show to Paul Oppé.[1] The Merediths who rent the house from the National Trust very cordial and grateful for our £100. I investigated their row of birch trees separating them from the next-door villa and called on the next-door people. The wife was clamorous and vulgar. She demanded the lot to be cut down because they took the sun from their kitchen garden. Talked of digging for victory, etc. All rot I thought, for the birches were planted long before their

[1] Paul Oppé (1878–1957), collector, and expert in English water-colours.

12

beastly house was built, and besides I could see no sign of a kitchen garden at all.

Tuesday, 27th January

Nancy at luncheon: 'I said to myself, "in the bloodiest war in all history it's no good being squeamish over one wounded moorhen". So I shut my eyes and twisted its neck.' Spot had mauled it.

Wednesday, 28th January

Went up to London to the dentist. Finished Cherry-Garrard's book in the train. His terrible descriptions of the cold affected me physically. They made me feel far colder than I actually was, so that I shivered all through luncheon at Brooks's, and by the time I arrived at the dentist's, felt sick. After he had finished with me, I was sick. On recovery I walked to Heywood Hill's bookshop. There was a strange bearded man wearing a brown fustian cloak and dictating a letter to Heywood at his typewriter. Anne[1] whispered mysteriously, 'He is the claimant to the throne of Poland.' But there hasn't been a Polish throne since the eighteenth century.

In the club I saw Tom [Mitford],[2] looking extremely wan and absent. He says he may not be going to the East after all; and he much wants to.

Walked across St. James's Park to Westminster and looked at Archer's baroque church in Smith Square. It is completely gutted by fire. Jamesey Pope-Hennessy[3] and I went over it the first winter of the war, and I recollect dragging him reluctantly inside on the plea that it would probably be destroyed. The shell is intact and with a little trained ivy would make a fine Piranesi ruin. Had tea with Lady Colefax in 19 Lord North Street. These are cosy little houses. She was sitting on a stool right in front of the fire so that the room was made distinctly chilly by her acting as a fire screen. There were tea things on a small table beside her. Bogey Harris, whose significance I am un-

---

[1] Lady Anne Gathorne-Hardy, wife of Heywood Hill, owner of the bookshop in Curzon Street which was, and is, a meeting place of writers and friends.

[2] Hon. T. D. Freeman-Mitford (1909–45), only son of 2nd Lord Redesdale. J. L.-M.'s oldest friend. Killed in the Far East on active service.

[3] James Pope-Hennessy (1916–74), biographer. Murdered in 1974.

aware of, came in soon after me. Lady Colefax talked of Aunt Jean
Hamilton and expressed disappointment with Sir Ian's[1] *Memoir*. It
failed to convey the peculiar magic of Jean. We talked of Stratford-
on-Avon, led there by mention of Marie Corelli. I said I remembered
her well like a plump, superannuated Nell Gwynne, her bosoms
lolloping over the plush edge of a box in the old theatre, sparkling
with diamonds (or crystals?) and swathed in ivory satin. I remember
black curls enveloping a great grinning outline. Lady Colefax is, I
should say, not malicious, only extremely curious, with a hunter's
instinct for lions. Hers is a scientific sort of snobbery. She is evidently
hell-bent on collecting scalps, and impatient with anything that may
deflect her from the chase. Although well born she has had to push her
way into circles that ordinarily would not have lain open to her.
When I left she told me to come again. I said perhaps I would see her
at West Wycombe. She said, 'No, here I hope.'

The nice thing about her is that she is totally without ostentation.
Because she is quite poor and inhabits a small house this is not allowed
to interfere with her mode of living. She gets people just the same, and
since she cannot give large parties at her own expense, she now expects
people to dine with her at the Dorchester and pay for themselves. In
other words it is interesting people she cares about, individuals and not
society with a large S. Her friends ring her up about people as one might
ring up Selfridges' Information Bureau. Mr. Harris said, 'By the way,
Sibyl, I have been meaning to ask you, who is Mrs. Benthall, the
mother of Sir Somebody Benthall?' 'Mrs. Benthall, *Mrs.* Benthall,'
she repeated with emphasis upon the Mrs. as though that non-title
were extraordinary, 'I am afraid I really can't help you there,' in quite
an agitated tone. Even Selfridge's can be stumped at times.

Nancy said that Bogey Harris was an old crone of Lady Cunard,
noted for his wit, when he deigned to give an exhibition of it.

Sunday, 1st February

After Mass went to Paul Oppé's through deep snow and falling flakes
with my two National Trust pictures. He was delighted with them
and pronounced the Rowlandsonish one to be charming and interesting. Said it was better than amateurish, but could not tell by whom.
As a matter of fact it *is* amateurish when you look carefully at it. He

[1] General Sir Ian Hamilton (1853–1947) of Dardanelles fame. His wife was
Jean, daughter of Sir John Muir, 1st Bart. She died 1941.

dates it about 1790 by the *vis-à-vis* in the picture, which was first introduced to the smart world in 1783. The scene depicted is obviously not of the smart world but the suburban world. The other he at once recognized as by William Payne. Neither of them the least valuable, the former worth about 8 guineas, the latter 2 or 3. He showed me his book on Rowlandson and told me a lot I did not know. Very friendly and helpful.

After tea went to see the Rosses[1] for a few minutes. They are going to Ireland tonight. I could not get a taxi and so missed my bus to High Wycombe. They let me stay the night at Eaton Terrace after they had gone. Michael looking very well and Anne most affectionate and sweet. They took me to Prince Vsevolode [of Russia] and Mamie's for a drink before they left for Euston. The Prince is very ugly and surely rather dull. She, still beautiful, is called Princess Romanovsky-Pav-lovsky, (a stage joke name) because she is a morganatic wife. Had gin and peppermint to drink, not very nice. Mamie does all her own house-work. He is fifth in succession to the throne of Russia; and his succes-sion is about as unlikely as the uncrowned King of Poland's.

To bed early, worn out, because I sat with Rick[2] [Stewart-Jones] until 2.30 a.m. last night. He suddenly turned up. He is sick of having being drilled and drilled for 2¼ years and believes he really will soon be sent to an Octu. About time too. Although I forget his very existence during prolonged absences, I find after ten minutes talk he is the only person to whom I can say just everything. His advice on all topics is invariably sound. His integrity lies deep down, his humour perpetually bubbles on the surface.

Thursday, 5th February

A horrid day in London. Cold intense, and a bitter wind blowing nasty wet snow — nice snow is dry — in one's face. I was extravagant and to console myself deliberately spent £3. Hailed a taxi at Marylebone, for as usual the train was late on arrival, and drove to *The Times'* Book Club to buy Dudley Ryder's *Diaries 1715–16*; and on to Claridge's 'Causerie'. Waited quite a bit and got a table to myself; had a delicious hors d'oeuvre mountain on one plate and some coffee for 5/–. Then taxied to the S.P.A.B.[3] office in Great Ormond Street. It is almost the

[1] The Earl and Countess of Rosse.
[2] Married 1951 Emma Smith, novelist, and died 1957.
[3] Society for the Protection of Ancient Buildings founded by William Morris, Ruskin and others in the 1870s.

only building left standing in this devastated area. All around, where whole squares and streets of houses existed a short time ago, are now empty blankets of snow. The meeting had already begun, with Lord Esher in the chair. They were discussing an invitation, received from I think the Lord Justice Scott Committee, for the S.P.A.B., Georgian Group and London Society to send representatives to list old buildings in London which they consider should not at any cost be sacrificed to post-war improvements: for instance, the Mansion House's future is threatened—George Dance! Our committee struck me after my long absence as a body of serious men facing up to their responsibilities. This is entirely owing to Esher now attending committee meetings as chairman, a thing he used not to do, but left to a vice-chairman.

The chief item on the agenda was Holland House. William Weir has made a detailed report on the condition of the house. He estimates that for £37,000 it can be rebuilt. It appears that the whole interior is gutted, and the staircase is rotting in the rain and snow. Everything else has gone except the walls, which in my opinion are no longer true Jacobean, for the windows, copings etc., were largely Victorianized. Others took the absurd view that this important house is once again pure Jacobean since the Victorianisms have been purged by the fire, which was the best thing that could have happened. I submitted that the chief point about Holland House was its historical associations, which have now gone for ever. Only Esher, Hiorns and I voted against its retention. Anyway the Ilchesters will never live in it again, if built up, and I feel sure the £37,000 will not be forthcoming after the war. The prospect of a twentieth-century Jacobean fake is worse than a Victorian Jacobean fake.

Friday, 6th February

Still perishingly cold and freezing hard. The drive coated with slippery ice. Dirty frozen snow is lying and even more snow falling today. We have had snow for a month now and since the New Year the weather has been most severe. Mercifully West Wycombe is a bit warmer and my new room, the Adam Room at the top of the stairs on the first floor, one of the warmest in the house. It faces south on to the colonnade. I am very pleased with it. It is an elegant room, the walls papered with a stiff olive green and hung with picturesque oils of the house and surrounding views by Daniell I think, done just after the building of the house. It is luxurious and comfortable. Judged strictly as a work of

16

art this house is indifferent; all the interior painted ceilings and the *grisaille* work on the walls are frankly bad. Yet the quality of the joinery is good. The general effect is charming.

Thank goodness I have at last finished Scott's lengthy journals of the polar expedition. There is no question that the man could write. I did not skip, not even the details of horse and dog management. Scott was a little bit of a poet and contriver. Nevertheless, instead of wanting to weep, I was irritated by his dramatization of the end of the story. His letters are too carefully heroic. What an unattractive, schoolmastery fellow. His sense of decency and duty hideous, and almost embarrassing. He was not at all unlike his successor Lord Kennet, who is smug, superior and condescending. I don't believe Kathleen Kennet[1] was ever much in love with Scott. I finished Leigh Hunt's autobiography tonight in bed. Hunt is a boring writer, though a nice man. He admits he was a vulgar snob when a young man. Endearing. He was unheroic.

I see that Beaverbrook is the new Minister of Production. Lady Lindsell[2] was saying in London on Sunday how much her husband, Sir Wilfred the General, loathed the Beaver, and loathed working with him. He would override the generals, give way to passions of temper and neglect detail, thus incurring a multitude of small mistakes. Not unlike Churchill in these respects. But these men are dictators and we are becoming rapidly nazified, let us face it.

Sunday, 8th February

Still freezing hard and the drive desperately dangerous and slippery. Eddy is here again, and Cecil Beaton came last night. He is quite grey, and darts like a bird. He is flagrantly twentyish. He must be very successful if money-making is an indication. I do not mean to be critical for he is an artist. Jamesey likes him and I find him very sympathetic though a little alarming. This morning on my return from Mass at High Wycombe I gave him an hour's typewriting lesson; and made him use all his fingers too. He showed promise. Towards the end we started gossiping, and then I saw how entertaining and sharp he is.

I much dislike the High Wycombe church. It is ugly and always so full I have difficulty in squeezing a way in; but this morning for the

[1] Kathleen (*d.* 1947), wife of 1st Lord Kennet and widow of Captain R. F. Scott (*d.* 1912) of the Antarctic. Sculptor.
[2] She was an aunt of the Stewart-Jones brothers and sisters.

first time I warmed up to something approaching devoutness. That was because I took my missal, followed the Latin and pondered over the beautiful succinctness of each word, so carefully, blessedly placed. In spite of the recollection of Nancy's blasphemous witticisms about 'munching' and 'munchers' nothing disturbed my devotions. I have not been to confession since the cave days under the Dover cliffs with my regiment. Bad.

Yesterday's luncheon revealed Helen in a new light, for the curate and his old mother came. H. said to us just before they arrived that there must be no witticisms and no house-party talk. I took this well from her for it is the sort of thing Mama would say. They were indeed an eminently 'bedint' couple, and H. said so poor that they undoubtedly hadn't enough to eat. The mother was sadly dressed for the terrible cold, was most humble and pathetic. Yet the two were proud in their reciprocal love. He was a facetious young man, with black, dusty hair badly cut, and a blue blotchy face. He wore a long, black cutaway coat. Eddy disliked him intensely and said he had aspirations to muscular Christianity, and with little encouragement would have been coarse, if thereby he could have impressed a sophisticated house-party with his broadmindedness; that he was the very worst type of C. of E. clergyman. But he was far too pathetic to be dislikeable. Helen made great efforts to entertain them, and induce them to have a square meal. Alas, they were far too genteel to be pressed to second helpings.

During a walk I asked Eddy if he would marry. He said that he never could, for how was he to find a woman prepared to undertake the rôle of nanny, housekeeper and hospital-nurse combined; that he [heir to Knole] had nothing to offer in return. He started denigrating himself in all sincerity. When I expostulated he replied naively, 'It's true of course that I am a very clever man.'

After dinner I took up my knitting—'the true sock' Clementine [Beit] calls it, which on St. Milne's Day, instead of liquefying, will unravel if there is to be a good harvest. Cecil had hiccoughs he laughed so much. Eddy took up his knitting, an endless khaki scarf. We were sitting side by side on a pair of upright Chinese Chippendale chairs before the fire, Eddy wearing his blue cloak with silver buckles, and his red velvet waistcoat with the Sackville coachman's gold livery buttons. I suppose we were an odd spectacle. Still, I wish Helen would not call us the two old bombed houses.

We talked about beautiful women, and it was interesting to listen to Cecil on the subject. He depreciated Tilly Losch, and said Diana

Cooper was probably the most beautiful woman he had photographed. Lady Goonie Churchill, that divine, mysterious, sphinx-like creature looked, he said, like a cream bun. Of Sarah Churchill, Vic Oliver's wife, 'Perhaps I should not tell tales out of school, but if her nose were only her own.' 'Well, whose is it?' Nancy asked. 'Gillies's,'[1] he said.

Monday, 9th February

The thaw has at last set in. Eddy and Cecil sat in the back of the National Trust car with a cabin trunk between them and a magnolia tree Cecil had been given. I dropped them in Chester Square. Cecil was telling Eddy that he did not touch up his photographs himself, but directed how each should be done. Special experts with very fine pencils spend hours on the negatives. No wonder he charges £50 for a sitting. He asked Eddy to sit for him with a walking stick.

After the Finance Committee Mr. Bond invited me to lunch with him at the Travellers'. We walked there. He was extremely friendly but upset me by saying that Esher was writing to poor Eardley that the Trust could not employ him any longer. When I remarked that I sometimes wondered whether there would be a niche for me in the National Trust after the war he said, 'You do not know the nice things they always say about you.' We ate gnocchi and mashed potatoes, sultana roll and coffee. Nigel Bond is a dear old boy. He was the first secretary of the National Trust, in the last century I think.

Friday, 13th February

Today is Friday 13th and we hear the news of the three German battleships escaping from Brest and, worse still, from our fleet by slinking up the Channel and through the Straits. It is the greatest sea disaster in some ways since the Dutch sailed up the Medway; and I hope to God there is no more glossing over it, but that enquiries are made and pursued. The English are sick of bad news being twisted to resemble good.

Saturday, 14th February

Wickhamford. Walk with Deenie [Doreen Cuninghame, my mother's widowed sister] in the afternoon to the Sandys Arms and talk with

[1] The eminent surgeon.

Maggie in her back room which smells of dusty plush and stale cheese, little Maggie with cheeks like the shiny crust of a cottage loaf, and a knot of hair on the top of her head like the twist of a loaf. She is big with the child to be born in April and heartily disgruntled by the prospect. 'Oh, Master Jim, I could kill that there Bert [husband] for what he's done to me—and at such a time too [the escape of the 3 German battleships].' I could also readily kill Bert for having taken away Maggie from us in the first place.

Sunday, 15th February

This morning after breakfast Haines and I took ten minutes thawing with a warm sponge the film of ice upon the Austin's windscreen. There were 15 degrees of frost last night and almost as many the night before.

After Mass in Broadway, during which I made plans instead of listening to the Archbishop's pastoral letter, which read like a legal document without punctuation, I motored to Hayles Abbey. Looked inside the tiny parish church. It is a gem, utterly unspoilt. Paved floor with medieval tiles from the abbey, un-stripped plaster walls with a deal of stencil work. Oak pews and oak Jacobean pulpit. Minute chancel with benches facing inwards. In this space there must once have stood an altar table, east to westwards. Some fifteenth-century glass panels in the east window placed there by old Andrews of Toddington, having formerly been taken to Toddington by a Lord Sudeley from the abbey. They are now home again.

I walked round the abbey. How I wish we could dispense with the museum like a hideous yellow squash court. It needs brushing out and there are flies under the glass cases. The paths need weeding and the grass cutting back. The restoration by the Office of Works of part of the cloisters is quite disgusting, all cement with carefully interspaced stone coping like a suburban rockery. Nevertheless there is still an atmosphere of sanctity about the abbey, and it is moving to read the lead plaque on the ground, 'Here Richard Earl of Cornwall lies buried.' I wonder where they chucked the Holy Blood of Hayles, so deeply venerated by generations of pilgrims. Did some rare and celestial flower grow upon the spot? And does it still?

I stopped at Didbrook and found the old priest Allen at home—after many years. In 1929 Johnnie Churchill and I were here. He has not altered a bit, is just as vague and forgetful of all names. He laughs

20

and sucks through his false teeth a spate of saliva as of old. I returned by Stanway. Stopped the car just to gloat upon the gatehouse and the gabled front of the house. With the yellow church this group is the most romantic, most moving thing I know. It stirs within me my deep, deep love, stiffly coagulated at times, for England. Nothing whatever inside the church.

Monday, 16th February

Off at 10 o'clock on a sort of tour, taking Deenie and Mama with me.

Went straight to Bewdley, to Dowles Manor, where I went in and talked to Mr. Elliott. Very frail and ill with rheumatism, he spoke of dying shortly and wants the National Trust to have the house and twenty acres of the valley as soon as he can get the consent of his elder daughter now in Ceylon. This may take six months or more. A complete picture postcard house, olde worlde black and white, the outside almost ridiculous. Mama at once said, 'What a dream! What a heavenly little house!' Certainly the stencilling inside is remarkable. It is of the date of the house, *circa* 1570 and covers both beams and plaster panels. On this account alone the building is important. So too is the mouth of this valley and the fact of its practically adjoining our Knowles Mill property. Walked by the trout brook to the mill and talked to the woodman's wife. Lovely rustling walk beside the water under trees.

Mr. Elliott said he was almost sure one room's panelling came out of Ribbesford [House]. Another room's panelling he bought for a song from the old Angel Inn, Bewdley. He has a fireback of the Herbert of Cherbury arms and coronet which is a cast from the one we have in the hall at Wickhamford. Papa allowed him to have the cast made many years ago. He asked why on earth we left the overmantel and other oak panelling at Ribbesford, which Grandfather brought from Crompton Hall. Why indeed? The overmantel was part of a superb four-poster at Crompton.

On to Harvington Hall where a garrulous caretaker took us round. Mama and Deenie delighted with this house too, and the secret hiding holes. Bad restoration work here, and the National Trust furniture very indifferent.

Tuesday, 17th February

Dined with Harold Nicholson and Jamesey at Rule's. Harold talked

21

much about Byron. The conversation arose from the present Jamesey brought Harold of a posthumous print of the boy Byron (bald at the temples!) reclining on a tomb in Harrow churchyard. Jamesey is always bringing suitable offerings like this, and H. was delighted. We discussed Byron's sex life of course. Lady Byron is said to have recorded in her diary that when she once told Byron he could not share her bed because she had the 'curse', Byron replied, 'Oh, that's all right! I can now sleep with Augusta.' Sounds improbable to me—I mean Lady Byron recording it. In Hobhouse's copy of Moore's *Life of Byron*, which Harold possesses, Hobhouse has pencilled in the margin that Lord Holland told him the reason why Lady Byron left her husband was that Byron attempted to bugger her; that Augusta was not the cause. Harold attributes the incest boasting to one of Byron's subconscious getting-his-own-backs on Augusta, who when he was a boy was much his senior in social sophistication. For it was Augusta who schooled Byron how to speak of 'Lady Jersey', not 'the Countess of Jersey', etc., and how to behave in London drawing-rooms—indeed who taught him correct manners which Byron was supremely backward in acquiring, if he ever properly acquired them, owing to Mrs. Byron's slipshod and provincial upbringing of her son. As late as 1823 Lady Blessington laughed at Byron's antiquated dandy airs and graces, and the pretentious bed he slept in under the Byron coronet, crest and motto.

Again in Hobhouse's copy, where Moore gives a highfalutin poetical reason for Byron's desire to be left alone in Greece, without Hobhouse's presence, a caustic marginal note gives the true reason. It was quite simply that Byron did not want another English gentleman, even his best friend, to witness his sexual aberrations, which were—in Hobhouse's words—a disgrace to his class and country. Harold has read a letter from Pietro Gamba, written in Italian after Byron's death, to Hobhouse as one of the executors, explaining the disappearance of some £300 from Byron's bedside at Missolonghi. Byron instructed Gamba to give it all to Luca Kalandrinos, the boy peasant with whom he was much in love at the time. This peasant, when an old man, used to meet once a year a Miss Hancock, the young niece of Charles Hancock an attorney, or banker, who became a friend of Byron in Greece and advanced him money. The old peasant had a fantastic suit of clothes which he claimed had belonged to Byron and of which he was inordinately proud. He used to wear it only on this anniversary. Years later Harold sent a drawing of the suit Byron was known to

22

have worn at the very end of his life to Miss Hancock, then a very old lady. This was in the 1920s when Harold was writing his Byron book. She replied that the clothes in the drawing exactly resembled the clothes she remembered Kalandrinos wearing. Harold immediately wrote again from England begging her to go to Kalandrinos's village, to try and find the cherished suit. Unfortunately his letter was returned undelivered for Miss Hancock had died in the meanwhile.

Harold spoke of Byron's lasting love for his school-friend, Lord Clare, and their dramatic meeting in Italy; of Shelley's reference to the concubines and catamites in the Palazzo Lanfranchi in Pisa. After the failure of Harold's delegation in 1924 to persuade the Dean and Chapter of Westminster Abbey to allow a bust of Byron to be erected in Poets' Corner, owing to Byron's flouting the marital rules of the Church, Harold walked away from the abbey and across the park with Lord Ernle. Harold said, 'I suppose the Dean and Chapter were, according to their rights, justified in refusing?' Lord Ernle who always denied in print the Augusta scandal, replied, 'Of course they were right, but they might have overlooked it.'

Sir Edmund Gosse told Harold that the Dorchester papers were destroyed on his recommendation. Gosse said to him, 'If I had been a little older at the time, I would have had copies kept.' Harold disliked Gosse very much.

It was my fault that we got on to politics. Jamesey and I always find ourselves in disagreement with Harold. H. upheld Churchill's speech in which he twisted the escape of the German battleships to our advantage. We walked in the pitch dark to have a glass of beer at the Charing Cross station bar. Then we parted.

Thursday, 19th February

Up to London again by the morning train. Found myself at a table next to Mr. Winant lunching with Lord Reith. I watched the American Ambassador closely. He is very dark, luminously so, very like portraits of Lincoln, and not untidily dressed as he is supposed always to be. Limpid black eyes, burning like coals, with black dashes of eyebrows beetling over them. Nervously passing his hand across his eyes and through his lanky hair. Smiling perpetually and knowingly. I liked the honest look of him but could not decide whether he were a stupid man or shrewd in spite of his gauche manners.

To my surprise Ralph Jarvis[1] walked into the dining-room. He drank coffee with me afterwards. He arrived from Portugal yesterday by air, having had breakfast at Cintra only yesterday morning. He has been away a year, secretary in the Lisbon Embassy, having been extracted from the army for the purpose. He encouraged me to come out. Said he was sure there was lots to be done. You have to flatter, he says, the Portuguese vanity and indulge their sentimentality to get on with them. They are very friendly though some are pro-German through fear of communism, and because of German propaganda which is subtler than ours. There are two German professors at Coimbra University. The British Council representative, who is non-public school, suffers from an inferiority complex. He is engaged on the compilation of a history of pornography at this particular juncture of our affairs! Ralph says the British Council is not to be despised. It is the only place where the young Portuguese of both sexes may meet and the boys take out their girls. Very oriental in their treatment of women in their own orbit.

Walked to the Epstein exhibition at the Leicester Galleries. Jacob and the Angel in alabaster. Strong, ugly and vastly arresting. One is awed and repelled by the Jew. I was struck by the number and variety of people wrapt in contemplation. There is undoubtedly a growing interest in works of art among all sections. Other virile busts and flower paintings, always chrysanthemums. I would give my soul to be busted by Epstein, and then would probably be sick at the sight of the thing. Some Dod Procters in the other room — insipid breakfast trays and still lifes. Almost old-fashioned because so comprehensible.

I took the 4.10 from Euston to Manchester and arrived at 10, worn out by the journey. At the Midland Hotel ordered supper, very expensive, about 10/-, of chill soup, golden plover with wet swimmy veg. presented on one plate, and coffee. Extraordinary people in the hotel, peroxide blondes decked with false gems, and middle-aged men with their ears sunk into the fat of their necks and the wire bridges of their specs into their noses. Rolls of skin over their collars.

Friday, 20th February

Telephoned to the District Bank to fix my appointment with them. Paid my hotel bill and went to the bank at 10.15. Motored with one of the sub-managers to Ashton-under-Lyne and picked up a surveyor, a

[1] Ralph Jarvis (1907–73), of Doddington Hall, Lincs. Merchant banker.

solicitor, another bank manager, and off we went to inspect Hen Cote cottage and Daisy Nook. Had been considerably put off by the names, but lo! the property was immensely worth while. Surrounded by Manchester, Oldham, Ashton, it is a blessed oasis. A deep gulley of some thirteen acres with a rushing yellow-backed burn through it. Much frequented by the inhabitants of these towns. There are wildish moors near by, and I decide it is just the sort of land the Trust should hold. My companions charming. Lancashire people are like children, friendly and warm, but inferiority-complexy about people from the south, which is so strange. They are always talking of Lancashire qualities, and seemed pleased when I told them that I derived from Lancashire, from these parts indeed. Worcestershire people never go on about Worcestershire qualities, I notice. We all drank tea in Hen Cote cottage, which is half-timbered, one-storeyed and peasantry. Our taxi driver came with us as a matter of course; was very communicative and kept spitting into the fire between his gulps of tea. I said, 'Don't put it out, chum. We need it.' Bitterly cold day, and a film of ice practically covering the burn.

Took only four hours in an express train back to London in order to dine with Jamesey. Had I not made this arrangement, I would have gone to see the cathedral in Manchester. Waited in Brooks's till 9, too late to get dinner there, and when Jamesey came he had no money. I was extremely tired by then, and cross. Walked to the Barcelona restaurant where we had to wait half an hour before we were served. A disappointing evening. Testily I tell J. he is becoming spoilt and too reliant upon his youthful charm. At once realize I make the mistake of admitting that he still has these qualities, not that he isn't perfectly well aware of them.

Saturday, 21st February

To Moss Bros. in the morning where I bought a maroon velvet smoking jacket for 8½ guineas and thirteen coupons. I still have a few coupons left till June.

Saw the Margaretha Trip portrait exhibited at the National Gallery, by Rembrandt, bought recently from Lord Crawford's collection. Looked at it a long while. The old lady reminds me of someone, I think old Mrs. Burgess of Farncombe, near Broadway. How ashamed I would be were Ben Nicolson to know that this is all I find to say about one of the world's great masterpieces.

At West Wycombe Sarah [Dashwood] had an 18th birthday weekend. After dinner we played telegrams. I could have been funny if I dared be vulgar, which one daren't be with the young. They of course allow themselves every licence.

Sunday, 22nd February

I cannot concentrate on sermons, however good. A kind young woman in front of me in church entertained a bored child by showing her pretty pictures of the Pope, Our Lord in colour from her missal, while the mother attended to her devotions. This unsolicited attention is the very height of saintliness. From High Wycombe I bussed to Bray Wick. Walked from there to Ockwells Manor.

I was last here in 1936. My host, Sir Edward Barry, now eighty-four, is as lively as ever. He has one servant. Sir Edward stokes the boiler himself each morning. The house is sadly dusty. We had a delicious English roast beef luncheon with Yorkshire pudding, not hard or spongey, but soft and melting. Rhubarb tart to follow. A gin and vermouth warmed me first of all. Today it is still bitterly cold and the ground frozen hard.

Sir Edward wants to sell. He owns 600 acres with a rental of £1,200 p.a. and is asking £75,000 because of the Ockwells glass and because an American millionaire offered him that figure ten years or more ago. He spurned Hill's offer from Mr. Cook[1] of £40,000. I fear I cannot help him unless he changes his tune. He took me round the house again. Although it is most important, it yet does not please. The herring-bone nogging was taken out and replaced before he bought forty years ago. The hall is undoubtedly fine and just as when Nash drew it in the 1830s. The long oak table of two planks is longer than the Baddesley Clinton table Baron Ash has at Packwood. He showed me an early fourteenth-century chest with English Gothic carving on the front. Several Elizabethan portraits of the Scotts who formerly lived here. Much good oak furniture. Sir E. is 2nd baronet and Baron de Barry in Portugal, which is strange.

At tea at West Wycombe the Eshers present with Dick Girouard who is staying with them. Esher talked about Tuesday's meeting and I told him I had for the past five years thought, as he at last is coming to think, the Trust must not expect mighty high endowments from country

[1] Ernest Cook, a rich, eccentric recluse and great benefactor of the National Trust, to which he gave Montacute House and the Bath Assembly Rooms.

house donors. We talked about colour blindness at tea. Lady Esher stated that every man who *was* a man was partially colour blind. We disputed this, and so it was put to the test. Lord Esher failed lamentably, so did Dick. I fear I didn't, for I pronounced the table-cloth to be egg blue. Whereupon Lady E. gave me a searching look. Helen, as though to affirm my virility in her guest's eyes, very kindly suggested that the cloth was sky blue.

Tuesday, 24th February

Packed all the relevant papers into my old black bag and caught the 9.6 from West Wycombe station to London for the Country Houses Committee meeting which I had to take by myself since Matheson is away ill, with a temperature of 104. Rather nervous how I was going to acquit myself this first time I have ever taken a meeting alone. But as a matter of fact all went fairly well. The old gentlemen are so fearfully ignorant of the intricacies of most items on the agenda that one need have little fear of them. Besides they one and all are *so* nice.

I had luncheon with old Mr. Horne at Stewart's afterwards. I suspect from things he let fall that he does not care for Matheson. He is in awe of him and M. snubs him, shouts at him and makes him feel dense. Now no one likes that sort of treatment, even when he is dense.

Went to see the income tax authorities. My hatred of them is so intense that I cannot be polite, which is unwise and stands me in no good stead. Then to the Leger Galleries to look at Dunlop's pictures. Several landscapes like water-colour, but in fact tempera smeared on to the canvas with a palette knife. The still-lifes have more life in them than the landscapes. I do not think he is an inspiring artist. In the next room were the works of a Welsh surrealist, C. Richards. He is a superb, confident draftsman with keen sense of composition. I enjoyed several of his fantastic designs in the way that I enjoy Chelsea china cabbages and cauliflowers.

Already there is a wooden gate at the end of the drive at West Wycombe. The iron gates were requisitioned for scrap about a fortnight ago, two days only after Helen had the notice served on her. They were very indifferent ironwork, about fifty years old, and are no loss. Rather the contrary.

Saturday, 28th February

In considerable discomfort this week in the lumbar region as well as the leg. Today was the worst day so far, owing to a two-mile walk with Miss Paterson last night to the farm.

The weather is still bitterly cold, with a biting east wind. Snow lying on the slope by the north front. We haven't been without it or frosts since Christmas. One of the severest winters, apart from that of 1939–40, I can remember.

Eddy for the weekend, and not very well; and a certain Christopher Bramwell from the Foreign Office, about forty, hugely tall, shaped like a pear, and ungainly, but affable. Rebecca West and her husband came to luncheon. Rebecca West speaks in a high, rolling, not unaffected voice which somehow does not become her, and does not give a right indication of her essentially masculine mind. She is handsome-plain, of big build, with uncouth legs and hands. And she is big enough to brush aside and defy all conventions that are a hindrance. Yet I get the impression that she has reached that comfortable stage of her career when few conventions are a hindrance. On the contrary she allows most conventions to enhance her established position. Nancy has arrived at this same stage, which is why she so often shocks me, accustomed as I still am to think of her running contrary to conventions in her old girlish, mocking manner. For example she said today, looking at me very seriously in the way people do when they know what they are about to say will meet with disagreement, 'It is clearly our duty to remain in England after the war, whatever the temptations to get out. The upper classes have derived more fun from living in this country since the last war than any other stratum of society in any other country in the world. No more foreign parts for *us*,' with a hiss on the last sibilant. Rebecca West seemed bewildered that we should all have been steeping ourselves in Antarctica, and when she rose to leave said she would write a short story about it.

The Beits[1] have got, in their newly rented house at Holmer Rise, a small portrait by Gainsborough of Madame Bacelli, dancing and holding with one hand a gauzy, flowered skirt with blue ribbons. She is an ugly horse-faced woman, who was the mistress of a Duke of Dorset. Nancy observed that her eyes were the same as Eddy's. Another picture is a striking oil by Jacques de Lajoue of a fantastic, rococo pillared building in process of construction, furnished with incongruous scientific instruments, magnifying glasses, cranes, pulleys—a kind of eighteenth-century *surréaliste* picture, very attractive.

[1] Sir Alfred Beit, Bart., M.P. Married 1939 Clementine Mitford.

I find May the kitchen maid on the bus and accompany her to Mass. She is very Irish, blarney, at ease and amusing. Like a perfect guest I keep her off gossip—which I long to hear—about the household. Waiting for the return bus I stand hunched against the bitter cold in a shop entrance. Suddenly a group of Salvationists march past and strike up a hymn with portentous solemnity and discipline, two stalwart matrons in blue bonnets goose-stepping at the fore. As they disappear round a corner an old beggar with crutches and a real wooden leg (which these days is a rarity) hobbles across my vision, briskly in step. I think what a Rowlandish scene this is in its English, laughable, humourless way. The strains of 'God Our Help' were stifled by a gust of piercing wind and a swirl of old bus tickets and dust.

May and I were both given a lift back to West Wycombe by a seedy, sandy, red-bearded, arty-crafty fellow and an Eskimo wife in a red riding-hood. They were both wearing sandals. I asked them how they could bear it in this weather! 'You get used to it,' was the reply. But why have to get used to it?

I have finished Siever's life of Dr. Bill Wilson, that goody-goody prig of the Wykehamist stamp. Doubtless he had charm for those other tough Antarctic creatures. He hated coarseness of speech and profanity, and must have been intolerable. There is a gulf between his generation and ours which is unbridgeable. I sometimes fear that I have drifted so far from the concept of a gentleman that I can no longer appreciate the genuine article when I read about it.

Before luncheon Nancy said, 'I must just dash to the Beardmore. I won't be a minute, you bet.' 'The what?' Helen asked. 'Don't you know,' we said, 'that the upstairs lavatory is called after the Beardmore Glacier. It faces due north, the window is permanently propped open so that it can't be shut, and the floor is under a drift of snow.' Helen doesn't find this a funny joke. After luncheon Eddy, Nancy and I huddle over a few green logs in the fireplace, Eddy trying to read *The Mill on the Floss*, I Jane Carlyle's letters. We turn to discussing H. and her extraordinary unadult character, her terror of being left out of anything that may be going on, her pique over preconceived plans going wrong, and a certain resentment over others enjoying something she fears she may be missing.

The guardian of the Wallace Collection (its pictures are stored in the house for the war) got out some of the Watteaus and Fragonards for us to look at. He arranged them in a row in the saloon. We had a perfect view of the lady incising a large S on a tree and the *scènes champêtres*, all of which suit the particular elegance of this house and park.

I motored to Eton in time to take Francis out to tea in the Cock Pit, where we ate the familiar bap rolls with jelly jam, whipped cream, and Austrian chocolate cake. Only the cream was ersatz, made from soya beans, and the cake tasted of straw rolled in dung. Then to evensong in College Chapel where the traditional ceremonial is invariable. The 'ram'[1] marches in the same deliberate, self-conscious manner. The same scrubby little boys sit demurely on the knife boards. In how short a time is contact with a younger generation completely lost. How can I be sure of what I believe these boys to be thinking about the service and each other, for I could never ask one, and no one would venture to tell me? Yet there they are, very well mannered it is true, but flashing across the nave confidential smiles that mean so much, ogling and making assignations without a word being spoken. Oh the squalid thoughts and the romance of it all at the time, I remember!

At dinner this evening Helen remarked on the beauty of a ring Eddy always wears. E. said, 'Yes, I have several spare stones for it which can be changed from day to day.' 'How many?' I asked. 'Forty-five,' E. said with a sigh. The ring belonged to Lady Betty Germaine. Nancy told a story of an American millionaire's wife who on meeting a parson's daughter wearing a small necklace of lapis lazuli remarked, 'I have a staircase made of those.'

Monday, 2nd March

Eardley and I motored to Princes Risborough to look at a wall at the bottom of the manor garden which is falling down. Afterwards Mrs. Vaughan, our tenant, showed us over the house. She is the widow of Dr. Vaughan, late headmaster of Rugby, a distinguished lady who has 'let herself go'. She is a mixture of Vita—perhaps the dark down on her upper lip suggested this resemblance, as well as her tallness and thinness—and Mrs. Ponsonby-Fane, the *châteleine* of Brympton D'Evercy. Very countrified, untidy and dressed in subfusc. She has the thinnest nose bridge I ever did see. It was like the edge of a pocket-knife blade. I could not take my eyes off it.

[1] The 'ram' is the procession of Fifth Form boys, led by the head of the school up the nave before services begin.

On the way home we saw Nancy sitting on a horse trough by the bus stop in the village, waiting for the Oxford bus. She is leaving after nearly three months and will be a great loss. I shall miss her terribly.

Wednesday, 4th March

After work this evening to London by train. Went straight to St. James's Court and there dined with Kathleen Kennet from whom I got a long letter on Tuesday. Lord Kennet was luckily in bed with bronchitis so we were alone. K. as outgiving as ever. The first glimpse of her showed how she is ageing. Her figure is noticeably spread, and not mitigated by the shapeless, sacklike garments she always wears. She is the worst dressed woman I know; and rejoices in a sort of aggressive no-taste in clothes and house.

For the first time I talked to her about the Antarctic expedition. She said Cherry-Garrard was a poor creature, an ugly youth of twenty-three who was only accepted because his family advanced £1,000 towards the expedition. If this is so and Scott truly addressed only two words to him throughout, then so much the less credit to Scott. But I don't altogether believe this. It appears that Cherry-Garrard submitted the first draft of his book to K., which she approved. One day while staying at his lovely Adam house in Hertfordshire, which she habitually did, she introduced him to Bernard Shaw. Shaw looked through the manuscript, and persuaded C.-G. that in a book about a great hero human interest was forfeited unless the biographer was candid about his subject's failings. C.-G. subsequently rewrote a great part of the book in which he dwelt upon Scott's deficiency in humour and so forth. He did not submit the redraft to K. She maintains that Scott did have a sense of humour. I said, 'I suppose he was a difficult man to live with, moody and hard to understand.' She said, 'Yes, he was rather moody. In this respect Peter[1] is superior to him.' Then in her gay manner, 'But I knew him.'

Shackleton, she said, was rotten; bad blood and no good at all. He had promised Scott, who for a long time could not get released by the Admiralty to go south, that he would not use his base; then straight away went and did so, leaving the hut in an appalling mess, 'but a disgusting mess in every respect', K. added with a meaning look which didn't mean anything to me. The two men never spoke to one another

[1] Now Sir Peter Scott, her son, artist and naturalist. Founder of the Wildfowl Trust.

again. Scott when pressed to appear on the same Albert Hall platform once gave a pretty-pretty speech on Shackleton's behalf, yet without exchanging a word with him in private.

Wilson, K. said, was a prig, just like a private school boy with no humour whatever. He was a good-looking, honest fellow whom the simple sailors could not see through. Mrs. Wilson is still alive, and K. described her as a drab female. Ponting was an artist who was all out for money; and somehow Alfred Bossom got mixed up in the purchase of the Antarctic film. K. cannot find bad enough words for him.

She said it is true that the whole lot of them never snapped, or nagged at each other. In this respect they were splendidly controlled. The only one of the party Scott disliked was Evans (Ted). He said so in no measured terms in his journals. However, K. thought it better to cut out the references.

Scott hated the cold, she said.

Amundsen was unscrupulous, and his going to the South Pole at all was a dirty trick. He borrowed the *Fram* from Nansen, thus depriving him of the means of making an expedition elsewhere, on the grounds of taking it to the North Pole. When at sea he turned round without a word to anyone, and sailed straight for the south. Nansen in a letter to K. wrote that the King and Queen of Norway on learning that Amundsen had reached the South Pole first, said how sorry they were, both wishing it had been Scott.

Birdie Bowers, a tiny man, with no legs to speak of, was wonderful. 6,000 applicants wrote for interviews, and K. was present at all the interviews held in a small, hired office in Victoria Street. Bowers's chits were so good and he himself so ugly and unprepossessing that K. persuaded Scott he should be accepted. A man with such physical disabilities and yet such testimonials, must be first-rate at the job.

She says that Peter is so exactly like Scott (although not so good-looking) that in her mind they are one and the same person. 'Peter inherits Con's uncontrollable urge for adventure.' She has just done a bust of Peter which she is sending to the Academy.

Thursday, 5th March

The reason for my coming up in the middle of the week was to attend General Pope-Hennessy's Requiem Mass this morning. Beforehand I tried seven shops for razor blades, and not one blade was obtainable. Damn it!

32

The Requiem was at the Chapel of Sts. John and Elizabeth Hospital, Grove End Road. In front of me a youthful figure was sitting, judging from its back view. When it turned its head I was surprised to notice Harold. He, Clarissa Churchill and I met at the church door. Jamesey conducted the three of us through an ante-chapel and got us a taxi. Harold was impressed by the service and interested in the ritual. 'All those bells,' he kept saying. 'I could not follow it through,' in an aggrieved tone.

Saturday, 7th March

There is a great stir in Brooks's about the member who has been asked to resign, and won't go. He doggedly makes use of the library every day and even insists upon privileges which the most hardened old members would not dare demand after half a century's membership. He has been so rude to the servants that in a body they informed the secretary they would leave unless he did. Now there is to be an extraordinary meeting in order formally to expel him. Such a thing has never been known to happen in the whole history of Brooks's. The offender is a vulgar, sinister-looking figure, who prowls round the club. When he leaves a room the other old gentlemen break into muffled whispers. They follow his retreating figure with their swivelling bald heads, and give vent to loud sneers.

I went to tea at the Kinnairds' house in Lennox Gardens. Tea was on a table in front of the fire and Lady Kinnaird on her knees with the toasting fork. Very friendly, but offered the butter half-heartedly, and when I said, 'I don't eat butter,' also half-heartedly, she did not press. I refused the sugar offered, taking out my saccharine, and again was not pressed. I was asked to take the honey from the comb with my knife to save dirtying a spoon. Lord K. wanted to know all about the National Trust and the country houses scheme. He lamented the servant scarcity and said it was a scandal elderly people should not be allowed a full quota of servants. Lamented education of the lower orders. I was a good deal entertained, and couldn't help liking them. All so unrealistic and old fashioned.

Sunday, 8th March

In the afternoon Rick [Stewart-Jones] and I walked in the sun. He wanted to look at the slum parts of Chelsea around Lott's power station. It is remarkable what vast areas there have been destroyed, and

33

yet the power station is unharmed. R. is fascinated by the problems of reconstructing these devastated areas when the war is over. It is slums in which he is really most interested. I am not at all. We looked at the Moravian Cemetery at the back of Lindsey Palace. There is a nice little cottage, and an old chapel, now a studio. Half-hidden by the long grass of a lawn are round and square stones on the ground, with inscriptions on them. The Moravians were buried standing up, the easier to scamper away at the sounding of the last trump.

Monday, 9th March

The sun was shining and the air almost balmy as I walked through Belgravia. For the first time this year I inhaled that familiar scent of London, which ought to be so full of promise and happy days. But alas, now it augurs despair, inevitable misery, and destruction. For the spring is a season one has come to dread. Yet the birds in the Green Park were singing oblivious of the future; and in spite of my awareness of it I found my feet skimming over the grass.

I once firmly believed in the permanency of human relationships. I suppose I read about their impermanency in books, but could not bring myself to acknowledge it. Now I know it to be a fact, just as every physical creation is transitory. The realization ought doubtless to strengthen my divine love, but I do not think it does.

Saturday, 14th March

I had a charming letter from Professor Trevelyan,[1] quite unsolicited, in which he said he did not know what the Trust would have done without me and how glad he was I had been invalided out of the army. Gratifying, but guilt-inducing. Matheson's illness continues. He is now removed to a nursing home for his temperature refuses to go down. I chose a delicious tweed at John Walls for a new suit. But I only have fourteen coupons left till next June. A suit requires twenty-six, although without a waistcoat I can manage with twenty-one.

I went to Heywood Hill's shop. Both he and Anne were away. Mrs. Willie King was taking charge for them. I enquired after her husband. She says he is the oldest subaltern in the British Army, a gunner stationed on Hadrian's Wall. He asked to join MI.5 so they put him into the R.A. He is delighted with the mistake, if it is one. She says he

[1] G. M. Trevelyan, O.M. (1876–1962), historian.

revels in army life and is blissfully happy. Certainly one would never expect this flimsy, weak creature, like the Chelsea porcelain of which he is such a connoisseur, actually to like the rough and tumble. But then I am constantly surprised by the attitude of friends to their war-time occupations.

I walked round St. Paul's Cathedral. It was full of little brown men, Burmese or Siamese, herded by kind English drago-ladies. The ambulatory and the transepts are closed to the public, and there is a great chasm where the bomb fell in the north transept. The inner screen whereon used to be the 'Si monumentum requiris circumspice' is totally destroyed. The Duke of Wellington's ornate monument is bricked up with iron stays from one side to the other. All the sculpture covered with dust and dirt.

I walked through the devastated area to the north of the cathedral. It was like wandering in Pompeii. The sun was shining warm and bright. There was not a breath stirring, only the seagulls wheeling and skirling over the ruins. Not a sound of traffic when I was in the midst of the isolation. From one spot there is waste land visible as far as the eye can roam. It was most moving. Unfortunately the ruins are not beautiful, too like scarred flesh, and as yet untoned by time. I do pray they will at all costs keep the Wren spires, even if they must clear away the shells of the naves. I walked past the ruins of Christchurch Newgate, St. Giles's Cripplegate, St. Vedast, St. Lawrence Jewry, St. Benet's, St. Mary-le-Bow (when I last saw this church about a year ago it still had its roof on though badly damaged. A subsequent raid has evidently finished it off) and so on. Walked to Finsbury Circus via the Guildhall. Noticed for the first time a good classical building, called Armourers' Hall I think. Past Liverpool Street, back via St. Botolph, little St. Ethelburga the Virgin, St. Helen's (these three unharmed), up Queen Victoria Street and back to St. Paul's where I took a bus to Brooks's. Exhaustion and tea.

Sunday, 15th March

Lunching at the old Gascoignes at Ashtead, Aunt Puss[1] politely praised the (rather dry) currant-cakey pudding. With considerable satisfaction Sir Frederick replied, 'Yes, we have had that pudding every Sunday since we were married.' That must be forty years ago.

[1] Lady Constance Milnes-Gaskell, mother of Charles Milnes-Gaskell. Lady-in-Waiting to Queen Mary.

The weather is mild, though rainy. The birds are very busy and singing their throats out as if in relief that at last the winter is over. There is no green on the trees, which are still winter bare, but the snowdrops have sprung up inches high in vast carpeted circles round the big trees on the drive. I do not recollect such a thickness of snowdrops before.

I went straight to the National Gallery and met Clarissa Churchill walking down the steps. She said she had failed to get in, having been told that only ticket holders would be admitted. I thought there must be some mistake. She had in fact gone to the wrong door. We bought tickets (1/- each) and just squeezed in. We had very bad seats right at the back behind the performers. Elena Gerhardt sang Schubert and Brahms songs, and Myra Hess played Schumann. No wonder it was a popular day. Elena Gerhardt came out close to where we were sitting. She is an enormous woman with so dropsical a belly that it looks like a pillow tied to her front not belonging to her person at all. She wore a black velvet dress like a monk's habit, tied with a black cord round her middle. She must be about sixty but still has a voice. When she walked in she was beautifully powdered, her grey hair teed up, immaculate. When she came out all the powder was gone, her face shining with sweat. She was mopping her forehead with a handkerchief. Yet she looked happy, fulfilled. Where we sat it was difficult to hear her clearly, and her low notes not at all. We ate sandwiches and drank cups of coffee in the canteen.

Clarissa walked with me as far as Brooks's. She told me that Randolph's wife had no intention of sticking to him; and that Mr. Churchill would be very sad if their marriage broke up. She said that General Pope-Hennessy's death was brought about by a stroke. A Colonel Someone was having tea with him and put him into a rage by remarking that Russian tanks were bad. When the visitor left the General went to Dame Una's[1] room, very upset, had a seizure and died four hours later. Cecil Beaton observed, 'Careless talk costs lives.'

A special meeting of members was held at Brooks's this afternoon formally to expel the member who has been rude to the servants and used bad language. The chairman announced that he had just received a letter from the member announcing his resignation after all, and promising never to cross the threshold of the club again. Great relief

[1] Dame Una Pope-Hennessy (*d.* 1949), wife of General Richard Pope-Hennessy, author, and mother of John and James.

was expressed by everybody at this end to their embarrassment. Later in the day, I passed the man, looking unconcerned and truculent under the arcade of the Ritz. Instantly I felt sorry for him and wondered why he had behaved like this. I can quite understand how, if one senses that one is disliked, one is impelled to make oneself detested.

Thursday, 19th March

Fairly warm and heavy showers with gleams of muslin sunshine intermittently. Today I start on my Lincolnshire tour.

I take two hours in starting, for that damned car refuses to work and Helen's, which she most generously offered to lend me, also refuses. In the end the National Trust car gets going and I leave at 11.45. On the way I look at the privet hedge at Whiteleaf Field which has been decently layered. I pass Ivinghoe Windmill, and walk across plough to inspect it. It stands in the middle of a flat waste silhouetted against the grey sky, with its black spectral arms now pinioned down its body. The Swan at Leighton Buzzard has no room for me, but the landlady is civil and indicates a tea shop a few doors off. I lunch there for 2/7 surprisingly well. There is a medieval cross in the centre of the street. Instinct told me to stop at the church in Lowick. Or was it the stone Gothic lantern on the tower? I was well rewarded, for in the north aisle every window was filled with medieval glass of kings, etc. The alabaster tomb of Ralph Greene (*d.* 1419) and wife most lovely. He is holding her hand in his and she is wearing the crespine headdress, netted stiffly and sticking out from both sides of the head. Also there is a table tomb to the Earl of Wiltshire (1498), again of alabaster, his bare head resting upon a heaume. There is a monument in the north aisle of a Lady Germaine, formerly Duchess of Norfolk, lying sideways, head on elbow, uncomfortable and Kneller-like. Her husband, also in marble, ostracized behind the organ case. Altogether a most rewarding church. This chance discovery brings a brimful cup of joy.

I arrive at Hambleton Hall late for tea. Old Mrs. Astley Cooper, now eighty-eight, the same as ever, rolling about in a huge bed like a stranded whale. Rather pathetic and lonely and so pleased to see me. We talked of Father Francis [Moncrieff] who has been made Prior and may become Provincial of the Dominican Order. Mrs. C. said that his pleasure at being made Prior slightly disappointed her. I liked this touch of her old acerbity. But she loves him. I put up at the George in Grantham. Good fare and comfortable, but uncivil people.

A goddamn awful day, cold and leaden. After breakfast I walked to the parish church. The blackout arrangements have made the inside dingy and dark. I was arrested by one large Georgian mural monument, and crossed over to look at it, and lo! it was Sir Dudley Ryder's, the Dudley Ryder whose diaries I have just enjoyed so immensely. I had no idea he was buried here. There was a Lenten service in progress in the choir; one curate with a cultured, gentlemanly voice reading from the New Testament, and one elderly devout lady in the congregation. I sat and listened to the lesson. I said to myself, this woman must be Miss Sedgwick. I followed her to the back door of Grantham House, where she entered. So I caught her up and asked if she were Miss Sedgwick. She took me into the garden and all round the house which she is leaving to the National Trust.[1] It occupies a large green area in the middle of the old town, adjoining the parish church—a strategic position.

In Tattershall I lunched at the Fortescue Arms. The host a very surly fellow who kept ejaculating 'Christ!' in an offensive manner.

Tattershall church may be the most beautiful I have ever seen. Perpendicular, it was built by the Lord Cromwell who built the castle. The nave windows are vast, and so are the clerestory windows, *and* there is no stained glass at all; just white translucent diamond panes. No pews either over the undulating flagged floors. The emptiness is Catholic and ancient. The castle is now filled with stacks of Natural History Museum fossils, neatly packed. The whole place reeks of mothballs.

Saturday, 21st March

Norton Place and Gainsborough Old Hall. The first an elegant seat built by Carr of York for Mr. Harrison, out of the prize money he received for making the best chronometer for the Admiralty, in 1770. A fitting and just reward for merit. The latter house is stacked, literally stacked, one on top of the other, with treasures belonging to Sir Hickman Bacon. They are not even covered with dust sheets; and are gathering dust and filth from the pigeons which scramble through the roof and roost in the great hall. There is a device in one bedroom, a

[1] Actually given by the Misses M. and W. Sedgwick to the National Trust in 1944–50.

hammer attached to the wall under the ceiling over the bed, which when pulled knocks loudly against the beam under the floor of the housemaid's room in order to wake her up.

Finding Lincoln Cathedral shut at 5 o'clock I walked disconsolately through the close. Met a canon's wife coming out of her house to post a letter. She was perfectly charming, took me into her house, gave me tea and lent me a book about the minster, and introduced me to her husband. They showed me their garden. I thought she was the perfect example of a Christian clergywife.

At Doddington I found Mrs. Jarvis picking snowdrops in the garden, and helped her. She is an old woman, witchlike in appearance, with a quiet, dry sense of humour. When she retired upstairs to rest I wandered round the house in the dusk. Doddington is one of the most appealing houses I know, Jacobean outside and Georgian inside. But the most sympathetic sort of Jacobean, plain, clean-cut surfaces and skyline only broken by cosy pin-cushion towers. And the deep rosy brick walls, the four great cedars, the detached gatehouse. What more could one demand of romance and seclusion? The rooms inside are very plain. Furniture walnut and mahogany, and lots of tapestry and needle-work fabrics. The house smells of sweet log fires and of Knellers and Lelys. Coney[1] cooked a delicious dinner of beetroot soup with cream, duck, raspberries from a bottle and cream again, burgundy and port. The top floor is full of children and so far the house has escaped requisitioning. It seems an isolated, far-away family home, struggling happily and comfortably.

Monday, 23rd March

Last Thursday, the very day I meant to call on Diana Worthington[2] on my way to Lincolnshire, it appears that Greville Worthington was killed by a sentry who fired at his car because he failed to stop when challenged to halt. Greville never heard the sentry and the bullet hit him in the back. He pulled up the car, collapsed and died. The girl with him was unhurt. He was to have married her, his divorce from Diana having just come through. Diana is very upset and miserable, for she never meant or wished to lose Greville.

Wilson Steer is dead.[3] I passed him in Cheyne Walk only the other

[1] Wife of Ralph Jarvis, and daughter-in-law of old Mrs. Jarvis.
[2] Lady Diana Worthington (d. 1943), daughter of 2nd Earl of Feversham.
[3] Philip Wilson Steer (1860–1942), Post-Impressionist artist.

Sunday. He was a big, burly, gruff man, always wearing a wide, black, untidy stock or scarf, walking painfully, grimly and determinedly, very much preoccupied by inner thoughts.

Tuesday, 24th March

Eardley and I hose and wash the National Trust car, each doing a side, thoroughly we think, with sponge and leather. When the car has dried I am horrified to find streaks of mud still on my side. I look shyly at Eardley's side. It is just as bad. I am pleased.

Chichester Cathedral is chiefly Norman, clean and spacious, yet inexplicably lacking sanctity. It is full of monuments, none interesting. There is a life-size figure of Huskisson, who was killed by a train in 1830. He is wearing a toga. What an extraordinary fashion that was. Considered ridiculously archaic no doubt at the time, it is in our eyes symptomatic of the early nineteenth century. In other words artists should never be afraid of their work appearing derivative and un-original. For whatever they produce inevitably retains the flavour of their epoch.

I arrived at Brede at 7.30 in time for dinner with Clare Sheridan.[1] A very pretty girl of twenty, Maxime Birley, was staying. I had not seen Clare for years. She looks a little older, is stout but magnificent. She was wearing corduroy trousers which did not suit her, but the next morning she wore a terracotta skirt with flowing shawl to match. She kept flinging the shawl about her person in an Isadora Duncan fashion. Clare is a pacifist, and we spoke of the war, and of spiritual values. I found that I agreed with her almost fundamentally. She is a big woman and she has the bigness to remain detached from the war. I remember once thinking that in the event of another war most of my friends would have the bigness to be so detached, but no, none of them seems to be, not even myself. Clare is. It is true that now Dick [her son] is dead, she can afford to be. Clare has woven a spiritual seclusion and wrapped herself in it like a cocoon. She is often a little silly, but she can be impartial and wise.

She thinks her cousin Winston ought to go. She praises the contrasting virtues of Stafford Cripps, who neither smokes nor drinks, and is impressed by the love of the people in his own village for him.

I slept in Clare's studio, surrounded by uncarved tree trunks and

[1] Sculptor, died 1970. Her mother, Winston Churchill's mother and Shane Leslie's mother were the Jerome sisters.

busts of Red Indians. Her shelves were groaning with her own books, translated into German, French, Danish and even Russian.

Thursday, 26th March

After breakfast, at which I was offered a goose's egg and, like an ass, refused it for fear of appearing greedy, we went down the park to look at Brede Place, now occupied by soldiers. It is a wonderful house and to my surprise not large. Nothing, save Dick Sheridan's five bathrooms and heating plant, has been added to the house since Henry VIII's reign, so Clare says. It is a very perfect late medieval house, with a wide view, yet remote. It has several panelled rooms. One small room over the porch has masks, somewhat negroid, in the cornice. Clare would sell Brede for £7,000, but there is little land—sixty acres at most—and no other form of endowment. Yet it would let if the Trust held it, I feel sure.

Left for Smallhythe. Miss Edith Craig[1] was in bed, but the two other odd old ladies were about, Christopher St. John and Tony (really Clare) Atwood. They were dressed in corduroy trousers and men's jackets, one homespun, the other curry tweed. Their grey locks were hacked short and both wore tam-o'shanters. They were charming to me and gave me a huge two-handled mug of coffee. In Ellen Terry's little house one feels that she might walk past one at any minute, and in her bedroom that she might appear sitting before her dressing-table brushing her hair.

At Bodiam Castle I walked on the leads of the gatehouse. At Batemans[2] the tenants were away. Rudyard Kipling's study has atmosphere. It is filled with his books, the sort of books you would expect him to have, histories of the British Empire, Meredith's poems. The house of grey Burwash stone and a great cluster of chimney stacks was evidently larger, and has been truncated.

Saturday, 28th March

The coffee-room at Brooks's was full. I was just going to withdraw when the Professor [Richardson][3] hailed me and told me to sit with

---

[1] Daughter of Ellen Terry. She gave Smallhythe Place near Tenterden, her mother's home, to the National Trust in 1939.

[2] Rudyard Kipling's home, acquired by the National Trust in 1940.

[3] Professor, later Sir Albert E. Richardson, P.R.A. (1880–1964).

him. He is a dear man, and a little dotty. I don't always understand his esoteric jokes, and insinuations. Besides he laughs so much at his own jokes that one can barely hear what he says. Yet he halts, peers at one and demands an understanding. He is always punning. He spoke disparagingly of Groping Ass and Meddlesome, his two *bêtes-noires*. He says all great architecture is derivative when it is not deliberately imitative. He claims to have discovered Wren's own working note-books, but will not reveal or publish them, for there is no one alive worthy to profit from them. He only reads eighteenth-century news-papers, of which he has an enormous stock, for he says the news in them is just the same as it is today. You merely have to substitute the names of countries occasionally, and not invariably. He read me some passages from Swift. Wants me to join the Council for the Preservation of City Churches. He asked who he could find to fill the chair of the Royal Fine Art Commission. Ronnie Norman has declined because he will not take a peerage which is essential to the office. Esher is not serious enough, he maintains.

At 2.15 I straightway joined the Hills at Miss Jourdain[1] and Miss Compton-Burnett's[2] where they were lunching. I arrived for coffee. This is a great occasion. Margaret Jourdain is patently jealous of Ivy Compton-Burnett, whom she keeps unapproachable except through herself, and even when approached, guards with anxious care. This is evident from the way in which the former diverts one's attention if she thinks one is talking too much to the latter. It is a selfish kind of affection, to say the least. The two have lived together for years and are never parted. They are an Edwardian and remarkably acidulated pair. The coiffures of both look like wigs. The hair is bound with a thin fillet across the forehead and over a bun at the back. Thin pads of hair hang down their foreheads unconvincingly. Miss C.-B., whom I consider to be the greatest living novelist, is upright, starchy, forthright and about fifty-seven to sixty. There is a bubbling undercurrent of humour in every observation she makes, and she makes a good many, apparently hackneyed and usually sharp, in a rapid, choppy, rather old-fashioned upper-middle-class manner, clipping her breathless words. She enunciates clearly and faultlessly, saying slightly shocking things in a matter-of-fact tone, following up her sentences with a lot

[1] Margaret Jourdain (*d.* 1951), connoisseur and author of books on furniture and decoration.
[2] Miss, later Dame Ivy Compton-Burnett (1884–1969), novelist. The two ladies lived in Braemar Mansions, Cornwall Gardens, S.W.7.

of 'dontcherknows', and then smiling perceptibly. She has a low, breasty chuckle. She has not unpleasing, sharp features, and her profile is almost beautiful. But she is not the kind of woman who cares tuppence for appearances, and wears a simple, unrememberable black dress (I guess all her clothes are unrememberable), which she smoothes down with long fingers.

The two were very entertaining about their refugeeing with the niece of an old friend near Chedworth. They hated the niece, who tactlessly referred to her aunt's impending demise from senility, and let them know what she would then do with the aunt's furniture and belongings. We talked chiefly of country houses. Miss Jourdain looks rather wicked and frightening, when she peers through her quizzing glass. Miss C.-B. says that Miss J. has too little occasion to use it these days, now that there are so few houses available with furniture to be debunked; that she lost a lens in the train, and it has hardly mattered.

Sunday, 29th March

I walked in the sun down the Long Walk from Windsor, past the Copper Horse to Cumberland Lodge for tea. Lord FitzAlan[1] very charming. He drank a large glass of sherry at tea-time. He is eighty-seven. He spoke with profound affection of Lord Lloyd's memory, and said he never knew a greater patriot or more honourable man.

Thursday, 2nd April

At breakfast this morning, just as I was in a hurry to be off, I cut the index finger of my left hand with the bread knife, rather deep. I drove with Eardley straight to Avebury. He took me round the Circle. He is madly keen on Avebury and rather peevish about my lack of enthusiasm and disrespect for the ugly stones which Keiller has dragged from the ground into the light of day. I cannot approve of the proposal to destroy the old village inside the Circle. I admit that the empty sections of the Circle are impressive where the terraces have been cleaned of scrub and are neatly cropped by sheep; but to remove medieval cottages and clear away all traces of habitation subsequent to the Iron Age seems to me pedantic and a distortion of historical perspective. We walked round the Manor garden. Eardley was bored by the

[1] Lord Edmund Howard (later Talbot), 1st Viscount FitzAlan of Derwent (1855-1947), Lord Lieutenant of Ireland 1921-2.

house because it is not classical and is romantic. Today's fashionable distaste for the romantic in English country houses is as overemphasized as was the Edwardians' for the classical and regular.

We lunched at the inn off cold beef and potatoes in skins, and a trifle (the very word makes me retch) which was surprisingly sweet and good. At Tilshead we walked to the Long Barrow. I agreed with Eardley that the scrub and untidy spruce trees ought to be eradicated in order to reveal the simple contours of the Barrow. The undulations of these tumuli along the backs of the downs against the sky are their only point and beauty. To hell with archaeology! Although the White Barrow is right off the road and miles from Tilshead a party of children was playing round a little russet tent they had pitched here.

At Stonehenge we looked at our land, part of which on the north side of the Amesbury road has been ploughed. I cannot see that this matters in the present circumstances, although the archaeologists make a clamour. Having bought tickets at the turnstile we walked up to and round the monument. Both of us in agreement that the wire fencing is most unsightly; its criss-cross pattern suggests an internment camp. If there were more of Stonehenge left it would lose its awe.

What a contrast with the finished refinement of Dinton House where we had tea with the old Philippses.[1] How splendidly proportioned, clean-limbed and precise this great house is, springing straight out of the rough grass and silhouetted against a crescent belt of beech trees. The stair hall with its trim brass balusters, dividing flights, yellow scagliola columns and circular top lantern makes me gasp with admiration. All my cravings for proportion, propriety and architectural solution of problems are satisfied.

Friday, 3rd April

Good Friday at Westwood. Ted[2] has given me the North Room next to the parlour, the room with a double bed and original blue-green and white crewel-work William and Mary hangings. The ceiling is divided into four compartments by two beams, the whole stuccoed about 1610 with pendants. The walls retain their plain plaster surface but the chimneypiece is stuccoed with floral designs. There are three

---

[1] Mr. and Mrs. Bertram Philipps who gave Dinton Park and Hyde's House, Wiltshire, to the Trust in 1943.

[2] E. G. Lister, under whose will Westwood Manor, Wiltshire, came to the Trust in 1960.

little children's masks over the fire, which was lit for me last night. I lay in bed with one candle guttering behind a glass hurricane globe (for there is no electric light in the house) and the logs flickering thin flames, seen rather than felt through the half-drawn bed curtains.

We strolled down the lane to Farleigh Castle. It is very tidily kept by the Office of Works, but the gatehouse and scanty remains have been thickly pointed with a black cement made of Brighton pebbles. I cannot approve of this pointing which the Office of Works use all over the country regardless of regional customs. It is certainly enduring, but unnatural and ugly and prevents wild flowers growing in the crevices. The chapel is hung with armour, for the cleaning of which the owner, Lord Cairns, recently paid an expert in advance. The best pieces mysteriously disappeared. There is Flemish glass in the windows. A panel depicts St. Colette doing penance for having prayed success-fully to be changed from a squat, plain lady into a comely, tall abbess. The iron grille, dating from 1411, round the early Hungerford monu-ment has at the four corners finials frizzled to resemble black hearse plumes.

Ted has received a photograph from Tom Goff who is A.D.C. to the Athlones in Ottawa of the whole Government House party including Princess Alice and himself knitting, and Lord Galway crocheting. When Tom went to Buckingham Palace the other day to attend to Handel's harpsichord the two princesses were playing to the Queen a duet they had learnt by heart. The Queen said to Tom, 'You are a lucky man to be able to do what you like.'

Saturday, 4th April

I have finished Froude's three volumes of Mrs. Carlyle's letters. I am struck by the Victorians' apparent concern for the health and well-being of their relations and friends, whereas we are really indifferent to the tribulations of our nearest and dearest, unless they are very dear indeed. Deathbed scenes bore us to tears.

Two young men to luncheon, one called Eric Knight who is half German, having a German mother and a German wife, the other in the air force and reeking of cheap scent. Knight with long, golden hair, a large nose and thick, ugly Yiddish lips, was unprepossessing but interesting when he talked of Russia which he visited in 1935. His impressions in that year were that the Soviet system was a laughable, and total failure. Nothing worked. Everything was tawdry and drab.

The people were corrupt and ready to commit any treason for money which all lacked. He spoke to many beggars, some of them educated old ladies who complained to him of their miseries in frightened undertones.

I must say my convictions regarding the Russian campaign are that the Germans are not yet in earnest. Although they miscalculated in assuming that the campaign would be over before last winter, they have been treading water since then, and merely keeping up their line. The Russian advance has been inappreciable. I foresee a renewal of the German onslaught when the mud has gone, and a terrible Russian defeat.

Tuesday, 7th April

Talked with Mama in her bedroom this morning.[1] She is full of complaints as usual. Papa has let the large cottage for only £2 although it is fully furnished; there are endless parties of people in the house; the garden boy is leaving, and the gardener, who is only forty-three, may be called up; and Gertrude is to be married in a fortnight. She is the only servant in the house now, and Colonel Riley, who is billeted on them, has to be waited upon, hand and foot. Mama is very distressed because Gertrude is due to have the curse the very day of her wedding, which could not be arranged otherwise because her young man has to take his leave when he is given it. Mama says the curse will come precisely at 11.55 a.m. that day, that it always comes regular as clockwork with strong, healthy girls, a thing I never knew before and can scarcely credit.

Wednesday, 8th April

This afternoon Sarah [Dashwood] ran into the office at West Wycombe calling for Miss Paterson. The tapestry room chimney was on fire. They rely on Miss P. for everything. I dashed upstairs and with Helen went on to the flat roof. Smoke was pouring from the chimneystack. I got a stirrup pump and soaked the stack with water. Within five minutes of the fire being extinguished the fire brigade arrived. They swarmed all over the house. I secretly enjoyed the incident. Helen was very scared, which was only natural, looked very white and issued and counter-issued orders snappishly in a confused way.

[1] This was at Wickhamford Manor, Worcestershire, where J. L.-M. was born and brought up.

After lunching by myself in a tiny, stuffy, Italian-serviced café near Covent Garden off sausages and golden roll, I went to the S.P.A.B. meeting. Very annoyed to find that it had been put off and I had come all this way to no purpose. But Mrs. Esdaile and Maresco Pearse were also there on the same misunderstanding. So we talked of the scheme to house all the amenity societies in Holland House. Mrs. Esdaile was pleased that I too was in favour, and particularly favoured the two advantages I put forward, that there should be a central library and a communal solicitor in the building. Rick and I have long advocated this and we go further in advocating amalgamation of the societies under one name as well as under one roof.

Thursday, 16th April

A tedious 2½-hour journey by a series of buses to Englefield Green. Mediterranean sky, and the chestnuts having burst their buds are in the fan-unfolding stage. All the trees along the Thames valley are shooting buds noisily. The green is almost too shiny, too polished.

I walked through Bishop's Gate into Windsor Park and was overtaken by Alathea FitzAlan-Howard on her bicycle. She is the FitzAlan's pretty granddaughter aged eighteen, frail and freckled. I arrived just in time for dinner for which there is no changing these days. Lord FitzAlan's son staying. It is the first time I have seen him, a tiny, rather wizened, insignificant man with a wooden leg. Magdalen[1] sad as ever, with heavy folds of tumbling, wispy hair parted in the middle of her head and looped behind anyhow. Two Grenadier officers came to dinner. They are guarding the King and Queen who are at present in Royal Lodge next door. One is called Lascelles and is, I believe, Blanche Lloyd's nephew, very good-looking and fair-haired, tall and the 'flower of English youth', a plant that always makes me stare and rub my eyes in admiration and envy. Both are on guard for a week, may not leave the locality, and sleep only half-undressed in the royal stables. Yet they look uncrumpled, immaculate. They seldom see the King. They had just been in a new stratosphere Wellington bomber. These bombers are being turned out at a small factory near by at the rate of two a week. They hope to reach 43,000 feet. This is

[1] Hon. Magdalen FitzAlan-Howard, unmarried daughter of Lord FitzAlan, d. 1974.

highly confidential. When over a certain height the crew collect in one confined cabin, where no oxygen apparatus is required, and a switch from the engine supplies them with what they need in the cabin. These machines fly blind by radar. The boys said the beauty and finish of the instrument boards were wonderful beyond words. Every convenience of the crew was studied and brought to perfection.

Lord FitzAlan is delighted with the Cripps breakdown in India and does not think it presages any immediate ill-consequences, but in the long run good results. He fears Cripps intends to be next viceroy. He talked to me after dinner in his study about the Stanley Baldwins. S.B. is by no means a fool; is on the contrary extremely astute, and far from obstinate as is generally supposed. His besetting fault is indolence. He confided in Lord F. that his reason for not rearming was that the country would not stand for it at the time.

Friday, 17th April

I was given the Chapel Room, a stuffy, old-fashioned bedroom, with a huge made-up, oak bed, very comfortable with two fat rich linen pillows.

Mass in the chapel at 9. One of the Jesuits from Beaumont comes three times a week to say Mass. The Blessed Sacrament is kept in this chapel which is well arranged and well furnished. It is not the usual makeshift type found in most country houses, like for instance poor Mrs. Cooper's at Hambleton. The floor is covered with a red plush carpet up to the walls which are simply panelled. The prie-dieux are well padded and heavy with plush. Rare vestments are kept in the sacristy. Alathea came in late and bare-headed. She hastily snatched a black veil from her prid-dieu and adjusted it as she knelt.

The ceremony was somehow extraordinary. There were Magdalen, Alathea, a lady's maid and one old woman from I don't know where, all under veils. Lord FitzAlan served in spite of his eighty-seven years, shuffling about and genuflecting like a two-year-old. The priest, Father Day, a son of the judge in the Parnell case, is a cripple with arthritis and can barely move with a stick. He crawls at a snail's pace, leaning heavily on the stick. I was in agonies lest he or Lord F. should collapse and have to be propped up. As it was each supported himself upon the other. Yet the scene was impressive and the recollection of it fills me with pleasure. I went to Confession and as usual had to rack my brains to extract the worst sins since I last confessed, which was at

48

Dover I believe. I find it hard to decide what are my sins. I was given 3 Paters, 3 Aves and 3 Reginas. Only Lord F. and I communicated. Lord F. handed me a clean napkin and I trembled lest the priest, who was creaking and groaning, should drop the wafer. The wafer dissolves so foamlike in the mouth, always adhering to the roof of the mouth first of all.

I drove to Egham station with Father Day, who is an inquisitive old man, wanting to be told everything, who I am (who am I?), how I spell my name, how long I have known Cumberland Lodge and what is my age. Not an agreeable priest, and his false teeth do not fit.

Saturday, 18th April

The Wintertons are here for the weekend. I met them with Helen in the village, and we walked back to the house for luncheon. Lady Winterton is a curious stick, frumpish, contradictory, prudish you will think. She makes surprisingly outspoken remarks which are quite uncompromising and often unconsciously funny. Lord W.,[1] who at twenty-one was the promising young man in the House of Commons, has at sixty not progressed beyond this unfulfilled stage of adolescence. He is tall, gaunt, willowy. He talks a great deal, has attentive manners of the old school, and indeed a schoolboy's charm. He is particularly sweet with children. At times he gets angry, for he is very retentive of anciently formed opinions. Apparently he senses every fluctuation of the moods of the House of Commons, and has known every politician and every great house in London since Gladstone's day. He has trustful, open blue eyes that rove around. You can tell by the movement of his mouth and his giggles that he is not a clever man. He sits bent over himself at table, and in his enthusiasms rubs his long hands together and shoots out an arm ahead of him in gesticulation and sheer joy of expression. When he laughs, which he often does over his own stories, he jumps up and down in his chair like some elongated doll on a spring.

Sunday, 19th April

Francis has been mowing the lawns round the house with the motor tractor, leaving the dead grass lying, so that there is a heavenly amber-sweet smell of hay, as in midsummer. I wish there were more wild

[1] 6th Earl Winterton (1883–1962), an Irish peer. Conservative M.P. for nearly 50 years. Lady Winterton d. 1974.

flowers here besides the dandelions, which I love and others disdain. I lay on the grass and peered closely into the head of one. It was like looking into the inmost recesses of the sun, aswirl with petal flames alive and licking each other. To think that each of the million dandelions in Buckinghamshire, which are taken for granted or ignored, is in fact a marvellous star of golden beauty. How blind human beings are to the best around them, and perceptive of the worst! I must admit that the dandelion's leaves are coarse and common, unworthy of the resplendent head.

After dinner Eddie Winterton poured out stories of the last war, the dance he gave in Cairo, and Lord Allenby's outbursts of temper over small matters, *viz.* with his A.D.C.s because they could not find his Easter eggs. They called him the Bull. E.W. thinks he was a great soldier. He said that Churchill had quarrelled with Roger Keyes and Lord Trenchard so that they could no longer meet; that recently Trenchard left Downing Street in the middle of dinner after Winston called him a liar, and that Mrs. Winston followed Trenchard down the pavement and begged him to return. Lord W. says that as a young man Winston's manners were worse than Randolph's, which seems to me incredible. He thinks Randolph will not achieve anything because he lacks the industry and application of his father. Lord W.'s aunt was Lady Blandford, sister-in-law of Lord Randolph. She told him that all Churchills were undoubtedly eccentric even when brilliant. Her husband, who died young, was more brilliant that Lord Randolph. Lord W. told how each of two women guests at a Hackwood house-party confided in him separately that Curzon loved only her. All sorts of gossip he reeled off.

Wednesday, 22nd April

Motored to London after work and gave a lift to a man from the Pedestal to High Wycombe. He told me he was a milkman and was only allowed five gallons of petrol a month to do his rounds. When the allowance ran out, he delivered on foot. At Brooks's Eddy S.-W. dined with me. He warned me not to make marriage an objective, declaring that the only successful marriages were chance ones.

Poor Rick [Stewart-Jones] told me that his mother has had a tumour as large as her fist cut out, besides other smaller ones. The ovaries too have been removed, but nothing else vital. Unfortunately some smaller tumours have had to be left and are to be treated with radium.

All were malignant. Di [Murray] rather to my surprise has found faith in some prayer centre people, always a desperate sign with intelligent people.

Thursday, 23rd April

Today at Bradbourne [Kent] that once most romantic, untouched, primitive Queen Anne home of the Twisdens, I was reminded of a meeting in a House of Commons committee room just before the war. A few of us were assembled to discuss how the East Malling Horticultural Research station could buy and establish itself in the place. For some reason Lloyd George joined us. He swept into the room like a whirlwind. When he settled down I observed him. He resembled a red turkey cock with a crest of white feathers. He gobbled and spluttered, was opinionated and rude. When this plethoric old bird announced that he did not care a damn about the beautiful Bradbourne, or for any country house for that matter, I hated him. Of course I was too insignificant for him to address a word to me. But I cast such intensive looks of hatred and indignation at him that he was obliged to notice them. He merely gave me a frown of irritation as though I were a tiresome fly. I was glad that I had at least caused him a fly's irritation.

My reception at the Wool House in Loose was just as Eardley foretold. The house has been divided into two since the war. Miss Hunt lives in one part; some people called Beeson in the other. The house is a hideous, pretentious, genteel over-restored fake, just like its inhabitants. A horrible property. I hope it gets bombed. Miss Hunt shouted a catalogue of grievances against the Trust for not carrying out repairs to the bogus half-timber which she had been obliged to attend to at her expense. It is true that plaster is falling off the panels, and you can see daylight between plaster and beams, most of which should never have been exposed. The Beesons came out of their part and shouted abuse at Miss Hunt, and then at me. I could not bear it and fled, without seeing the museum of African flints and trophies.

Drove down Watling Street, by Gravesend and Deptford. This unconfined, Thames estuary is rather exciting, sprinkled as it is with drifting pylons, factory chimneys and distant gasometers gleaming in the sunshine across the river, with squadrons of bombers flying overhead.

Wickhamford. Up at 7.10 with Deenie to prepare breakfast. This early hour is quite unnecessary, but Deenie fusses inordinately and is in deadly terror of my father. We made porridge, coffee and toast. Papa came down at 8.45 to ask why breakfast wasn't ready — why indeed? — and at that moment the toast, which we had forgotten, burst into flame and, when I had blown it out, emitted black smoke and a stink. The vicar, who had had communion in the church all by himself, came in to talk while we cooked; then Mrs. Haines, then Mrs. Mansfield for a gossip before starting housework; then Haines carrying tins of evil-smelling paraffin. While we were seated round the kitchen table the milkman's wife ambled in to fill the jugs and pass the time of day. Papa took all this informality quite well, though looking very stiff and starch as my grandmother used to look at her croquet parties.

Miss P. told me in the office that the Bath Assembly Rooms had been gutted by fire in the Bath raid on Sunday night. It has upset me dreadfully that so beautiful a building, hallowed by Jane Austen and Dickens, should disappear like this in a single night. Eardley, who was staying the weekend with his mother, came in for the full brunt. He says the Circus has a crater in the middle of the grass, and all its windows are blown out. Two houses in Royal Crescent are burned out, the abbey windows are gone, and the fires and destruction have been devastating. There were no defences, no A.A. guns were heard, and the Germans dived low and machine-gunned the wardens and A.R.P. workers in the streets. This is a reprisal raid for ours over Lübeck. Both raids are sheer barbaric bloody-mindedness, anti-culture and anti-all that life stands for. I positively want not to survive the war when things like this can happen.

At 11 Ted Lister called for me and I took him to Holland House. We walked in at the gates and right up to the house where we talked to the caretaker, who had been on the spot when the house was burnt about a year ago. It is a shell. The only apartment remaining, though badly damaged, is oddly enough the Jacobean staircase, with one of the Jacobean doorways leading to it. The Spanish leather under the stairs is still hanging in festoons from the walls. A sedan chair and a small lacquer chest, half-burnt, are left. The painted panelled room for

52

Charles I which I remembered Lord Ilchester once showing me is gone. We could just distinguish where it had been, and I saw traces of one painted pilaster. The library and everything else irretrievably gone. I am glad I once visited the house, and danced in it, in its heyday. Ted and I walked along the terraces, through the old walled garden and northwards through the park, and down a long lime avenue. The grass was long and unmown, but the trees were fresh and re-budding, quite indifferent to the terrible indignities of last year. The tranquillity made it difficult for us to realize we were in the centre of London. How important it is to preserve what remains of this sanctuary.

I was an usher at Peter Scott's wedding but did precious little work. Kissed K. [Kennet] at the reception but had only a quick word with her. Peter shook hands warmly, and thanked, and God-blessed, which I thought nice of him, considering that I have not given him a present — yet.

At tea on the train a small boy without his mother sat at my table and ordered and ate five chocolate cakes. I wondered if I ought to stop him ordering a sixth, and didn't. I spent twenty minutes with Mrs. S.-J. in her Reading nursing home. She is a pathetic little spectacle, shifting about on the bed from side to side, looking white and ghastly ill. She said that she longed to leave her body. 'I am just about to be sixty, and the children say I am still needed. But I don't know.'

Thursday, 30th April

I sent Lord Esher a cutting from *The Times* of today quoting a Wilhelmstrasse statement that they will make a point of bombing English country houses, those haunts of bloated plutocrats and aristocrats, especially the famous 'Tudor' ones. I think the Germans have now plumbed the depths of human degradation by a positive intention to destroy monuments of art.

In King's Bench Walk I was joined at 10.30 by Harold and Jamesey who had been dining together. Jamesey was bright, affectionate and entertaining. He was ebullient and furious about our senseless destruction of the old town of Lübeck, where he said there were no military or factory objectives of any kind.[1] The 'Baedeker' reprisal bombing was consequently brought about by our foolish philistinism. Even Harold did not deny that this Lübeck raid was a mistake on our part.

[1] James's statement was in fact totally incorrect. Lübeck-Blankensee was a legitimate military target.

I had no idea of this which puts an entirely different complexion on the whole business. Jamesey said we were worse philistines than the Germans, who do at least care for their own monuments whereas the British are bored to tears by theirs. Harold agreed. Then J. and I became provocative. Harold remonstrated with us in an aggrieved, shocked tone once or twice. He says that when we are with him, it is like a sunny day until a magnifying glass (James, I suppose) is applied to shavings. Jamesey asserted that all civilized people desired a compromise peace. Harold hastened to contradict him with a vehemence which suggested to me that he was in secret agreement. I backed Jamesey up. Harold admitted to me later that Singapore was a bad business; also Hong Kong; that our people were demoralized, and did not fight.

Friday, 1st May

In bed during the night I thought—for I could not get to sleep—I am mentally deficient in some respects. My mind is like a ravine with dense patches of fog. I get along all right until suddenly—blank! I become muddled, fuddled, at a loss for words, even thoughts, and quite inconsistent and irrational; often silly and sometimes hysterical.

At breakfast Harold said, 'Jamesey asks me at times, "Did you not realize in September 1939 that this war would mean the end of the world?" Of course I realized that it meant the end of it for us, but not for the vast majority.' I replied that since I did not belong to the vast majority his argument had no appeal for me.

Caught the 10 o'clock from Liverpool Street to Cromer. Met Harry Strauss[1] on the train. I told him what I thought about the bombing of Lübeck. He answered that the Baedeker bombing would have happened anyway, sooner or later—an inept reply. He seemed distraught and although polite in rising from his seat to shake hands, he was not listening to much I said. He is a worthy man, and earnestly loves the country*side* (I find myself writing this awful word, although 'country' is what I mean). Strauss is small and dark, with straight hair in a line across the forehead as though it were a wig.

I waited half an hour or so in Norwich. Walked from the station to the cathedral, but saw no signs at all of bomb damage, and none to the cathedral and close.

I was met at West Runton by the local committee, headed by the

[1] Later Lord Conesford, died 1974.

54

rector, on the station platform. I jumped down hatless and unimpressive. We discussed on the site of the Roman camp (in reality a Napoleonic beacon) with a representative of the Ministry of Supply, the erection of a saw mill on our property. I capitulated, with the committee's concurrence I think. The rector motored me part of the way to Felbrigg. I walked down a lane and along the drive carrying my bag.

It is frightfully cold in Norfolk. There is a bitter wind. The trees are still in bud and hardly green. Ketton-Cremer[1] was not in when I arrived but his manservant, Ward, gave me tea. I learned later that only Ward and his wife 'do'. K.-C. spends most nights at his mother's house, and the daytime here. Then Ketton-Cremer came in. He is big and shapeless, ugly, mild and podgy. He carries his head on one side, and is wan and delicate. He is donnish, extremely cultivated and an urbane and polished writer. He is a trifle ill at ease rather than shy, yet punctilious, methodical and determined. If one let fall ill-considered opinions, he would not leave them unpicked-over, I feel sure. Toryish, if not prejudiced in his views of conduct. Yet open-minded and friendly in a cautious way. Very courteous too. His conversation, though measured and correct, is informative and agreeable. Oh, a most sympathetic man! No wonder Christopher Hobhouse was fond of him.

Saturday, 2nd May

After inspecting our mill at Burnham Staithe I walked to Burnham Market. No food at the Hoste Arms, but at the Nelson I got beer, sausage rolls and hot meat rolls. There were evacuees toping at the bar and recounting their bomb experiences in London. 'The wife said to me, she said, did you ever? Me and my kiddies,' etc. Slightly drunk on a pint of bitter, after my walk, I joined in the conversation and found myself recounting my experiences (they were non-existent) of the Germans and their atrocities. 'Would you believe it,' I said, 'they cut out the heart and began . . .?' 'Well, I never,' they said in a chorus of delight. Cockneys are good-hearted people. These particularly deplored warfare against women and children. Yes, I said, and put in a plea against the deliberate bombing of our cathedrals and churches, to test their reaction. Reaction: 'One in a hundred may care for such old-fashioned places. They are all right to see now and then. It's flesh and

[1] R. Wyndham Ketton-Cremer (1906–69), man of letters and biographer. He bequeathed Felbrigg Hall and estate to the National Trust.

C

blood what matters. For myself, the whole lot can go. Hear! Hear!'
All most good-natured and honestly meant. Philistines!

The old cottages in this part of the world are faced with smooth
flints, or large pebbles picked from the shore, and washed smooth by
the sea. They give a cream to the strawberry brick walls. Sometimes
they look like Easter eggs stacked in a pile by children. All along the
coast to Cromer there is a great structure of iron barricading, covered
with barbed wire in defence against the invaders, if they should come
this way. The bus with a trailer containing gas kept breaking down,
which delayed my return to Runton, whence I had to walk four miles
back to Felbrigg.

Sunday, 3rd May

After luncheon walked with Ketton-Cremer round Felbrigg park,
now mostly under plough. By the lake we were joined by Rick who is
posted at Sheringham for a month's course of gunnery. He was very
dirty in his battledress, but bronzed and shiny with health. Also rather
smelly — tommy-gun oil and sweat — I could not help noticing. He
stayed to tea and departed on his borrowed bicycle. He told us how the
A.T.S. all swore, and that now he did not discriminate between a
gunner and an A.T. in daily intercourse and speech. When Rick had
gone Ketton-Cremer read me his will from beginning to end, asking
for comments. Since the will covered foolscap sheet after sheet, and
like all legal documents had no punctuation whatever, and the fire in
the hall where we sat was hot, I kept dropping off. Politely K.-C.
would throw me a deprecatory glance, and continue: 'And such Trust
moneys may be invested in or laid out or applied in the subscription
or purchase of or at interest upon the security of such stocks funds
shares securities or other properties holdings or investments of whatso-
ever nature and wheresoever as my Trustees shall in their absolute
discretion . . .' Pause, and another interrogative glance. 'That sounds
perfectly satisfactory,' I would say with too little conviction before
nodding off again.

Saturday, 9th May

Over a cup of tea in Brooks's I opened the *New Statesman* and began an
article by Raymond Mortimer on the Royal Academy exhibition. I
read that there was one gallery devoted entirely to pictures by Wilson

Steer and Sickert, that there was a Vanessa Bell of the Queen and princesses, someone else of the Prime Minister and a Moynihan of Eddy Sackville-West. I was so excited that I did not even finish the article or my tea, and rushed to the Academy before it shut, bought a catalogue and went the rounds. Nowhere could I find any of the sixty or so pictures by the most eminent contemporary artists mentioned by Raymond. The beast had, by way of skit, written a mock review of all those artists' works which he would have liked to see exhibited. I was furious with him.

Monday, 11th May

I went to see Miss Davy, Lord Astor's private secretary at the back of St. James's Square. She is a dear lady, dressed in a well-tailored coat and skirt. Lord Astor has decided to make over to the National Trust, with as little delay as possible, Cliveden House, contents and grounds with an endowment of £200,000, and a hospital in the park, providing another £3,000 to £4,000 p.a.

Churchill's broadcast last night, in which he announced that the Germans had already lost more men on the Russian front than they lost in the whole of the last war, and that the Russians had evidence that the Germans might use gas, gave my stomach a twist, and made me think rapidly and desperately all last night.

Thursday, 14th May

Mr. Forsyth the architect met me at Marylebone station at 10.5 and drove me in a respectable Austin saloon up the Great North Road to Norfolk. Mr. Forsyth is so scrupulously polite, correct, pudic and imperturbable that I feel ill at ease. He listens deferentially and nods his head to every inanity that I utter. He clears his throat continuously and speaks in a low voice for fear of being assertive. Conversation in the car is constrained, and dull. He has a queer straight profile with returning Roman nose, like a face cut out of cardboard. No flicker of changing mood alters his dead-pan expression. Never looking to left or right he drives straight ahead hour after hour. I shift uneasily in my seat. I long to let out an expletive like 'Fuck!' just to see how, or even whether Mr. Forsyth would react. Instead I say timidly, 'Mr. Forsyth!' He inclines his granite profile one inch, and says, 'Yes, Mr. Lees-Milne,' with Uriah Heep-like humility. I say, 'If you don't stop this

57

instant and let me get out, I shall burst my bladder.' He is absolutely appalled. I look him full in the profile. I detect a grey flush on the one cheek visible, and a bead of sweat on the brow. He stops the car in silence. As I get out I say in a jolly way, 'Don't you want to pee too?' He actually scowls, and replies, 'Well, I wouldn't put it quite like that,' yet gets out himself. Long after I am relieved, and back in my seat, I see him through the mirror still at it at the rear wheel of the car. Quite clearly he was in just the same straits as I was. Silly ass. I fear I have so shocked him that he will never think the same of me again.

At Attleborough we look at the magnificent fifteenth-century screen in the church. Later we lunch by the roadside on ham sandwiches, national loaf and chocolate.

On arrival at Blickling we are greeted by a sea of Nissen huts in the park in front of the Orangery, and a brick Naafi construction opposite the entrance to the house. The sudden view of the south front takes the breath away. The front is undeniably noble and impressive. We walk round the outside. Then Lord Lothian's secretary, now our house-keeper-caretaker, conducts me round those staterooms on the first floor that are not occupied by the R.A.F. The furniture, which has now been removed to Henley Hall for safety, is under dust sheets. All the best pictures have been removed too. The R.A.F. are in Miss O'Sullivan's bad books for they have needlessly broken several window casements, and smashed the old crown glass. They have forced the locks of the doors into the staterooms, out of devilry. This sort of thing is inevitable.

We stay the night at Rippon Hall with the Birkbecks. He[1] was Lothian's and is now our agent, a genial, simple, woolly bear type, very friendly and co-operative. Over coffee I was handed a vinaigrette of saccharine, early nineteenth century, on the lid of which I noticed Newstead Abbey engraved. 'Oh,' said my hostess, 'that was given by Byron to Mary Chaworth. I thought the engraving was Westminster Abbey or something.'

Friday, 15th May

At Melton Constable we were welcomed most kindly by Lord Hastings,[2] who is living in the stable wing, lateral to the main block. He is

[1] Christopher Birkbeck (1889–1973).
[2] 21st Lord Hastings (1882–1956).

a sort of Edwardian stage peer with a purple visage. He wears his hat at a roué's angle. He is vastly proud of the place and has recently celebrated his family's 700th anniversary of their lordship of Melton Constable, unbroken from father to son, which is remarkable. He prefaced his reception of us with a resumé of his family honours and connections. His ignorance of the house's architecture was however startling. He kept dogmatizing pompously, and wrongly, about this and that feature. The house is ruined to my mind by the 1880 additions. They could easily be pulled down so as to leave the lovely 'Wren' block intact. But Lord Hastings prefers them to the original house. A pity that it has lost its roof balustrade and cupola. We looked at the church in the park. It contains a Caroline family pew hugely out of proportion to the nave, and an ugly war memorial to the men of Melton Constable. It is headed by the name in large letters of The Hon. — Astley, followed underneath by the names in smaller lettering of the humble privates and gunners of the village.

Sunday, 17th May

Sir Courtauld-Thomson's[1] proposition is an extraordinary one. He wants to make over Dorney Wood and the 250 acres in which it stands to the National Trust now, reserving a life interest to himself, aged seventy-seven, and his sister, aged seventy-nine, with an endowment of £30,000, and on his death to leave a further endowment of £170,000, a preposterously large sum. The house is to be used as a small Chequers either by the Prime Minister or a Cabinet Minister recommended by the reigning Prime Minister. Mrs. Churchill is lunching with Courtauld-Thomson on Monday to look at the place and report to her husband. If the Prime Minister approves, the National Trust and the Government must fight out the problem of holding and administering the endowment. The house is not up to our standard, although a fairly pleasant red brick building, now swathed in, rather dribbling with, great bunches of wonderful wisteria. The central part is possibly of Queen Anne time. Lorimer's additions are indifferent in C.-T.'s opinion which I felt free to corroborate. The outbuildings, motor-house, etc. have been faked about in half-timbering to look olde-worlde. The green fields close to Burnham Beeches, in which the house stands, should be preserved. There are several good contents, a

[1] Sir Courtauld-Thomson (1865–1954) was created Lord Courtauld-Thomson, 1944.

large collection of mezzotints and engravings, much late eighteenth-century imitation bamboo furniture (beech really), very pretty.

Sir Courtauld is a weird person. I do not quite understand him. Matheson thinks he is after a peerage, and I think he may be disingenuous. He appears to be a very kind old man and devoted to his faithful retainers, whom he pats on the shoulder and orders about gruffly with a twinkle (to the gallery) in his eye to fetch and carry—for their own use and recreation. For instance he sternly ordered his man, who had been unwell, to fetch a chair from the garden house, place it on a certain spot on the lawn and there sit himself down and rest, without moving until he was told.

Eddy said this evening that I was very bad in keeping my friends apart, that I did not like them meeting, and that this was 'one of my small perversities'.

Friday, 22nd May

I was the last to leave the office for the Whitsun holiday, and motored to Wickhamford. Immediately outside the West Wycombe gates a young hitch-hiker hailed me. He told me he had walked throughout the previous night from Oxford to Marlow solely to buy some books, which I thought most laudable. Outside Halls, the shirtshop in Oxford High Street, Auberon Herbert was standing on the pavement. He dragged me off to tea in his rooms in Oriel Street. He said Gabriel [Herbert] was coming to stay the night with him, so I said I would stay too. He had just been staying with the Zogs at Parmoor. He said Queen Geraldine was a real beauty and the little Crown Prince, already a prodigy of learning at the age of four, knew four languages. The Queen's grandmother, a dreadful old American matron, lives with them, and never draws breath for speaking. King Zog is frankly a cad. He wants to buy *The Times* newspaper and told Auberon, 'And I won't give a penny more than ten million for it.' The princesses were present and he overheard them openly speculating on his sexual potentialities. Auberon, who speaks Albanian, understood every word. Champagne flowed before and during every meal. The King enjoys diplomatic status, does nothing but nurse his majesty and take tiny, Parisian walks.

Auberon, long, lanky, pale, with his square, low-eyebrowed little face, has much charm. He burbles rather than speaks words, which proceed from his mouth like water from an air-locked pipe.

60

Mrs. Stewart-Jones has been brought back from the nursing home. They found she could not stand the radium treatment and since her chances of recovery are now nil, they have chosen the melancholy course of making her as comfortable as possible in her own room at Cheyne Walk surrounded by the family. She has two nurses and is not expected to live more than three weeks at most. Rick said goodbye to his mother yesterday morning while she was well enough to talk to him, and both were happy. He and I dined together and talked of everything except her condition. I slept in my old room on a lielow, R. in the bed, and was reminded of that evening in September 1938 when we expected war, and the situation was reversed, I in the bed and R. on the lielow. How intense was the agony of unhappiness then.

Thursday, 28th May

Lord Lytton talked about transferring Knebworth to the Trust, as I expected. He betrayed no misgivings about Knebworth being unacceptable on historic or architectural grounds. Since one cannot turn down a man's offer without first seeing the place, I persuaded him to let me go over the property with him in order to report to the committee. Graciously he consented. He is tall, immaculately dressed in a black suit with a long, thin gold chain round his neck, the end of the chain hidden in a waistcoat pocket. He has silvery hair, curling at the back, handsome regular features and a stick-like manner. He is rather pompous, dry, fussy and I should guess, difficult.

I lunched in Cornwall Gardens with Margaret Jourdain and Ivy Compton-Burnett. Ernest Thesiger[1] was the fourth person. He is an old pansy, affected, meticulous, garrulous and entertaining. I had not met him before. We were introduced in the dark hall. M.J. 'So you have met on the way up?' E.T. 'I knew at once he was the sort of young man you would rope in.' M.J. 'He is quite a new acquisition.' We sat in a high-ceilinged, pitch-dark dining-room, with one window opening upon blank walls and a fire escape. We ate lentil soup, white fish with sauce and steamed potatoes, a rhubarb and ginger tart, Morecambe shrimps and biscuits. Margaret Jourdain opened a large bottle of Cidrax, poured out Thesiger's and my glasses and was about to pour her own when Miss C.-B. shouted, 'Margaret! Remember at

[1] Ernest Thesiger (1879–1961), actor.

breakfast it was decided that you were to finish the opened bottle of flat Cidrax.'

She makes very acid comments in a prim, clipped manner, enunciating sharply and clearly every syllable, while casting at one a sidelong glance full of mischief. We talked about servants. She agreed that today fewer servants managed to get through double the work, doubly efficiently, to what a greater number did a generation ago. They are better fed and housed, she said. Her parents took care to have excellent food themselves, whereas their children were thrown the scraps. While today children are given pheasant and all that goes with it, in her day they were given the chips and bread sauce, but no pheasant. For supper she used to be given the crusts cut from her parents' toast. She has an insatiable appetite for chocolates, and Ernest Thesiger told her she was intemperate in some of her habits. Miss Jourdain gave us cherry brandy, but did not offer any to Miss C.-B., who took some for herself. She swigged it all in one gulp instead of sipping, declaring that it was excellent and she would have some more. Miss J. intervened and would not allow it.

Talking of sham marbling as a form of wall decoration, Miss C.-B. said, 'I'm all for shams. So long as they are good ones, what do they matter?' Miss Jourdain said of Freya Stark, who is at present broadcasting from Cairo under the direction of the Foreign Secretary, that hers 'is the voice that breathed o'er Eden'.

Saturday, 30th May

I picked flowers to take to Mrs. Stewart-Jones in London. When I reached Cheyne Walk after tea, I learned that she was dying and not expected to last many hours. All the family were wonderfully calm and resigned. Di took in my flowers and about 7.30 came to tell me I could now go in to see her, for she was having a lucid moment. I went in. She lay in a bed by the window at the far corner of the room. Rick was at one side of the bed, offering her a drink of water from a spoon, Edward[1] holding her hand at the other side, and Di sitting by the window smiling at me. I went to the end of the bed and blew her a kiss, to which she replied by raising her hand to her lips very feebly. I was struck by the change in her appearance, particularly by her sunken eyes and the sharp, thin line of her jaw. She was propped against raised pillows. Di said to her, 'Jim has brought you these

[1] Edward Stewart-Jones (d. 1972), brother of Richard and Diona Murray.

62

flowers,' and to me, 'Tell her you have brought them for her.' So I said rather foolishly, 'I hope you like them. They came from the garden today.' Edward raised the bowl of roses and honeysuckle and handed her a rose to smell. She understood perfectly and looking at it, said, 'Lovely' in a slow, painful way. This was, I believe, the last word she spoke. She looked at me a little and smiled, then closed her eyes and remained so quiet for a few seconds that I thought she must have died. I saw Rick glance at Edward who did not move a feature. Then she took a deep breath and held her hand to her breast. I noticed how swollen her hands were, and blue. Rick gave me a chair to sit on, but I felt embarrassed by seeming to be curious in just watching her die; and wondered if she were aware of us all listening to her awkward breathing. So I quietly slipped away.

I slept that night in my old room, Edward on the lielow on the floor, R. in the next-door room where Di and Eff were also sleeping. At about 1.30 I heard R. leaning over Edward and whisper something like, 'She is unconscious.' Then I went to sleep again.

Sunday, 31st May

I am only glad to be here at this particular moment because for once in my life I am able to help others. I can wash up — for we eat upstairs by ourselves — run messages and I hope, cheer at times. Nanny brought me a cup of tea at 8 and when I asked how Mrs. S.-J. had passed the night, she answered, 'She left at 1.30 in her sleep quite peacefully and looks happy and beautiful.' People always say these words, and I wonder if they are ever true. At breakfast there was no reference to what had happened so that I wondered if indeed it had.

Rick was particularly anxious for me to go and see her, so I did. When I opened the door the wind through the wide open window blew the bed clothes about gently. Mrs. S.-J. lay on her back as though asleep, with her head visible on the pillow. The room was unnaturally quiet. A screen had been put round the head of the bed, my lupins on the side table, and photographs of all the children, including my Peter Scott drawing, around her. Her handbag by the bed and a handkerchief on the topsheet. It was difficult to believe she was not just asleep as I tiptoed up as though not to wake her. Her grey hair had been platted and the wind was fanning the loose wisps very gently which gave a further impression of life and only sleep. I looked very closely at her dear little head. The colour was fairly natural, but the features were

c*   63 very sharp and the eye sockets sadly deepened. R. had also said how young and beautiful she was looking; but somehow I did not like the hard line of her tight shut mouth which was not at all characteristic, for in life she had the sweetest, most innocent face conceivable. The outline of her tiny body under the thin covering of the sheet was pathetic.

Monday, 1st June

Matheson met me at Brooks's. He prefaced the interview with the remark, 'If I may say so, I think you have done extremely well in my absence.' I replied, 'Well, that remains for you to find out when you return to the office.' How can he have the slightest indication whether I have done well or ill, yet?

Today Rick went to a memorial service for his mother at Leckhampstead, which the villagers had organized on their own. The church was packed with the inhabitants of Leckhampstead and the neighbouring villages. On the way down R. bought sixty cream buns at Newbury, and after the service entertained all the schoolchildren and their parents in his mother's house. He said it was one of the most satisfactory days of his life and just what his mother would have liked.

Saturday, 6th June

A cloudless, grilling day, wonderful to live through. Miss Compton-Burnett and Miss Jourdain came down from London to lunch. I met them at High Wycombe station where they inadvertently left the return halves of their tickets. Away from her own house Miss C.-B. is not quite herself, but at luncheon when we were discussing what we ought to do with the Germans at the end of the war, she came out with a startling, 'I am actuated by a healthy spirit of revenge.' She was wearing a beige governessy dress, beige stockings and a beige straw hat to match. She was very spruce and upright. After luncheon I conducted Miss Jourdain round the house. Miss C.-B. sat all the time on the edge of a Windsor chair, wearing her hat and clutching her parasol as though just about to leave. Walking up the drive they both carried their parasols open although under the trees. Eddy said they looked the epitome of late Victorian, middle-class respectability. Helen noticed how nothing escaped them, how their beady eyes looked through her, up and down, through her, letting nothing slip, quietly curious, missing nothing.

64

Miss C.-B. remarked to Eddy (apropos her greed), 'I like Manchester. One gets such good teas there.'

I asked her at luncheon to which county she belonged. She said, 'Wilt-sheer', for her father had a house there when she was a child. I think the Hills told me she had a brother, whom she adored, killed in the last war, and two sisters, each of whom committed suicide in the same room within an interval of some three years.

Her opening remark to Eddy was, 'We are such cowards. We both hate air-raids and are frightened to death of bombs.' To me she said, 'We could never possibly win a George Cross.' 'You never know,' I answered, 'the most unlikely people have done so.' She said, 'We might be the cause of someone else getting it through our being in the way for them to save.'

Sunday, 7th June

Eddy was staying last weekend at Victor Cazalet's, where King Peter and the Queen of Yugoslavia were guests. They brought no retinue, no valet or maid, only one lady-in-waiting. The King had an enormous Cadillac in which they drove to the cinema in Cranbrook. The King washed up after dinner, or rather carried some glasses into the pantry and made a gesture of washing up, *pour rire*. Eddy liked the Queen, who is stout and simple, and intelligent. He did not much care for the King, whom she addressed as 'Son'.

Wednesday, 10th June

After dinner I went down to Miss Millbourne's cottage in the village where Captain Hill and William Weir were dining. I guessed that Miss Millbourne had been sitting on the empty chair because it felt warm when my bottom touched it. Weir is a splendid old man, and so Scotch that often I cannot understand what he is saying. Now that Troup is dead he is the father of the S.P.A.B. committee. He is the foremost expert at repairing old buildings alive today. He told us he knew William Morris intimately, and in Morris's lifetime looked after Kelmscott for him. He also worked under Philip Webb whom he considers the greatest architect of his time. Weir helped Webb build Clouds for the Wyndhams. Mr. Wyndham wanted Morris to do the interior decorations; and Weir was present when Morris visited Clouds during a weekend while the guests were lounging about the

65

hall in armchairs. Morris was provoked to say: 'I see this is already a home for incurables.' Weir said there was no one quite like A. R. Powys[1] for distinction of manner, appearance and scholarship.

Weir is always eager to impart the knowledge he has gained throughout a full working lifetime. He gave Hill and me several hints which we put down on paper. For re-leading roofs he advised the use of 'cast' rather than 'milled' lead, in sheets no larger than 7 ft. by 3 ft., in order to avoid excessive expansion and contraction; and the use always of old lead for re-casting. He said lead will perish if laid on oak, owing to some form of acid in oak. Even the lead casings of electric light wires will so perish, whereas they will not if laid on pine. With regard to beetle, he said the bugs begin eating the damp parts of wood where there is sap, which is usually on the ends of timber resting in the walls. The bugs then work their way to the dry wood in the centre. Beetle won't attack pine, and never pitch pine where there is resin. The time to de-beetle is in May and June when the creatures fly out to mate, returning to lay eggs at the end of their three years' existence. He considered Heppels Fluid far the best antidote for beetle, although too strong for furniture. It is apt to take away varnish and polish.

Saturday, 13th June

I took a bus to Knebworth where I was met by the agent and motored to Knebworth Manor. Lord Lytton pompous, courteous in a keep-your-distance manner, patrician and vice-regal. He was wearing rather precious country clothes, a too immaculate tweed suit, a yellow-green shirt of large checks loose at the collar, and that gold chain round the neck again. He has truly beautiful blue eyes. If one did not know otherwise one would suppose him to be what my father calls 'effeminate' by the well cut, yet long silver hair deliberately curled over the nape of his neck.

We walked through the gardens to Knebworth House. It is undeniably hideous. The old house was rebuilt by Bulwer Lytton in 1847, and if only Lord Lytton had not recently removed the gargoyles from the absurd turrets and the heraldic animals from the terrace, it would be a perfect specimen of a Disraelian patrician's Gothic mansion. The whole outside is stuccoed in a base way. The Jacobean grand staircase and the Presence Chamber upstairs are terribly shoddy. The only room

[1] Brother of T. F., John Cooper, and Llewelyn Powys. He was for many years Secretary of the S.P.A.B. He died in 1937.

that I liked was the Palladianized great hall. Lord Lytton has had the paint stripped off the wainscote. He said it was the first stripping to be undertaken in England. At present the Froebel Girls' College is installed in the house, which becomes them. Lord Lytton is determined to return to the house after the war. I insisted on going round the estate for he offers the whole 3,000 acres in endowment. My view is that the estate is more worth holding, because of its nearness to London, than the house, for all its historic associations.

We had tea with Lady Lytton who is still a beautiful woman. The tragedy of Antony Knebworth[1] hangs heavily upon her.

I got back to London late for dinner to find Jamesey waiting. We dined at Brooks's over claret and returned to his flat in Chester Square where I stayed the night. We talked of Bulwer Lytton and he lent me a book about him.

Jamesey said he wanted to sleep with a woman, and expressed misgivings. I said it was as easy as falling off a log. The moment these words were out of my mouth I realized how discouraging the simile must have sounded.

Sunday, 14th June

I went to Dorney Wood to tea with Sir Courtauld-Thomson who wanted to tell me all about his luncheon with the Prime Minister yesterday at Chequers. To his delight Churchill insisted upon motoring to Dorney Wood there and then in spite of the fact that he habitually rests every afternoon. Mrs. Churchill and Miss Thomson motored in the Thomsons' car, Sir Courtauld with Churchill in his. The car is armour-plated and the windows are bullet-proofed, an inch thick. Churchill had a tommy gun beside him which he played with throughout the journey. He was wearing his siren suit and smoking endless cigars. Sir C. said he was in the best of form; and Sir C. was flattered to death at engaging the Prime Minister's attention from 1 till 7 p.m. Churchill has evidently approved the scheme and told Lord Portal he must accept the offer without to-do. Sir C. expressed some anxiety over the endowment and death duties, and Churchill said quite calmly but firmly, 'Then I shall have an Act of Parliament passed.' Although a quondam Chancellor of the Exchequer Winston showed childlike ignorance about death duties.

[1] Antony, Viscount Knebworth (1903–33), was a paragon about whom a memoir, *Antony*, was published in 1935.

At the White Hart in Lincoln I met Lord Brocket who motored over from Burghley. He drove me in his blue two-seater Rolls-Bentley up the Roman road to Norton Place. Here we met Major Hoult, his agent, and his nephew, a Colonel Trevor (younger than me), in the Commandos. We motored round the whole property. Lord Brocket went conscientiously into every cottage and over every farm building. We spent two hours doing this. The outcome was that he did not agree with Captain Hill that the estate is 'derelict'.

At 5.30 we left for Culverthorpe, giving lifts on our way to R.A.F.s and W.A.A.F.s. Brocket is breezy and good-natured, although he does 'buck' a bit. He has a slightly tiresome seeing-the-sunny-side-of-every-thing manner. He is amusingly conscious of his nobility, and explained at great length his Irish descent from the O'Cains, whoever they may be. His crest of a cat rampant figures prominently on the radiator of his car. However, he is condescending enough to include me among the well-bred. He did not care much for Culverthorpe. I think it is lovely although in a deplorable condition owing to the troops stationed in the house all the war. The splendid hall has been partitioned into an orderly room and officers' mess with passage in between. The capitals of the columns have been boarded up, and the Wootton panels shrouded under canvas. I noticed a great crack in the Hauderoy painted ceiling over the stairs. Many glass panes are broken and the surrounds of one window are blackened by a projecting stove pipe.

We reached Ayot St. Lawrence at 11 p.m. The whole village, olde worlde and rather horrifying, particularly the Brocket Arms, belongs to him. Much to my surprise he banged on the inn door. I saw he had been leading up to something. It was to be a pretty piece of patronage. The publican opened the door and there was a great deal of, 'Oh, your lord-shape! You must come in. My friends would be honoured to see your lord-shape,' for it was after closing time. We were ushered into the saloon bar, I keeping well to the rear like a bad smell. The publican clapped his hands, and announced in an awful voice, 'This is Lord Brocket.' B., still wearing his cap at a jaunty angle, beamed, bowed and received the homage of a dozen demi-mondaines and flash-alfs during an impressive hush. Trying to be inconspicuous I was pushed forward. I must say B.'s friendliness is unfeigned. He introduced me to all and sundry, and shook hands with them in a hearty fashion. The peer charmingly condescending. We were supplied with 'gin and It' and cheese rolls. There was much forced hilarity, B. nudging me and laughing a bit too much. With more ushering, the other way round, and 'Good night, Lord Brocket! Good night your lord-shape,' we swept out, having caused a stir, and left them all astounded.

We got to Brocket at midnight. The big house is filled with expectant and parturiating mothers from the East End, so Brocket keeps a room at Warren House across the lake, a little seventeenth-century bailiff's house. Here we drank tea and ate sausage rolls. I asked him outright how closely associated he really had been with Hitler. He said he had only met Hitler three times through H . . . (whose name I forget), his link with the Nazis. He knew Ribbentrop quite well, and liked Goering, who was 'the only gent of the party'. In fact Brocket has faint hopes even now that at some future date terms might be reached through Goering. I asked him if he had believed Hitler to be honest. He said, 'No, not exactly.' From the first he thought him repellent and abnormal. For instance, in 1938 Hitler foretold that something dramatic must happen on 1st October that year. H . . . told Brocket that to make sure the Führer's presentiment was fulfilled the leading Nazis felt obliged to arrange that something—no matter what—should take place for face-saving reasons. The democratic press had infuriated Hitler by saying the Germans were massing along the Czech frontier, whereas they were not doing so. The democratic press was Hitler's bugbear, and he told Brocket that Chamberlain ought to put the English press lords in a concentration camp. Brocket replied, 'I agree. Only you will have to put your press controllers in camps likewise, and we shall all be happier.' And Hitler added, 'I will put them in the same camp.'

Brocket greatly admired and liked Chamberlain. The truth is that although Brocket is a fundamentally nice man, he is stupid. Chamberlain ought not to have been so intimate with a man of his calibre. One infers that the fleshpots of Brocket and Bramshill were a bait. At any rate Chamberlain made a confidant of Brocket who found himself in an exalted position undeservedly. Then he was made a scapegoat. B. told me that because he was so frequently in Germany and was so closely connected with the leading Nazis Halifax used him as a channel through which to communicate to Hitler and Ribbentrop the views of the Government. He assured me that he constantly warned the Nazi leaders that Britain would fight, if only with her fists, were the Germans to march into Poland. The Nazis just would not believe this threat. Hitler never relinquished his belief that Chamberlain had bluffed him at Munich by pretending that Britain was in a position to fight, if sufficiently provoked, nor his subsequent conviction that such action was quite impossible. Hitler harboured a grievance against Chamberlain ever after.

Brocket's nervous breakdown at the beginning of the war was brought about by the aspersions thrown at him from all quarters. He confesses that he has not yet recovered, and cannot walk any distance, and is suffering from a weak heart. At all events he was graded Class 4 and rejected for military service. At the end of these confidences he said we must be on christian name terms; but I don't for the life of me know what his name is. I feel rather sorry for him. He is by no means dislikeable.

Sunday, 21st June

I sat reading all morning while Brocket interviewed his men of various kinds. He is a very keen and enthusiastic landowner, and flits from one country seat to another. We motored across the park to the pub for luncheon, and ate cold but excellent lamb sandwiches and drank shandy. He is too breezy with yokels in the bar. It don't quite ring true, embarrasses me a lot and them a little, I dare say.

Brocket told me that the ironwork clairvoyée, gates and railings, came from the Grove, Chiswick, and are a pair to and contemporary with the Devonshire House gates now in the Green Park. They certainly are fine, in spite of the addition of the Brocket cat rampant, an excusable vanity, and quite in the tradition of the new nobility.

I returned to West Wycombe while the 9 o'clock news was blaring. Helen and Gerry Villiers, listening-in in the dining-room, were very depressed about the fall of Tobruk. It is a great disaster and seems unaccountable. It has been a terribly hot day. Lovely days will always be associated by me with international crises, like the ghastly fall of France, and indeed the outbreak of the war, and then the Battle of Britain.

Thursday, 25th June

I attended an interview with the Chief Medical Officer of Health at the Ministry about the Cliveden hospital problem: whether or not the Government will give an assurance that they will rent the hospital after the war, if it is made over to the Trust as endowment. Both Sir Wilson Jameson, the Chief Medical Officer, and Sir John Maude, who is Secretary to the Minister, gave an assurance that the hospital *would* be used right enough, although they could not provide a rental figure, or affirm whether one would be forthcoming. This is not altogether satisfactory. When I saw Miss Davy afterwards, she said that Lord Astor was adopting the attitude of 'take it or leave it' (Cliveden). We must make up our minds at once. This is hardly fair, for the Trust cannot commit itself to accepting a property of such size without carefully weighing income and expenditure.

Friday, 26th June

I found a mural tablet in Oxford Cathedral which fascinated me. I looked at it a long time, and it gave me a strange aesthetic kick. It is quite small, of a Viscount Brounker and his lady, *circa* 1645, in relief. The two of them are reclining, he with his head on his hand, a bland, round, moustachioed head, like that of any bluff, extrovert Brigade officer today, caught in a quick moment of questioning the vanities of his profession. His wife has the seraphic, resigned look of the wise little woman who already knows the answer.

I sat in the shade of St. Mary's looking across at the Radcliffe Camera, meaning to wait until my appointment at 11.45 in New College. Evidently my watch had stopped, for I suddenly awoke to the fact that it was 12.15. I ran to the Warden's House. Mrs. H. A. L. Fisher was quite unconcerned about my lateness. She is a hirsute, plain, very untidy elderly lady, wearing no stockings (at her age!) and showing black, wiry legs emerging from shabby, down-at-heel slippers. She was packing to leave, and was very abrupt, efficient and self-assured. Not at all my sort of woman. The house not my sort of house either. Only the small panelled room over the porter's lodge was worth a glance, apart from the Restoration stairway with continuous newel posts. Though coarse, this is the outstanding feature.

I dined at Braemar Mansions, where there was a lot of plain cooking to be got down. Basil Marsden-Smedley the other guest, a very loosely knit man with one withered arm. Miss Compton-Burnett was so defeatist about the news that Miss Jourdain rebuked her. Miss C.-B. complained that Miss J. on the other hand always thinks the war will be over in three days' time. Miss J. hotly denied this, and the two contradicted one another. Miss C.-B. said of Tobruk, 'If *she* is of no use strategically, why do we endeavour to hold *her*?' She told another story against their friend at Chedworth, laughing so much that she

71

could barely get the words out. The friend is so unpopular in the neighbourhood that her only social intercourse with the local colonels, vicars and doctors is achieved through blood transfusion parties. She goes to one after another, where they all lie prone on sofas and the floor in most intimate positions, and are publicly 'cupped' in turn, and refreshed with tea afterwards.

Speaking of Dorothy Wordsworth Miss C.-B. said she was 'sadly' in love with William, who reciprocated the passion. It was definitely incestuous, she affirmed. Miss J. denied this. Miss C.-B. said that she knew Virginia Woolf to speak to when they met, but that was all. She thinks she was not a great novelist, but a great writer in other respects. She did not enjoy *Between the Acts*, which betrayed muddled thinking, and was 'too flimsy'. We talked of diaries like Pepys's which had been expurgated in the nineteenth century. When unexpurgated editions came out these days, she was invariably disappointed. There was never much revealed after all. She said that Charlotte M. Yonge was 'a potential strayer'. It amused her that in *Cranford*, when Lady X after her *mésalliance* with the doctor, explained that the two of them had long had an 'understanding', the ladies of Cranford found the word coarse. The Duke of Windsor had had an 'understanding' with Mrs. Simpson right enough.

Saturday, 27th June

I drop a pound of truffles on Miss C.-B. first thing, to assuage her passion for chocolate.

I look at the picture of the week on show in the National Gallery. It would be an excellent plan never to show more than one picture at a time. I look greedily, intimately into the Pieter de Hooch courtyard, examining the details of the pump, the Flemish bond of the brick walls, the plaster flaking away, the worn steps. The scene might be any old woman's backyard today.

I dine with Johnnie Churchill[1] and his new little wife. Pam[2] and Derek Jackson join us in the neat little flat. Derek is positively pro-Nazi. What a catching disease Mitfordism is! There is Derek, a gallant man older than me, a rear-gunner in air-force blue, awarded a D.F.C., in private life a brilliant scientist, saying that we can't win the war, that he loathes the British lower classes who have forced us into this un-

[1] John George Spencer-Churchill, artist and old friend.
[2] Hon. Pamela Mitford, married 1936 Professor Derek Jackson.

necessary war (absolute tosh!), and that the Germans know the best way of treating them, which is to crush them under heel. We argued. I think he cannot be absolutely in earnest, but is probably more so than a stranger might suppose possible.

Before the Jacksons came Johnnie told me about his experiences at Dunkirk. He said it was hell, but not such hell as an ordinary air-raid on London. He did not see many of our people die, but he did see Belgian civilians cutting off the heads of German parachutists; and he watched unmoved German airmen burning to death in their planes. He felt very savage, yet exalted. Although only a camouflage major he was put in charge of a whole company of men whose captain, a Highland officer, had been removed for cutting off the fingers of German prisoners for their rings.

Sunday, 28th June

I walked from the station to Clandon where Noel and Giana Blakiston are living among the stored documents from Noel's Record Office. Otherwise they and the two children have this enormous house to themselves. They live in the small room on the right of the hall, and dine in the servants' quarters in the basement. The house is dirty and in decay. We went on to the roof. One chimney stack had a name and the date 1790 carved on the brick. The lead on the roof is thin in places and needs recasting, and relaying. The hall and most of the downstairs rooms are stuffed with records. After tea Noel and the children gave a play in a toy theatre, with scenery of Clandon made by themselves. The words were written by Noel in Pope couplets, very cleverly. The Blakistons are sweet people.

There is a kind of grotto at Clandon, the roof picked out in hewn flint and brick, interspersed with the bottoms and necks of wine bottles.

Wednesday, 1st July

To London for an S.P.A.B. meeting to discuss the society's policy about the rebuilding of churches and other monuments after the war. Esher was in the chair. There was, as I expected, considerable difference of opinion, and some members like Mr. Hiorns bored us very much with long, irrelevant dissertations. Lord Esher was clearly not in favour of any form of rebuilding, it seemed to me. I do not go as far as this myself and think that each case must be judged according to its own merits and the state of its damage; that certain churches like St. James's, Piccadilly, where more than the outside walls have survived and where detailed and measured drawings exist, should be rebuilt as they were. Finally a sub-committee was appointed to elaborate the memorandum drafted by John Macgregor.[1]

Macgregor said that the original moulds for the plaster cornices at the Assembly Rooms, Bath, were known to exist, which favours the argument of those wishing to rebuild the Rooms.

Friday, 3rd July

At the Jardin des Gourmets we had a modest dinner, with only lager to drink, and the bill was £1 11s. 6d. for two. It is monstrous! You pay 7/6 table cover, for the mere privilege of sitting down. In fact the new limit of 5/– for every meal seems to be evaded and the price of meals to be increased if anything.

Monday, 6th July

After cashing a cheque at the club and buying Turkish cigarettes at Benson & Hedges I went straight to Miss Davy, whom I now treat like a beloved, old-fashioned aunt. I showed her the figures of our estimates for running the Cliveden property. She believes that what is worrying Lord Astor most is the question how much rental the hospital may command, for if it yields £3,000 p.a. endowment, why should he hand over unnecessary capital to produce that amount. She said to me, as aunt to nephew confidentially, 'As a matter of fact Lord Astor in giving away £200,000 is actually losing only £150 a year.' It is fantastic how high taxation is.

I went straight to the Georgian Group meeting and sat next to Dame Una. Professor Richardson made her and me into a sub-committee to deal with the affiliation of schools, which Mrs. Esdaile's son, a schoolmaster at Stowe, is sponsoring. Dame Una is very much *en deuil* like a French war widow. I put her into a taxi and went to Horne & Birkett.[2]

Mr. Horne took me to lunch at the Law Society, a kind of club. We had a perfectly horrid luncheon, and the cabinet pudding with sweet custard nearly made me sick. Had I only not taken the custard I could

[1] A pupil of William Weir and leading architect-restorer of ancient buildings.
[2] Messrs. Horne & Birkett, Lincoln's Inn Fields, the National Trust's solicitors. Mr. Horne was the operative figure in the firm.

have put the pudding into my handkerchief while Horne was not looking. We then walked across Fleet Street to Withers & Co., solicitors to Major Fuller of Great Chalfield. On the way Horne, to my surprise, pointed with his stick and said: 'That is where Clifford's Inn was, and where I used regularly to have tea with my old friend, Samuel Butler.' I asked him what he was like. He said he was a little shrivelled man with a scrubby beard and eyes that twinkled mischievously. He had been at school with Horne's uncle and was an old Salopian. He lived with an odd sort of servant. Butler and Horne watched the Coronation (King Edward's) together.

The Withers' solicitor was stout and pompous. Afterwards Mr. Horne said, 'That man would have browbeaten me if I had been just an insignificant little attorney instead of a solicitor of standing.' I was impressed.

From 4 till 6 we were closeted with the Brettingham agent, a fairly handsome bounder. This man cast glad eyes at me. He did this once before. He is very genteel and familiar in an uncertain sort of way.

Old Ted Lister took me to *Iolanthe* which began at 6.45. We sat in the front row of the stalls. Ted adored it and chortled so loudly that I was embarrassed. 'We couldn't help ourselves,' they sang. And the Fairy Queen commented, 'But you seem to have helped yourselves liberally.' In the interval I rang up Cheyne Walk and was told that Q. had been trying to get hold of me. I had a sharp pang, for this information made me wish I were with Q., drinking wine and flirting with her in some expensive restaurant instead of with old Ted in Schmidt's (whither we went to drink dark beer and eat Frankfurter sausages).

Ted gave me this example of how women stink and men do not. Mrs. Jenkins was playing the harp one hot afternoon at Westwood, and smelt horribly. Then her daughter sang and she stank so much that Ted had to put his handkerchief to his nose and rush to the window to avoid being sick. Then the son played the harp and the nostrils could detect nothing amiss. However, Ted would not risk a repetition of mother and daughter's performances, and moved the whole party on to the lawn.

Thursday, 9th July

I met Sir Courtauld-Thomson by appointment. He is going to see Lord Portal[1] tomorrow about Dorney Wood, having asked Sir John

[1] 1st Viscount Portal (1885–1949), industrialist. Minister of Works 1940–42.

Anderson, who is a member of Brooks's, what sort of a man Portal is. The reply was that he is a very cautious man who before making a decision endeavours to fathom peoples' motives.

I stepped out of Truefitts straight into Heywood Hill's shop, and the horrid, pungent Brilliantine which they put on my hair nearly asphyxiated everybody. Nancy said that if there had been a window that opened, she would open it. She told me she had refused to go to Deborah Cavendish's[1] ball or to any party because the news was so bad, and this attitude had annoyed Helen who is staying with her. Tom [Mitford] is in Libya and may at this moment be fighting for his life. He is in the armoured division, she thinks diverted there from India in order to reinforce our troops. She also refuses to use her electricity for hot water, and this too annoys Helen quite a bit. The public, she says piously, have been asked to save electricity.

Friday, 10th July

Matheson, Eardley and I attended an absurd Trust meeting at Watlington [Park], absurd because there was not a single committee member apart from the chairman. When it was over Esher sent Eardley and me out of the room in order to discuss with Matheson the staff reorganization. Eardley and I stood in the hall straining our ears to catch what Matheson was shouting to Esher, who is a little deaf. I crept down the passage as far as I dared. I nearly reached the keyhole but Eardley made me giggle so much that I had to come away for fear of betraying myself.

Saturday, 11th July

On my way to stay with Midi in her cottage on the Buscot estate I had an hour between buses to spend in Oxford. I wandered into the Sheldonian Theatre. An old, bent woman sold me an admission ticket and would follow me, sitting and breathing heavily whenever I stopped to look at the ceiling. This irritated me profoundly and I asked acidly if visitors were never left alone. She said No, they weren't. Thereupon I lost my temper, and walked straight out. In one way and another the Sheldonian leaves something to be desired.

After luncheon Midi and I bicycled to see Margaret Douglas-Home,

[1] Lady Andrew Cavendish, now Duchess of Devonshire. She is the youngest daughter of the 2nd Lord Redesdale.

living in another cottage, but in Buscot village. It is a single sitting-roomed workman's cottage, and her children play in the street with the other village children. Margaret got the George Medal a year ago for saving two children, one after the other, from a blazing house in the East End during a blitz. She told Midi she did not do it out of courage but anger with the children's mother for making a scene in the street. She had to break one child's leg to release it from a fallen beam. She gave her name as Mrs. Hume and walked away. But her identity was discovered. After tea we bicycled over the fields and across the river to Kelmscott [Manor].

The old, grey stone, pointed gables are first seen through the trees. The house is surrounded by a dovecote and farm buildings which are still used by a farmer. The romantic group must look exactly as it did when William Morris found it lying in the low water meadows, quiet and dreaming. It is like an etching by F. L. Griggs. The garden is divine, crammed with flowers wild and tangled, an enchanted orchard garden for there are fruit trees and a mulberry planted by Morris. All the flowers are as Pre-Raphaelite as the house, being rosemary, orange-smelling lilies, lemon-smelling verbena. The windows outside have small pediments over them. Inside there are Charles II chimneypieces, countrified by rude Renaissance scrolls at the base of the jambs. The interior is redolent of Morris and Rossetti, yet not the least nineteenth century, which speaks loudly for their taste. Most of the rooms have Morris wallpapers, and contain many framed drawings by them both, of Mrs. Morris and the children. The room in which Morris worked has a great four-poster. Rossetti's room is lined with the tapestries which, when the wind blew them about, worried him and induced nightmares. I like bad old tapestries to be chopped about and treated as wallpaper. They make a superb background to pictures. I leant out of the casement window, unlike the Lady of Shalott, and gazed across the flat, meadowy landscape and the winding river which looked so comfortable and serene. I do not remember experiencing such sweet peace and happiness as during these two hours.

Old Miss May Morris stupidly left the house and contents to Miss Lobb, the woman she lived with. On the latter's death six months afterwards everything was sold. Interested friends bought back what they could. All Mrs. Morris's clothes went and were last seen tossed about by farmers' wives. We saw the room where Miss Lobb died, while eating veal pie and shouting at the top of her voice.

Midi and I went for a long walk through hayfields, talking chiefly about her circle of women friends. She says there is nothing they will not discuss with her and each other unashamedly. They tell her how often they sleep with their husbands, what they do in bed, and whether it brings on palpitations. One of them says her husband, although little over forty, cannot sleep with her more than once a month because all his life he has had too much sex. I just don't believe this reason is the true one. There can't be any man of that age incapable of sex at least once every night in the year. What I do know is that husbands do not talk together about their wives in this fashion.

Wednesday, 15th July

Sir Courtauld-Thomson told me he had seen Lord Portal who was courteous and business-like, that six architects from the Ministry of Works have thoroughly surveyed Dorney Wood, and that he still wants the National Trust to accept the property and the £30,000 endowment now in his lifetime. He will leave by will two separate funds amounting to £200,000 in all, one for Government expenditure on the Minister of the Crown who is to enjoy the house, and the other for the Trust to buy additional land round about, as it comes into the market.

At Brooks's I ran into Eddy [Sackville-West], Raymond [Mortimer] and Roger Senhouse,[1] who on seeing me said, 'What a svelte figure he still has!' Eddy said, 'I should think so too at his age. But I must tell you he's blind as a bat and out of vanity won't wear his spectacles.'

Q. dined with me at the Mirabelle in Curzon Street. Together we drank a couple of bottles of *vin rosé* at 18/6 the bottle, the whole dinner costing £4. It was an absurd evening. We both got rather tipsy. On leaving the restaurant at midnight we had to walk down Curzon Street to sober ourselves. Linked arms we swayed. I told her Brocket had written me a letter saying, 'Stop brocketting me.' And Q. said 'And don't start brocketting me either.' In the taxi I thought what is happening now must have happened a hundred, no a thousand, no a million times. How bored taxi drivers must get at nights. Or are they merely revolted? And I also thought, women have legs, and tongues like conger eels.

[1] Roger Pocklington-Senhouse (1899–1970), bibliophile, translator, and co-founder of the publishers, Secker & Warburg.

I got to Lapworth station in the evening and was met by Baron Ash[1] in a smart trap drawn by a small grey pony. I was very tired but could not sleep for thinking of dear Hamish[2] reported missing in Libya last month. I read the news in an evening paper while sitting on the platform of Wolverhampton station. It seems a short time ago that I spent his last weekend with him before he sailed away. We motored to stay a night with Diana Worthington and Dig Yorke[3] at Weston. We sat on the terrace beneath a wall covered with pears. I remarked upon the pears. The two girls sighed, and said how sad it was there was no one left now to pick them.

Friday, 17th July

After luncheon Baron and I drove in the pony cart to Earlswood Moat House[4] in pouring rain, he holding the reins, I an enormous carriage umbrella over our heads. It was an old-fashioned sort of outing. Baron would hold the reins very high, flourish a whip and cry appealingly, 'Now then, laddie! Whoa, little laddie!' nervously, without admitting it. He continually expressed the hope that I was not nervous. I wasn't in the very least.

The Moat House is a yeoman's house built in 1480 and altered in 1550. It has been owned by the Misses Smythe's family since 1743. It is an archaeologists' gem because of its high rich roof and ceiling timbers. It is wonderfully uncomfortable. There is no telephone, no water — but a pump in the garden — no heating, no light, no bath, and no water closet — but an outdoor twin earth closet also in the garden. The two old Smythe sisters gave us tea, stone cold, and delicious rye bread and butter, in a cosy, pitch-dark parlour with a bright fire in an open grate. Grate and fireback depict the fable of the fox and the grapes. I noticed a small oak chest and some rude country oak chairs at the top of the newel staircase. The two sisters must be unique, for they are absolutely of yeoman stock, certainly not gentry, although educated. They spoke slight Warwickshire dialect. Both were dressed in subfusc, buttoned up to the chin. One had a patch over her eye. They were very sweet, and very old-world. They own a house in Wimbledon, which is

[1] Donor of Packwood House, Warwickshire, to the National Trust, 1941.
[2] Hon. Hamish St. Clair-Erskine, M.C. (1909–74).
[3] Wife of Henry Green (Yorke), the novelist.
[4] A small house given to the Trust by the Misses J. and M. Smythe, 1929–40.

79

strange, and said they both haunted the British Museum reading room. The intellectual one is reading the eighth volume out of nine on the *History of the Crimean War*. She was very solemn about this. Their garden is a wilderness, and shrubs are growing over the windows, which are festooned inside with the thickest blackout curtains of flannel.

Saturday, 18th July

From Warwick station I was driven to Charlecote Park. It is the second time that I have been here; the first was in 1936, which shows how long negotiations have been dragging on. On that occasion I was sent to consider and report upon the merits of the house. Sir Henry Fairfax-Lucy, military, dapper and arrogant walked me quickly round the park and garden. It was a rainy day I remember. On returning to the porch, whence we had set out immediately on my arrival, Sir Henry stretched out his hand and bade me good-bye. In those days I was shy. Nervously I asked if I might see inside. The reply was, 'There is absolutely no need. Charlecote is known to be one of the great, *the* greatest houses of England. Good morning.' So without disputing I went off with my tail between my legs. On my return to the office I was told I had been a fool.

Now as for Sir Henry Fairfax-Lucy, I have today found out about him. He may be a pompous ass like Justice Shallow (who was supposed to be Sir Thomas Lucy), but underneath the strutting, the peppery, the arrogant, surface a kindly old man lurks. In fact I am rather sorry for him, because I think he is a little odd. He is obstinate and muddle-headed because of his oddness. I believe he struggles to be reasonable, and just cannot manage to be. His ideas do not co-ordinate. His lisp is like that of a peevish child eating pap.

We went inside the house this time; and then round the park, again in the rain. He showed me the complicated boundaries of the land he proposes to make over. But he kept contradicting himself so that neither he nor I knew at the end of my visit what his intentions were. Although most indefinite he was most exacting. He was also very cheese-paring, reducing the total income the Trust should receive to shillings and pence as well as pounds. I thought he was rather touching when he urged haste—how is this to be achieved with him?— if we wanted the transaction to go through. 'I don't want to say anything unseemly, but Lady Lucy is very seriously ill.' The place is of course hers, not his.

Sunday, 19th July

I read in the paper that the new Lord Knebworth has been killed in Libya. This will be a devastating blow to the Lyttons, and I dare say will dish the scheme for Knebworth after all.

Monday, 20th July

I stayed the night with the Price Woods at Henley Hall outside Ludlow. Mrs. Wood and her head housemaid helped me go through the Blickling tapestries in search of moth. I unrolled them on trestle tables out of doors and brushed them with hard bristle brushes. Then spread them loosely on the lawn and yew hedge in the sunlight. Then spread them flat and sprinkled them with napthaline flakes, rolling them up with wax paper, and tying them round with newspaper outside. This operation took all afternoon.

I was struck again by the selfishness of the Woods. They have eight servants in the house, wearing uniforms as in pre-war days. When Colonel Wood suggested having someone to stay, mentioning a name, his wife retorted, 'We can't have sick people to stay here.' She said to me, 'If there is any threat of evacuees I shall spread out the art treasures and furniture into more rooms.' And she added, 'We are keeping it very dark. We do not want *them* to take away our cars. We have two Rolls Royces and one Rolls Bentley laid up.'

Wednesday, 22nd July

To my surprise the dentist did not pull any teeth out, but said the cause of the trouble was an old stopping. This he removed and replaced. As I write the toothache is as bad as ever.

Nancy lunched with me at Fleming's Hotel. It was a mingy meal for which I paid 18/-. To my joy she said that Hamish was a prisoner of war, slightly wounded.

At luncheon the waiter asked, 'Will you have cream with your gooseberries, m'm?' 'Yes, rather,' said Nancy. 'Delicious chalk.'

By the evening my toothache began again, and was far worse than before. I had a terrible night without any sleep at all. Each time I nodded from utter exhaustion, I was woken by the pain. It kept recurring in spasms with such acuteness that I had to get out of bed and walk up and down the room, holding my head. The only relief was sipping cold water and rinsing it round the bad tooth.

After another terrible night, during which I kept sponging my face with cold water, for rinsing the mouth ceased to be effectual, I went to London again. The dentist took out the temporary stopping of Wednesday which was pressing on the nerve, and substituted gutta-percha. Now there is no pain at all. An extraordinary thing is how quickly humans like animals forget that only hours ago they were in agony. When free of pain one cannot sympathize with the pain of others. The person in pain becomes a bore, and the painfree person hates him.

The committee today raised my salary from £400 to £500 p.a. Eardley's to his, and my disgust, was raised a mere £25 p.a. He is going to write to the committee refusing it.

When the others had left the office this evening Matheson became confidential. He told me the committee had agreed to engage a head agent to be paid £1,200 to £1,500 a year. This man would gradually replace our local agents and local committees. Meanwhile he must visit all the properties and formulate plans for their management. He went on to say he wished to see the Trust's organization put on a new footing before he left when the war was over. To my great surprise he thought I should take his place, and the committee thought so too. It is surely gratifying to be told this, but honestly I do not know that I should care for the responsibility of secretaryship: and certainly not if it meant relinquishing my country houses.

Another breeze with Helen this morning. She was very annoyed that the National Trust would not consent to register as a householder in order to acquire twenty-five hens, in other words to keep her twenty-five hens (already acquired) for her. We cannot because it is illegal. So she said, 'Then you National Trusts will have to go without and watch us eat eggs, that's all.' I replied, 'Rather than do that, we will go elsewhere where we shall get eggs.'

I saw Robert Donat in *The Young Mr. Pitt*, and was moved to tears. I feel very ashamed when cheap patriotism makes me weep. It is not a true emotion. The most casual sights make me weep, Queen Mary with her parasol, a military band playing, and even a kitten being removed by a kind policeman from the middle of a road.

At 6.30 Jamesey and I met at the New Theatre for the last performance of *Othello*. Our seats were at the back of the dress circle, with no more than an inch above our heads. The heat was stifling, our neighbours smelt. We left after the second act through sheer exhaustion. Shakespeare is like *The Times*. One must feel strong before plunging into either. Noël Coward and *The Daily Express* require less effort. We dined at a Turkish restaurant in Frith Street off vine leaves cooked in rice, sour milk and sugar.

Sunday, 2nd August

Jamesey says that if knowing famous men and keeping diaries is all that is necessary to acquire fame, he wonders more people do not keep them. Cecil Beaton, he says, writes such a diary, and J. has read parts of it. I didn't ask if he had cribbed it, as he cribbed Harold's, or if he was shown it.

I lunched with James and Dame Una in her new house in Ladbroke Grove.

After luncheon she and I went by bus to visit Clarissa Churchill, who is living in a gardener's bothy in Regent's Park. We found Clarissa alone in this tiny bothy, very pale and white, and listless. The Dame and I walked round the garden of Hanover Lodge along the bank of the Paddington Canal. She told me how depressed she was about the conduct of the war. She believed that people were beginning to lose faith in their leaders. She experienced a sense of frustration in all people she met on committees. She said it was a positive fact that our leaders were muddling along, without policy or plan. She is amazed at the Government's decision to evacuate large towns like Brighton in order to bring people back to London. She only hopes the reason may be to provide billeting space for American troops who will lead the second front. In fact the news is so depressing that one can only dismiss it from one's mind, and not read newspapers or listen to the wireless.

I have finished Mrs. Gaskell's *Life of Charlotte Brontë*. It leaves out a lot one would like to know; yet the picture she paints of that churchyard at Haworth and the moors behind the rectory is a superb drop-scene to the lives of those queer sisters.

I had tea at Dorney Wood. Sir Courtauld wished to tell me of his interview with Lord Zetland. No very fresh particulars except that he has made up his mind to give Dorney Wood and the preliminary £30,000 endowment without conditions of any sort, reserving no life interest, but taking a lease at a peppercorn rent from us as soon as the deed of gift is signed.

Wednesday, 5th August

I wanted to see the mausoleum at Blickling, so Forsyth and I walked across the park to it. It is a squat pyramid designed by Joseph Bonomi in 1793. Very solid and well constructed with openings on four sides, and an escutcheon and coronet over the entrance. The whole is surrounded by thin iron railings. We found that the padlock had been forced and the gate opened. Also the extremely heavy and large door of the mausoleum was ajar. It too had been forced and even bent. Considerable strength must have been required to do this, and possibly the use of one of several tree trunks lying in the bracken. The floor inside is paved. The interior is, somewhat surprisingly, circular with a domed ceiling which reverberates. Within three deeply splayed recesses are sarcophagi of marble, the central one the 2nd Earl of Buckinghamshire's, the side ones his two countesses'. The left sarcophagus had been hacked with a blunt instrument, and the marble coating prised off the side. Evidently the culprits are the R.A.F. boys who have tried to break open this sarcophagus, believing they would find inside the body of the second countess, who is reputed to have been buried wearing all her jewellery.

Thursday, 6th August

My birthday. I am thirty-four, though I pretend to be thirty-three.

It is wonderful being, if not totally, then chiefly responsible to the committee for Blickling. I am in love with the house, garden, park and estate. Birkbeck takes me round the woods all the afternoon, showing

84

me his new plantations. In spite of the R.A.F. station, Blickling seems to be at the furthermost extremity of East Anglia, even of England.

Friday, 7th August

Spent the morning in the attics with Miss O'Sullivan[1] looking at the portraits which belong to the Peter the Great Room. She showed me the tower and described the route which the black dog takes across the staterooms. Miss O'Sullivan, the most matter-of-fact of ladies, has seen this ghostly creature once. I had a long talk with Miss James the housekeeper, and decided to keep her. She seems a friendly woman in spite of her grand talk of the responsible jobs she has had in the past, at Blenheim, Clandeboye, etc. She told Miss O'Sullivan that at Blenheim she over-ate to the tune of putting on two stone.

I took a bus from Aylsham to Norwich. An old man with a nose the size of his hand and covered with blistered bubbles of skin, got in. A revolting sight. I changed in Norwich for Haddiscoe, where I arrived at the wrong time. There was no one to meet me but the stationmaster, who was most helpful. I had a late tea with Kathleen [Kennet] at Fritton, for I am to stay with the Kennets for the weekend. Lord Kennet arrived shortly after me. We dined off rabbit, claret, nectarines and raspberries. I am already getting a few spots from all this fruit. Lord K. showed me his books. Evidently I said something disparaging. His old bound editions are as great treasures to him as houses are to me. I must concede this. But I do resent Lord Kennet's superciliousness. He is so morose too.

Saturday, 8th August

I stroll about with K. in the morning after being given breakfast in bed. I find myself strangely tired and long to be left alone with the book I have picked up here, Geikie Cobb's on the Ductless Glands, instead of embarking upon intense conversations with K. so early in the day. I give up, for one must pull one's weight a bit in other people's houses when one has been such a fool as to visit them. So I pick raspberries with K. and converse. A Major Jack Abbey comes to luncheon. He is gossipy and wet. In the afternoon I feel really ill and heavy, owing to my epanutin, I suppose. I sleep hard until tea-time. Peter Scott and his

[1] She had been private secretary to Philip Kerr, 11th Marquess of Lothian, who bequeathed the Blickling estate to the National Trust, 1940.

new wife, Jane, come unexpectedly after tea for two nights' leave. At dinner I feel horribly shy with them and hardly speak. This family makes one feel inferior and excluded. I have an admiration for their prowess, and at the same time despise their intellects. They are more intelligent, less intellectual than I am. In fact they are thorough middle-brows. K.'s great failing is to blow the trumpets of her family until one is deafened and wants to run away from the din. It's true they always do the decent, and the right thing. But they appear priggish and self-righteous.

We drank champagne for dinner to celebrate Peter's arrival, so surreptitiously, so ostentatiously unostentatiously produced by Lord K. Peter showed us his latest drawings of Jane, also some photographs of earlier drawings of his, including the one of me, which I must say looks better in photograph than in the original. Kathleen was enraptured with the drawings, and cried, 'Look, [Augustus] John could not produce anything finer than these!' None of them has any understanding of art whatever. Then Peter talked of his sea exploits; and I marvelled. He explained how bomb effects are greater on sea than on land. He has certainly done gallant things. His adoring wife is only nineteen. She is a little too skinny and lank to be really beautiful yet. Beauty may come. I am not surprised that she worships Pete who must be romantic in her eyes. For this philistines' ideal of manhood, no, this god, is of course attractive. He is stocky, sturdy and square to be sure with a small bright face and a turned-up nose. There is something great about the sweep of his brow. He is untidy in his dress. His blue eyes twinkle and when he smiles he can be fascinating; and his short, deep laugh is unforced.

Sunday, 9th August

The others sail spasmodically on the lake in their beastly boats, but the water bores me and I don't go near it. When we all meet the fun is not furious and the conversation not sparkling. I feel discontented and unwell. Indeed I wonder why on earth I ever came. With K. alone it would have been fun. Wayland[1] I find no more sympathetic than his father. When at last I can leave for my train I am relieved and happy. Dear K. accompanies me to the station in the Austin 7 and kisses me fondly when the train steams out. She herself said it was a pity my visit coincided with Peter's.

[1] The present Lord Kennet.

I was very touched to find on my return a cable of birthday greetings from my dear brother Dick in Egypt. To think of his bothering to remember while on active service!

Tuesday, 11th August

While I was walking through the Ritz an umbrella hooked my arm from behind, and there was Peter Derwent.[1] This was my first sight of him since the war. He was looking far thinner, younger and more handsome than formerly. I commented on his thinness and he replied, 'It would be difficult to be otherwise these days.' He has returned from Berne once and for all and hopes to join the R.A.F. He said how sorry he was about Robert's [Byron] death, adding, 'But then we have all had our private troubles,' his only reference to his wife's death in Switzerland. He said what a long time ago it seemed when we four — the other two being Robert and Michael [Rosse] — founded the Georgian Group. Yet it was only five years ago. He seemed unhappy, lost and hopeless.

Wednesday, 12th August

I caught the 8.45 from Waterloo for the Isle of Wight. From the train window Portsmouth looked devastated, with hardly a house intact, yet all the buses and trams were running. The sergeant examining credentials allowed me on board, having looked cursorily at Matheson's letter and my identity card. All harbours are beautiful. Here the width of water, the great chimneys, the cranes and dock buildings, camouflaged in a slipshod, garish way, were no exception. There was much activity of speedboats with barrage balloons floating above them on strings; much leisureliness of warships, grey or camouflaged in sea colours. There were spiky things sticking out of the water along the shores to prevent landings, I suppose. It was a fine and wet day in fits and starts. I noticed some huge floating fortresses out to sea. The docks and harbours looked the only part of Portsmouth not destroyed.

At Newport I was met by Sir Vere Hobart who peered closely at me and said, 'Brigade tie?' It was not, because I never wear one. *Ergo*, he must be rather blind. But he was wearing one. He is a small old man who can't pronounce his 'r's or 'th's. He started off with a long exposition on the pronunciation of surnames, *vide* Hobart, which is always Hubbard, except in Tasmania. Hobart was founded by his relation,

[1] 3rd Lord Derwent (1899-1949), diplomat and man of letters.

D

87

Lord *Hubbard*. Did I know this? No, but I might have guessed, had I thought. 'Where that fellow Sir George Arthur left his name, Port Arthur. Did I know?' Yes, I actually did because he was my relation. This retort took him aback, and rather annoyed him. Was I going to like Sir Vere Hobart? And how was I going to stick two nights at Gatcombe House? I wasn't at all sure.

Sir Vere bought this property some six years ago. I cancel my erstwhile unfavourable opinion of the Isle of Wight, for the landscape here is beautiful, not flat and uneventful. From all sides of the house spread steep downland hills with distant prospects, and afar off is visible the white crest of a sea cliff near Ventnor. The property extends to 800 acres.

Gatcombe is in good condition, it is built of ashlar; a large square box of 1751 to be exact, with regularly spaced windows. At the back of the house is a huge double chimney for the contending winds. Otherwise only two top-heavy chimneys remain, since Sir Vere has had all the fireplaces blocked up and the chimney-stacks removed.

The inside of the house is ghastly for Sir Vere has painted the wood-work burnt sienna. There is a very nice oak staircase with moulded handrail, continuous to the top of the house. The handrail ends on the ground floor with an abnormal clenched fist over the newel. The dining-room has an ornate rococo chimney-piece, with central carved basket of flowers, also painted burnt sienna. The breakfast-room stucco ceiling is like its walls, salmon pink.

Sir Vere is a genealogist and archaeologist (below ground), two things I detest; also a big bit of a bore. But he is kind to his old grey-haired wife, who is surprisingly commonplace. They seem devoted. They are loquacious on the subject of the parson, with whom they have quarrelled in the true squirearchical tradition. In consequence they patronize the church in Newport, and have constructed their own vault in the garden, out of reach of the Gatcombe graveyard.

After tea the Deputy Mayor—of Newport I suppose—came to drink sherry and meet me!

Thursday, 13th August

Breakfast at 9 and Sir Vere luckily not down until 10.30 so I had some peace. Lady Hobart met me in the hall and told me how delicate Sir V. was. She is obviously anxious about his state of health. She launched into a long, sad story of his first wife's death from a sudden accident while he was ill in a nursing home after a serious operation. This was only seven years ago. I suspect it was suicide on the first wife's part by the way she spoke, but I didn't like to ask outright. She told me how from that day she took him in hand and looked after him. 'Poppy, he said to me,' etc. A touching old thing, shining clean with her white hair, domesticated and shuffling around like a dear old cat. She is very pussylike and motherly.

After luncheon we motored to Newport to see Sir Vere's solicitor. I was made to read the relevant codicil to his will which contains his wishes for the future of Gatcombe. Meanwhile covenants.

I think Sir Vere is a nice old boy really, though a little pigheaded and full of his own importance. His interminable narratives about the Hobart lineage are enough to drive one to drink.

Friday, 14th August

I met John Summerson in Warwick Street and we lunched at the Majorca restaurant. He is with Walter Godfrey running the National Buildings Record. All their photographs are stored in the Bodleian and All Souls, Oxford. After the war John expects the Record will take over the Royal Commission survey. It appears that the Courtauld Institute have given it all their architectural papers.

At 3 the dentist. My old tooth extremely tender when he removed the temporary filling. I always sweat the moment the drill touches my teeth, if not before. I caught the 4.15 to Bradford-on-Avon, changing twice and arriving at Ted's at 8.20, worn out. Yet we sat knitting until long after midnight.

Saturday, 15th August

At 8.30 Christo [Ted Lister's Bulgarian servant] brought me a pot of tea and two thin slices of bread and butter. Otherwise nothing to eat until 1 when Ted got down to breakfast, which he calls brunch. I was ravenous by then. The purpose of this visit was to settle the restrictive covenants which I have persuaded him to give over the house and property of some sixty acres. Ted is considering leaving Westwood to the Trust in his will, if it can be arranged for his cousin to live here. His chief consideration is undoubtedly the house, for I don't think he much cares about his cousin or any relation. The truth is he cannot bear to dwell on the likelihood of his ever dying.

We went conscientiously round the house, and I made copious notes of each feature in each room, which he particularly wants mentioned in the deed, plaster ceilings, plaster friezes, plaster over-mantels, stone fireplaces and doorways, panelling, notably the portrait panels of the Kings of England in the Kings' Room, and so on. Each time I come here I am overwhelmed by the perfection of this house. Everything Ted has done to it is in the best possible taste and proves his astonishing, instinctive understanding of the late medieval and Jaco-bean periods. He has restored the interior porches, the late Gothic mullions and glazing bars, the stucco and stonework, with a restraint and sensitivity which I have never experienced in any English country house of these early dates. Even the patchy rendering of the outside walls, washed over with a primrose to russet harl, rough and broken, with an occasional rambler rose lolloping over the upper windows, is contrived to perfection.

I left on Sunday under something like a cloud. He is a very touchy old man and was cross with me for venturing to question his allegation that Helen Dashwood had allowed some myrtle trees at West Wycombe to die. He claimed that they derived from a myrtle wreath brought to England from Catherine the Great's floral tiara by Sir Francis Dashwood, who was an envoy to Russia in her time. He sulked and left the dining-room, and there was a noticeable coolness right up to my departure.

Di [Murray] tells me that every preparation is being made for the evacuation at twenty-four hours' notice of the south coast towns to London, presumably to make room for troops with which to invade the Continent. She is on an Evacuation Committee to receive the un-housed. She also says that convoys of barges are to be seen taken down the roads to the south coast.

During the last few days I have been reading Byron's *Don Juan* for the third time. I remember the first was in 1927 during Mama's and my voyage to Genoa, when I was confined to my cabin in the Bay of Biscay, feeling wretched. Even then I was able to perceive the wit of it. Now I still find myself gasping aloud in admiration. There is nothing like it. I am also in the middle of Symons's Life of Baron Corvo, a most nauseating figure. Even reading this book makes my flesh creep. It is the aroma of the soiled priestly habit that makes me feel sick, the very vicious creature masquerading as deeply devout. I must take warning. I met Symons at Lady Cranbrook's in the thirties. He was a horrid, sinister character too.

As I left the drive in making for the bus stop this morning, a khaki car hooted at me. Helen was in the company of her American beau, Colonel Jingle Bubb (this is his real name), being motored to London. They offered me a lift which I accepted.

At luncheon Esher sat himself down at the table next to mine and began talking about the country houses scheme. He was disappointed that so few houses were coming to the Trust. I said I thought they would come with a rush once the war seemed to owners to be nearing an end. He asked how the new office arrangements were working out. I said I was sorry I had decided to take a fortnight's holiday at a stretch lest, on my return, I found all my jobs filched by the secretary. Esher said the only way was to be quite determined, and take them back again. This is all very fine for a chairman, but not so easy for a subordinate.

Helen's second American beau, General Acres, nearly died as the result of standing in a wasps' nest while shooting at West Wycombe last Sunday. He was stung in fifty-two places and his heart all but stopped beating. I don't believe Helen minds a bit.

Friday, 21st August

This afternoon I came upon Rick talking to a lodger who is a Commando and was in the Dieppe raid this week. He is young, bronzed and incredibly tough. When introduced he shook my hand in a vice-like grip. I felt so shy in his presence, and humble, and inferior, that I could find nothing to say. Nor did I much care for him. He casually remarked that a man in his troop had shot two of his officers for cowardice, one at Dunkirk and the other during a recent cross-Channel raid.

Sunday, 23rd August

John Russell wants to write a biography of Henry James. He showed me a suitcase of his letters which he had been lent by Philip Morrell's sister. After a time I get used to John's stammer and hesitations. I do not look at him while he is speaking and try to appear unconcerned. I took him to Old Battersea House. Mrs. Stirling[1] was bedecked in

[1] A. M. W. Stirling, author of *Thomas Coke and the Building of Holkham*, 1908.

jewels and gems. When she walks across the room it is like a chandelier which has been let down from the ceiling and, without collapsing, mysteriously manages to move. I like the old lady, but John was rather bored. She told me that her brother-in-law, William de Morgan,[1] used as a boy to spend his holidays with Lady Byron, who was a friend of his parents. I find Mrs. de Morgan's pictures infinitely more sympathetic than most of the well-known Pre-Raphaelites. Hers of the five mermaids rising from the sea, their tails visible through the green waves, lacks the nauseating sentiment of Burne-Jones, and is arcane in subject, as well as opulent in treatment. Her use of gold is more lavish than Botticelli's.

Jamesey urged me to return to London and live with him. Very sweet of him, but he knows, and I know, that it would not work. We walked across St. James's Park in the moonlight. He accompanied me as far as Chelsea Hospital, remarking on the beauty of the Belgravia houses, their flat unfussy façades so placid in the moonlight which tonight was soft and misty.

Monday, 24th August

The National Gallery picture now on show is Turner's *Frosty Morning*, an early work *circa* 1813 between his frankly Claude Lorraine and later rainbowy periods. This is a Wordsworthian interpretation of dull, cold, still nature, with the rising sun's glow just beginning to steal over the hard fields.

Tuesday, 25th August

Wickhamford. In the morning I clip the yew hedge by the lawn, destroying the silvery spiders' webs as I advance like Atropos with my shears from end to end. I think 'Who the hell am I, wilfully, mercilessly to wipe out a whole world of insects? I am as bad as Genghis Khan, as bad as Hitler.'

Mama told me that Lord FitzAlan and Magdalen came to tea here, and were a great success with Papa. The Horsfield children were in the garden for the afternoon and told their mother when they got home that there was a real lord at the manor, so old that he should never have been allowed out: and that Magdalen looked like a fish with a red neck.

[1] William de Morgan (1839–1917), artist and potter.

This morning while shaving and listening to the news I heard the announcement of the Duke of Kent's death. I felt a sharp shock and could think of nothing else for some time. I only once saw him in the flesh, when he made a nervous speech at an S.P.A.B. dinner. He was sitting next to May Morris, an upright, smiling old dame very self-possessed, with a small, curly head. The Duke had a boyish figure and complexion.

Lily Horsfield complained that people in the Evesham streets would stop to condole with her over her son Hugh's death. If only they wouldn't, she said pathetically.

Thursday, 27th August

A grilling hot day. I work in the garden all morning, sweating into my blue aertex shirt. While plum-picking in the evening, Deenie said, 'My dear child, I believe you stink.' I laughed and said I was sure I did, for I knew I did, yet the fact that I had been detected worried me a little. Even when the circumstances may be excusable, one does not relish this particular charge.

Friday, 28th August

Mama and I have been sorting out old trunks in the loft above the motor-house. We came across some of my drawings done at the Ashmolean where Albert Rutherston was teaching. To my surprise a few of them were not too bad. The discovery has inspired me to sketch again. This evening I drew the house across the pond, and recaptured the immense joy of using my eyes as hard as I could. Eyes get wasted, like muscles, for lack of intensive exercise.

Saturday, 29th August

I had a row with Papa after dinner. He expressed idiotic views about the Duke of Kent. Said that he was a worthless fellow and 'no better than a pansy', a phrase I abominate. I could not tolerate this silly imputation by someone who knew nothing whatever about the prince. I blew up. Words flew, as of old, as of old. I cannot, alas, stay here more than two nights without allowing myself to be provoked beyond endurance.

Tuesday, 1st September

Today Helen's mother, Mrs. Eaton, and her aunt, Miss FitzRandolph, and young John Dashwood, arrived back from Canada. It has taken them over three months to work their passage. Helen had moved all hell and pulled all strings. She was determined to get little John back so that he might go to Eton. He is a funny little boy, plain and perky like his father, hunched like a flea, and with a large load of fun. The two old sisters are typical transatlantic matrons, *soignées*, white faced with mauve hair, who talk in unison. They are kind old things, in awe of Helen who snubs them mercilessly. They flew in the clipper from New York, after waiting there for weeks with very little money allowance, and being sent back to Canada once. At Lisbon they stopped only two days, whence they proceeded to Ireland. They are delighted to be back. Helen has engaged an old, old maid called Clara to look after them. She wanders about the large house like a lost sheep and is so pitiful to watch that she wrings my heart.

Thursday, 3rd September

Lady Hermione Cobbold rang me up, and I went to meet her and her husband at their farm near Stokenchurch. She is Lord Lytton's eldest daughter and has inherited Knebworth's part of the estate at Knebworth. Both expressed themselves averse to the idea of the Trust, saying they could never live in a place made over to the Trust. He is a landowner as well as someone important in the Bank of England.[1] They want to keep the estate to farm, and asked if we would accept the house and gardens only, if he found endowment funds from his own resources. I told them straight what I had not dared tell Lord Lytton, that I thought it doubtful whether the committee would accept the house on its own merits without the estate. She quite understood, and said Lord Lytton was surprised that the Trust was even interested in the house. Lady Hermione has beautiful deep, violet eyes, is shy, proud and farouche, and I think means to be friendlier than her manner allows her to appear.

Friday, 4th September

Jamesey arrives at Brooks's like a whirlwind and whisks me off to dine

[1] Now Lord Cobbold, Governor of the Bank of England 1949–61.

94

with Dame Una. He has come from Cecil Beaton, full of gin and excitement, for he has just been paid by Batsford's £300 in arrears for his book, and another sum in advance for his next book, having been £200 in debt when I last saw him. Says he had a wonderful 'grouse' luncheon with Charles Fry who complained that it is more profitable for publishers to give away money to authors than to keep it, because it is all taxed.

John Pope-Hennessy is at Dame Una's too. He is less forbidding — though God knows still frightening enough — and has grown very distinguished. He has a bull-terrier puppy called Jason, which is boisterous and delicious. Dame Una talked against John's gramophone about Lady Blessington. She was Dickens's first friend, and a real charmer. No woman would go to her house because of the Count D'Orsay scandal, but the Dame thinks her feelings for D'Orsay were purely maternal. He was her stepson-in-law, and she mothered him. At least there is no evidence whatever to the contrary. She talked also of Letitia Landon,[1] about whom I know nothing except that she died of an overdose of prussic acid, six months after her marriage, against which all her friends had warned her. Dame Una has been to Canonbury, which she found fascinating, and quite unaltered since the early nineteenth century. I asked if it had been bombed much. 'Not at all,' she said in that concise way of hers.

Sunday, 6th September

Miss O'Sullivan and I walked to the Blickling mausoleum through the park this morning. She is a weird, embittered woman, whom life has obviously treated unkindly. It is sad how many people there are whose natural goodness can only be brought to light by persistent delving beneath an unpromising surface. So often one has not the time, or energy, or circumstance for the operation, and consequently a false impression of a person may remain with one for a lifetime. During our walk we talked about the war. Miss O'S., who is a regular churchwoman and churchwarden at Blickling, said that the English did not deserve to win, for it was idle to presume we were fighting for the Christian ideal; and that the young, having been brought up without any religious instruction to fend for themselves, which meant to make money, were spiritually barren. These sentiments are, I dare say (although I am not absolutely sure), irrefutable. I told her that I was

[1] Letitia Elizabeth Landon (1802–38), poet under initials L. E. L.

still fundamentally a pacifist, and only decided to join the army and fight when I realized – not till six months after war had broken out – that no amount of pacifism would stop the war, and the only way to stop it was to win it, which involved the killing of as many Germans as possible. She replied that my decision showed lack of principle.

Tuesday, 8th September

At 2 o'clock I left my attaché case at Etchingham station and walked to Hurst Green village, where I telephoned Lady Milner.[1] She pressed me to come and see her, saying she remembered me and knew how fond of me Lord Lloyd was. Fortified by these kind words and two apples which I bought at the village shop, I continued my four-mile walk to Great Wigsell where she lives. A glorious early autumn day, the sun shining bright as I tramped, stick in hand, across fields and through woods. The country is remote, unspoilt, rich Sussex landscape.

Great Wigsell is similar in size, date and type to Bateman's. Both were built in the early seventeenth century of hard ironstone, and fittingly commemorate the solid integrity of the prosperous, non-armigerous stock who lived in them. Great Wigsell is more regular than Bateman's, and has pointed gables and tall chimneys. It is surrounded by barns and outbuildings, and has several forecourts enclosed by old stone walls, so that the garden is divided into separate compartments. It is a very rural and tranquil place. I found Lady Milner talking to her gardener by the front door. She is oldish, over seventy I would guess, with a broad, lined face and a robust and spread figure. She is very sharp. She reminded me that ten years ago I lunched with her and Sir Edward Grigg[2] in Manchester Square. I remember the house best.

Lady Milner is a sister of Leo Maxse and editor of the *National Review*. She was married first to Lord Edward Cecil, and secondly to Lord Milner. We talked of George Lloyd to whom she was absolutely devoted. She told me that a day or so ago three of the most distinguished journalists were in her house. They all agreed that the worst turning

[1] Viscountess Milner (1872–1958). Violet, daughter of Admiral F. A. Maxse, married firstly, 1894, Lord Edward Cecil, and secondly, 1902, Alfred (Viscount) Milner. Editor of *National Review*, 1932–48.
[2] Sir Edward Grigg, 1st Lord Altrincham (1879–1955), administrator and politician.

points of this war had been Munich, the fall of France, and the death of Lloyd. She thought G. Ll. would not have died if Lady Lloyd had not let Clouds Hill, so that during the severest blitzes, when he was over-worked, there was no retreat for him to go to. She last saw him two days before Christmas 1940, when he already looked desperately ill. At that time I was in hospital after Dover. She then asked him what he honestly thought of Churchill after sitting with him in the Cabinet. G. Ll. said he had come to think more highly of his brain, but less of his character. She believed that Churchill was jealous of Lloyd, because he does not like having able men about him; that he was never loyal to Lloyd, even during the thirties when Winston was flirting with the Navy League yet refusing to commit himself to rearmament; and that in earlier days still, when Chancellor of the Exchequer, he had positively discouraged rearmament. This I cannot dispute, for I do not remember.

She said Pétain had always been bad, and the last volume of Poin-caré's *Memoirs* bears this out. He was always terrified of communists (ever since his experiences with the Communard in 1871), and shot his officers and men whom he suspected of communism in the last war. I said I liked to think that Weygand was not sitting on the fence so much as biding his time when he could most usefully throw in his weight with the Allies. Lady Milner said No, he too had become quite rotten. She instanced Lloyd's experience with Weygand, who was with the French Government when Lloyd was sent by Churchill to Bordeaux in June 1940. Weygand was insolent and forgot his manners. By then he was firmly convinced that England was also beaten, and when contradicted by G. Ll. became angry and offensive. He was reproachful and accused England of having let France down. Yet he contradicted himself by asserting that it was necessary for France to go through a cleansing process, and suffer for her sins. Lady Milner said that when in 1936 she was with Weygand in Paris, she asked him what he would want of England if France were again involved in war with Germany. His answer was: 'Only six divisions.' She was astonished, and made him repeat this.

She said that G. Ll. gave her a full account of his visit to Bordeaux immediately after his return (as indeed he did to me), and she published it, without mentioning his name, in the *National Review*.

As for G. Ll.'s biography, she thinks Lady Lloyd will do nothing until the end of the war, and that Colin Forbes-Adam[1] may be the right person for it. Lady Ll. asked Thomas Cadett to edit his speeches

[1] Colin Forbes-Adam published *Life of Lord Lloyd*, 1948.

(at the time she was asking me for my advice), and horrified him by suggesting that he should rewrite the unrecorded ones in the way she believed G. Ll. must have delivered them! Cadett declined. Blanche Lloyd was hurt and withdrew the offer. Lady Milner said one should beware of wives dictating their husbands' biographies. When Alfred Milner died she consulted F. S. Oliver[1] whose advice was, 'Do not write his biography yourself, but collect his papers, and edit, and publish these.' She did so.

She said G. Ll. was the only person she respected so much that she would have gone to him from wherever she happened to be, at a whistle. One day the two of them agreed that they had consistently upheld the same policy and had never been wrong. She said too that there was absolutely *no* able man in England today. This convinced me that, clever as she is, she lives in the past and is out of date.

Hugh Whistler rang up during our talk. She said he was a great ornithologist, and they discussed birds for hours on end. During Dunkirk the rooks would never settle in her trees, and strange birds, never seen by her before, flew from France across the Channel. When the *Gneisenau* and the *Prinz Eugen* were chased down the Channel last year, the gulls flew over Great Wigsell at a great height all that day.

We barely had time to talk about Bateman's, and the local committee of which she is chairman. She thinks Mr. Parish[2] a most unsuitable tenant, with no respect for the Kipling association. She was an intimate friend of the Kiplings, and bought Great Wigsell to be near them. I had tea with her and her sister, and walked back to Etchingham.

I met Mr. Parish at the station, pretending I had come down from London on his train. I purposely disclosed nothing about my Great Wigsell visit. Mr. Parish, though of good family—his great-grandfather Parish having been at Eton, and his mother a Cotterell-Dormer of Rousham, he was at pains to tell me—is a curiously brash man. His neon light smiles, switched on and off like the illuminated advertisements in Piccadilly Circus during peacetime, are calculated to assure one of his good intentions. But since they are accompanied by a staccato clicking of his too regular, too snow-white dentures, the effect is on the contrary, predatory. They, the teeth, strike fear in the beholder (and auditor). Yet I found him extremely friendly, if a trifle sinister. Lady Milner said he exactly resembled the butler in *Dear Brutus*, who is sinister indeed. Mrs. Parish, slightly 'bedint', is a sister of Lord Luke

[1] Author of *Alexander Hamilton*, 1906, and *The Endless Adventure*, 1930–5.
[2] Clement Woodbine Parish (1888–1966).

and Lady Laurie—'my sister, the Lady Mayoress, you know.' I didn't.

Before dinner Parish took me all round the Bateman's property, which to my eyes looks in apple-pie order. He refers to the local committee as 'those old bitches'. He has the grace to admit to having made a few mistakes. He has spent a lot of money on Bateman's, and positively enjoys showing the house to visitors at all hours, even on Saturdays and Sundays. I think we should be grateful to him.

He gave me a delicious dinner of partridge and Château Haut-Brion claret, 1920, with brandy afterwards. I slept in the oak four-poster, too short for my legs, in the little room at the top of the stairs.

Wednesday, 9th September

Read in the train a fascinating diary written by Myles Hildyard, a friend of one of Parish's sons, both of whom escaped from the Germans in Crete last summer. It is written in a straightforward, not unpoetic way, and is thrilling and charming. I would love to meet Hildyard who seems an angelic person, sensitive, sympathetic and of lion courage.

My plans went wrong today for I was to have gone to Gravesend. This fell through. At Brooks's I read Churchill's speech in *The Times* verbatim; then went to the London Library where Mr. Cox[1] told me it was a fact that Rommel had been killed in an aeroplane and the Foreign Office would not release the news, for some unspecified reason.

Went to the National Gallery where Mrs. Heath at the canteen would shake hands and talk while endeavouring to serve others. I saw this would lead to awkwardnesses, and slunk away. Looked at Bellini's *Agony in the Garden*. The boy angel holding a chalice in the sky has a pot belly and heavy shape for a cloud to bear. The sunlight is wrong, and illuminates the side of the castle which is away from the sunset. The other picture on view is a recently acquired Giotto, the *Gift of Tongues* on a small panel. For a picture painted *circa* 1300 or earlier it is remarkable how the figures are in the round, how three-dimensional they are made to appear by the scantiest of curves.

I met Harold walking outside the Gallery, looking vague and a little wan. When he noticed me he at once became his jaunty self. He said Lady Milner was terrifying to meet, and absolutely wrong-headed. I went to the Leicester Galleries. I admire Paul Methuen's[2] pictures

[1] Frederick James Cox, on the staff of the London Library, 1882–1952. He remembered Disraeli taking out books.

[2] 4th Lord Methuen, R.A. (1886–1974), artist and owner of Corsham Court.

more and more. There was a line wash by him of St. Paul's which I coveted.

Friday, 11th September

Mr. Fortescue and his wife came to luncheon at West Wycombe. He is an Eton master and I was up to him for German during one half. He is now Francis's classical tutor. He is a tall, dirty, uncouth creature, very intelligent and a good linguist. He visits Iceland for the Government because he speaks Icelandic. He surprised us by saying he hoped that after the war the custom of wearing Eton clothes and top hats would be discontinued. It is curious how today people want to abolish uniforms as though they are something to be ashamed of, or are emblematic of servility. But we are all servants, whether we are generals, bishops, cooks or Etonians. Helen and all of us, Francis included, fell upon Mr. Fortescue at once. Francis claimed that it was more economic to wear Eton clothes for, being black, they don't show the spots, and last longer. The seats of the trousers can be patched *ad nauseam*, since they are concealed by the tails.

Tuesday, 15th September

Mr. Brown, Lord Hesketh's solicitor, summoned me in a peremptory fashion to his office. He wished to inform me of Lord Hesketh's irritation with the Trust for taking so long a time in making up its mind to accept his lordship's generous offers. He demanded the appointment of a special committee on which he, Mr. Brown, would be pleased to serve, in order to deal immediately with these pressing matters. I had business with Mr. Brown when Rufford Old Hall first came the Trust's way, and recall the spirited manner in which he would button-hole Lord Crewe, who performed the opening ceremony in 1936, and who ignored Mr. Brown as he would have ignored a distant buzzing midge. Mr. Brown is a subservient attorney with a high opinion of himself for being on close terms with his client, to whose colossal wealth he much likes to refer. He intimated that Lord Hesketh, if not irritated further, might make more munificent donations to Rufford; but that he was leaving Easton Neston and several other important houses, of which I know Gayhurst to be one, not to the National Trust, but to some family trust. He confided in me that Lord Hesketh has lately had a stroke and may not live long, and that Lady Hesketh now leads 'a cotton-wool existence'.

Lady Throckmorton[1] asked me to Coughton [Court] for the night, to go through the list of family heirlooms with her. She is living in the south wing only. The rest of the house is empty, in expectation of American officers, or nuns.

Lady Throckmorton is delightful: plain, unfashionable, intelligent and downright. *Très grande dame.* She has worked in Coughton's interests for thirty years, upholding its Catholic tradition, without becoming a Catholic herself. It is entirely owing to her that Coughton is to become Trust property, in the face of seemingly insuperable obstacles raised by the entail and the hostility of the Throckmorton family.

Coughton is a thoroughly romantic house, but I must say the late Georgian front is gloomy. There is something unconvincing and drab about thin rendering which peels. The central Perpendicular tower and the half-timbered wings are beautiful, as well as picturesque. The family associations — the papistry, recusancy, Gunpowder Plot, and intermarriages with other ancient Catholic families — are thrilling.

Wednesday, 16th September

All morning Lady Throckmorton and I went round the house, she dictating to me notes on the contents which she considered ought to remain in the house, on loan by her son Robert to the Trust, under a form of covenant. In fact her one idea is to push the deal through now, while Robert is abroad and before he returns to alter his mind. She has been given absolute power of attorney, and she means to exercise it.

In spite of her dowagerial correctness Lady T. is amusingly mischievous about people. She said that when Madame de Navarro[2] died, Toty her son wrote that he was sending her some jade earrings which his mother had often worn and cherished. Later there arrived the cheapest pair of jet earrings which the housemaid might have bought to wear at the funeral. Either Toty knows no difference between jade and jet, which is quite probable, or somebody else substituted the jet for the jade. The daughter, whom Madame detested, went to her mother's funeral dressed in Madame's own black hat and dress, which Lady T. easily recognized.

[1] Lilian, mother of the present baronet, was granted by Royal Warrant, 1927, the title of Lady Throckmorton, her husband having been killed fighting in World War I.
[2] Mary Anderson, American Shakespearean actress, married Antonio de Navarro, and lived in Broadway, Worcestershire.

On my way home I went into Birmingham Cathedral, by Archer. The roof has been quite burnt away, and is replaced with temporary corrugated iron.

Friday, 18th September

While I was sitting at breakfast in the coffee-room at Brooks's Lord Spencer entered in evident ill-humour, and grunted a good-morning. I spoke not a word until he remarked, 'I see the National Trust has come into another property.' 'Oh, which one?' I asked. 'Polesden Lacey,' he said. One of Mrs. Ronnie Greville's[1] executors had told him. I was not surprised and had wondered since her death if this would be the case.

Rick and I walked for hours round and round Chelsea in the moonlight. In the course of a rather distracted conversation he told me that, while dying, his mother, whom they thought asleep, overheard their despairing talk, and surprised them by asking in a frightened little voice, 'What are you going to do with me?' This haunts him. Clearly one should never speak confidentially to others before the dying.

Sunday, 20th September

Sat with Henry Andrews at luncheon. He is Rebecca West's husband. He says his wife does not take naturally to housework, but is conscientious and slow. He and she make their bed every morning.

I walked to the Temple. It is curious to see cabbages growing round the empty plinth of King William's equestrian statue in St. James's Square.

Found John Summerson in the Temple directing a number of pupils who are making measured drawings. Since more than three-quarters of the old buildings are already destroyed it seems a little late in the day.

Monday, 21st September

At Sheffield I walked from the station to the Grand Hotel for an expensive, indifferent businessman's luncheon. There has been much destruction of the town, large stores burnt out and great untidy open spaces, which at first I took to be the usual Midlands squalor, then

[1] Margaret, daughter of Rt. Hon. William M'Ewan, brewer, who married 1891 Hon. Ronald Greville. She was a rich hostess.

realized to be caused by bombing. The executors to the late Miss Watt told me the trustees definitely offer Speke Hall [Lancashire] to us straight away, with an endowment of not more than £10,000, either in land or cash. In waiting for my train on Sheffield platform I went to the Gents'. I could not believe my eyes in reading the *graffiti* on the walls. Invitations to buggery, and long accounts of what boys like done to them, completely illustrated, dates asked and answered, names and addresses given, etc. Are they just bad jokes? Are they serious? Or the repressed fantasy longings of respectable clergymen? And are similar *graffiti* to be found in the Ladies'?

The train to York was so crowded that I was obliged to stand on the concertina part connecting one coach with another. The floor beneath me twisted and swayed like water skis.

Tuesday, 22nd September

After a visit to the Treasurer's House I caught a bus to Wetherby, crossing Marston Moor. Mr. Foster met me and took me to lunch at the small priest's house at Stockeld, where he is living at present. His agent and accountant were present. Stockeld Park is now a maternity home. The place was bought by Mr. Foster's father in the nineties from the Middletons, a Catholic family. The chapel is by Detmar Blow. The house is eighteenth century and was greatly added to *circa* 1900 and decorated by Gillow. But the central elliptical staircase with iron, crinoline balusters and apsidal recesses leading to various rooms on each storey, is striking. A beautiful walled garden, woods and estate of 1,700 acres of fine, spreading country. I stayed to tea and the agent after many questionings motored me to Farnley, of which estate he is also agent.

Farnley Hall near Otley is on a splendid site above Wharfedale. Both the Horton-Fawkeses very friendly, and absolutely easy. Until recently he was an Eton master. Farnley is an enormous house. On arrival we found husband and wife cooking the dinner for they have no servants at all. One part of the house is early seventeenth century, wainscoted with chopped-up panelling, mostly taken from old beds. The dining-room panelling is painted with minute hunting scenes of horsemen and hounds, about 1820, by one George Woods. Tacked on to this house is a large block by John Carr. The furniture, made for the Carr block is stacked away, for until a month ago Farnley was also a maternity home. Chippendale came from Otley, so I wish I could have seen the furniture. Turner in his early years was patronized by a Fawkes, and his room is shown. There are still some forty of his water-colours of the park, lodges, and even of the interior of the house. Most of them are put away but I saw one of the present Mrs. Horton-Fawkes's room, wherein nearly all the furniture is discernible. I helped clear away after dinner, and dried to my hosts' washing up. I wish all my visits were as fun and as carefree as this one.

Wednesday, 23rd September

Bussed to East Riddlesden Hall. The house is perched above the Aire with a romantic view across the river to the hills in the west, but hugged by beastly development on the Keighley side.

Lunched late at the Victoria Hotel, Keighley. Yorkshire people are all friendly, unlike the gruff Lincolnshire folk. I went to Haworth Parsonage on pilgrimage. The bus climbs an interminable hill all the way from Keighley. The village street is still cobbled, and excessively steep. The women wear clogs. The church has been rebuilt, but the pathetic Brontë mural tablet has been preserved. In the churchyard is an impenetrable forest of tombstones. The Parsonage lies on higher ground overlooking the forest, not below grave level as I had supposed, but seemingly healthily if coldly situated. The moors stretch away from the very back door. Alas, the house was given an annexe round about 1880, also plate glass for square panes. The rooms, though small, are airy. The contents now exiguous. I walked on the moors which are windy, weird and inhospitable, and saw the heather and the black crags. It is surprising how many habitations up here are perched on the highest skylines. A pity, for they rob the contours of much of their weirdness. However every untouched contour, and some of the built-up ones, and every rock, almost every tuft of blasted heath I saw must have been known by the Brontës like the backs of their hands. The museum should be better arranged. Yet one is allowed freedom to roam in it, which is something.

Thursday, 24th September

In my York hotel I heard a siren in the night. At 9 in the morning I climbed to the top of the Minster tower. It was a fine autumn morning but too misty to see far. I was entirely alone up there, and free, my pleasure spiced with that persistent fear of heights. I get a crinkling of the toes, a tingling of the instep. When I descended a verger said I ought not to have gone up. 'There was no notice to that effect,' I said. 'No,' he said, 'but a live bomb was dropped close to the tower during the night, and has not been de-fused yet.'

I reached Catterick Bridge hotel at midday. After luncheon bussed and walked to Moulton Hall. Always the best way to approach a house is on foot. It is a beautiful, compact little house, built in 1654, with curved and pedimented gables in the Kew Palace style. There is plate glass in the windows. A peculiarity is the rusticated ashlar bands, each alternate one being fish-scaled. Nothing left inside beyond a superb Charles II staircase, pierced and scrolled with baskets of flowers and fruits on the newels, and carved pendants from the soffits. Pretty little garden with yew and beech hedges.

Mrs. Pease kept me waiting, and appeared a little sombre. She is an elderly, grey, good-looking widow, dressed in black. She soon melted. She thinks she may leave the house in her will.

I walked back to Catterick, five miles. I stopped to look at Moulton Manor from the gate. The owner appeared and showed me round. The house was built by the same family a little earlier than the Hall, and is only a few hundred yards from it.

Friday, 25th September

I took a bus from Newcastle, standing all the way, and arrived at Wallington at 7.30 in the rain and dark. Matheson and John Dower met me by the stables and carried my bag. I was tired and depressed all day, and found the Trevelyan[1] family overpowering in spite of the kind welcome they gave me. Lady Trevelyan came out of the drawing-room in a sweeping, stately rush, shaking my hands warmly and exuding cordiality. When I went into the dining-room Sir Charles rose and shook hands in the same hospitable way. I don't quite know why, because they are dyed in the wool socialists, this should have surprised me. A newly married daughter Patricia, big with child, is living here; so is another daughter Pauline (Mrs. Dower). Her husband, the aforementioned John Dower, is working on post-war National Park schemes, is very left-wing, and from his connections and position is, according to Matheson, important.

Lady Trevelyan speaks succinctly, carefully and measuredly, using

[1] Rt. Hon. Sir Charles Trevelyan, 3rd Bart. (1870–1958), President of the Board of Education 1924, and 1929–31. Lady Trevelyan was a daughter of Sir Hugh Bell, 2nd Bart.

the north country clipped 'a', and is distinctly 'clever'. Gertrude Bell was her sister. Lady T. is handsome in a 'no nonsense about appearances' manner, and looks as though she may have been the first woman chairman of the L.C.C. I don't know if she ever was this. She is authoritarian, slightly deaf, and wears pince-nez. The two daughters are abrupt and rather terrifying. Mrs. Dower paints water-colours, competently. After dinner I am worn out, and long for bed. But no. We have general knowledge questions. Lady T. puts the questions one after the other with lightning rapidity. I am amazed and impressed by her mental agility, and indeed by that of the daughters, who with pursed lips shoot forth unhesitating answers like a spray of machine-gun bullets. All most alarming to a tired stranger. At the end of the 'game', for that is what they call this preparatory school examination, they allot marks. Every single member of the family gets 100 out of 100. The son-in-law gets 80, Matheson (who is also a clever man) gets 30. I get 0. But then I am a half-wit. Deeply humiliated I receive condolences from the Trevelyans and assurances that I shall no doubt do better next time. I make an inward vow that there never will be a next time.

Saturday, 26th September

A beautiful sunny but frosty morning. Breakfast at 8. Having slept well and eaten well, I felt fit for anything. In fact having girded my loins I was prepared for the worst. As it turned out I enjoyed the day. Matheson and I spent morning and afternoon tramping, map in hand, round the entire estate, to Chesters Farm and the distant moorland in the north; and to Scots Gap in the opposite direction.

After tea Sir Charles took me round the house. He is seventy-one, rather old and slow, white-haired and bent, with a large nose. He is very like Professor Trevelyan, but less grim. Although an advanced socialist, he has lost his old fanaticism, is courteous, and not absolutely humourless. I quite like him.

The saloon is one of the loveliest rooms I have seen. It has a high coved ceiling, of which the ground colour is the original egg blue, with rococo plaster motifs in white. Under the cornice the walls are painted a Naples yellow, verging on terracotta.

Friday, 2nd October

I have again developed a streaming cold. Since doctors have done nothing to alleviate or cure, far less prevent the common cold, how can one have faith in them when one suffers from more serious complaints? Surgery has of course progressed, but medicine is pure quackery. When I think of the contradictory way in which doctors have treated my complaint over the past two years, the agonizing lumbar punctures, the torture chamber wracks, the psychoanalysis, the conflicting drugs, how can I have the least confidence in their ridiculous profession? The best one can say for doctors is that they are not all rogues, like all lawyers.

Feeling wretchedly ill and not knowing whether I am treading on air or land, I enter the London Library. I tease Mr. Cox over his misinformation about Rommel being killed in an air crash. 'Ah!' he says, 'but now we read what applause he received at Hitler's meeting in Berlin, he will surely be bumped off.'

While I was having tea in Brooks's Ben Nicolson[1] walked in. He looks older, more poised, more aware of the world around him. He said he was going to the Middle East immediately. He was to have flown this morning in a stratosphere bomber which to his delight was cancelled at the last moment, for he was not looking forward to this mode of transport. He felt sure he would feel ill, sick and frightened. Nigel[2] is also leaving shortly with his battalion, and Harold is very sad at losing them both.

A. H. said this afternoon that Charles Fry[3] swore to her he had slept, at different times, with three of her cousins, two sisters and a brother— a good record. This reminds me that Randolph [Churchill] once told me O. M. boasted to him of having what he called 'stretched the cock over three generations,' i.e. slept over an interval of years with a grandmother, her daughter, and her granddaughter. I don't know who they were. Jan, Angela Kinross's mother, came to tea with the Hills, where I am staying. It appears that Angela has had her illegitimate child, a son, before her divorce from Patrick is through. She has entered his birth under the father's name, although he is still married. Legally speaking however, the child could be the Hon. Something Balfour, and if Patrick were killed he might have a claim to be Lord Kinross unless the Balfour family disputed the title.[4]

[1] Harold Nicolson's elder son. Editor of the *Burlington Magazine* since 1947.
[2] Harold Nicolson's younger son, writer and biographer.
[3] Partner of B. T. Batsford, publishers.
[4] In fact in an exchange of letters between lawyers, both Lord Kinross and his former wife established the fact that the child was not his.

At Englefield Green I called on Mrs. Whitbread about her house, Burford, in Shropshire. She was unnecessarily modest about it, trying to rake up some Norman associations, whereas from the photographs it appears a decent George I house. It is extraordinary how quite intelligent people think that a house's site mentioned in Domesday is a better qualification than its architecture by Wren.

In pouring rain I walked to Cumberland Lodge. Soaked to the skin and my feet squelching in my shoes I sat talking for half an hour with Lord FitzAlan, who was lying in a vast four-post bed, gazing straight ahead, not at me, but the chimneypiece.

Standing with Alathea on Egham platform this morning, I was greeted, coldly enough, by the awful adjutant of my old regiment. The sight of this man, who can now do me no possible harm, made my knees quake. I could hardly pull myself into the train. Strange how such encounters can affect one physically. I would sooner 'go over the top' any day than meet him again.

Michael Peto who lunched with me said I had the most enviable life of anybody he knew. It is true and in the circumstances I do not deserve it. He is still absurdly optimistic, and assured me that the Germans would crack and the war would be over by the next Armistice Day. How can he be so foolish? I reminded him that in 1939 he assured me it would be over by March 1940.

Helen gave me a lift into High Wycombe in her taxi. At the traffic lights she leapt out, and into a green bus bound for Windsor, as it was waiting to cross, leaving me aghast at her promptness and agility, and under the obligation to pay the taxi fare. She is a woman of resources.

I went to Farrer & Co. who told me that Lord Mount Edgcumbe was toying with the idea of leaving Mount Edgcumbe and Cotehele to the Trust. Mount Edgcumbe house has been burnt out and all its contents destroyed during a raid on Plymouth. There is a lot of land which is of great importance to Plymouth. Lord Mt. E., over seventy, has a poor life; his successor is another old man whose only son has just been killed in this war, and the ultimate heir is a New Zealander whom he cares nothing for and who won't come to England. Farrer, in show-showing me over 66 Lincoln's Inn Fields, said the house has been the Farrer family office for 150 years, which is surely remarkable.

At 2.30 I attended a meeting of Mrs. Ronnie Greville's executors – Lords Ilchester, Bruntisfield and Dundonald, and Terence Maxwell. Lord D. asked me what relation I was to Aunt Dorothy. He said she was a real eccentric. The meeting lasted till 5. A most interesting and complex subject, involving an estate of some £2 million. Mrs. Greville has left Marie Antoinette's necklace to the Queen, £20,000 to Princess Margaret Rose, and £25,000 to the Queen of Spain. Everyone in London is agog to learn the terms of Mrs. G.'s will. She was a lady who loved the great because they were great, and apparently had a tongue dipped in gall. I remember old Lady Leslie once exclaiming, when her name was mentioned, 'Maggie Greville! I would sooner have an open sewer in my drawing-room.'

At Brooks's I had tea with Lord Ilchester who wanted to talk more about Polesden. He said John Fox-Strangways [his son] is expected home any day. He is among the first six officer prisoners to be ex-changed for Germans. He is now in New York where he has had an operation and a plate inserted in his thigh, which was shot through. Lord Ilchester was alarmed last week by finding Ministry officials walking round Melbury Park measuring it up for a possible hospital. He had had no warning of their visit.

Saturday, 10th October

Eddy and I went to the Arts Theatre Club to see *The House of Regrets* by a very young Russian, Peter Ustinov, son of Nadia Benois. It is a brilliant play about a White Russian family in some North London suburb before and during the war; quite in the *Cherry Orchard* tradition. There is too little drama, but it shows acute observation, exact feeling, humour and pathos. I was very much moved by it.

Monday, 12th October

In Salisbury I had a quick snack and walked to the cathedral. The setting of this and the setting of Durham Cathedral, which I saw last month, make them far and away my two favourite English cathedrals. The aspirant verticality of this spire literally takes the breath away. On entering the close, I gasped. But I was also transfixed by what I saw happening on the spire. Two boy steeplejacks were suspended from the very apex in cradles on ropes. I suppose they had been doing repairs to the stonework. Now they were playing the fool in swinging across one another, so that their ropes crossed and became entangled. With hoots of laughter they pressed their feet against the spire and swung themselves back again. An old man on the grass below shouted to them to stop. He clapped his hands, which made the pigeons fly off the clerestory. I felt so apprehensive that I rushed inside the cathedral in order not to witness the ropes break and the boys crash to the ground. Then I talked to a workman painting the jambs of the great west doorway. He said he was applying linseed oil to the Devonshire marble shafts, the pale greeny-yellow outdoor shafts, as a weather protective; and he pointed out the surface of the marble he had not yet painted, which was pitted all over. This treatment had been neglected, he said, for twenty years, at least.

By appointment with Sir Henry Hoare[1] I was at the County Hotel by 2 o'clock. I gave my name to the porter and sat in the dreary lounge to wait. A young R.A.F. sergeant came in and sat down. I looked up and saw a face of ineffable beauty which smiled in a most beseeching manner. The sergeant took out a cigarette, offered me one and was about to introduce himself when, damn it! Sir Henry Hoare was announced.

Sir Henry is an astonishing nineteenth-century John Bull, hobbling on two sticks. He was wearing a pepper and salt suit and a frayed grey billycock over his purple face. He had a very bronchial cough and kept hoiking and spitting into an enormous carrot-coloured handkerchief. En route for Stourhead I sat in the back of the car beside him and behind an old chauffeur of immense, overlapping fatness who had an asthmatic wheeze, like a blacksmith's bellows. Sir Henry talked about his bad knee, and told me he had lost a knee-cap. I found myself shouting, for he is rather deaf, 'Do you find it much of a handicap having no knee-cap?' After the third repetition I decided that my remark was inept.

Lady Hoare is an absolute treasure, and unique. She is tall, ugly and eighty-two; dressed in a long black skirt, belled from a wasp waist and trailing over her ankles. She has a thick net blouse over a rigidly upholstered bosom, complete with stiff, whaleboned high collar round

[1] Sir Henry Hoare, 6th Bart. (1865–1947). Gave Stourhead to the National Trust, 1946–7. He and Lady Hoare died on the same day, 25th March 1947.

the throat. Over this a black and white check jacket, evidently reinforced with stays, for it ends in tight points over her thighs. The sleeves are exaggeratedly mutton-chop. She has a protruding square coif of frizzly grey hair in the style of the late nineties, black eyebrows and the thickest spectacle lenses I have ever seen. She is nearly blind in one eye. She is humorous and enchanting. She adores the memory of George Lloyd and is quite convinced that he was the greatest Englishman of this century.

The Hoares took me round the house, which is packed to the brim with good things, and some ghastly things like cheap bamboo cake stands and thin silver vases filled with peacocks' feathers. On the grand piano an impenetrable forest of silver photograph frames. The house was gutted by fire in 1902 and rebuilt by Sir Aston Webb from old photographs and records. There are some rococo chimneypieces brought after the fire from another Hoare house in Northamptonshire. Only the Regency picture gallery and library in the projecting wings were spared. All the contents however were saved, including the wonderful suite of furniture by the younger Chippendale. I was given to read his bills from 1795 to 1812, and the *Stourhead Annals*, kept fairly regularly from 1792 to the present day.

For dinner we had soup, whiting, pheasant, apple pie, dessert, a white Rhine wine and port. Lady Hoare has no housemaid, and only a cook and butler. But she said with satisfaction, 'The Duchess of Somerset at Maiden Bradley has to do all her own cooking.'

We ate in the little dining-room at a long table, Sir Henry with his back to a colonnaded screen, Lady Hoare with hers to the window. He spoke very little, and that little addressed to himself. She kept up a lively, not entirely coherent prattle. She said to me, 'Don't you find the food better in this war than in the last?' I replied that I was rather young during the last war, but I certainly remembered the rancid margarine we were given at my preparatory school when I was eight. 'Oh!' she said. 'You were lucky. We were reduced to eating rats.' I was a little surprised, until Sir Henry looked up and said, 'No, no, Alda. You keep getting your wars wrong. That was when you were in Paris during the Commune.'

The purpose of my visit was to talk over Sir Henry's offer to leave with the estate the live and dead stock of the Home Farm, valued at £15,000. He told me that Rennie Hoare, his heir, would almost certainly not live at Stourhead, and this saddened him. The Hoares have reigned fifty years here. Their only son was killed in the last war, and both of them live on his memory.

They are the dearest old couple. I am quite in love with her out-spoken ways and funny old-fashioned dress. She is humorous in the gentlest, kindest manner conceivable. They have had soldiers in the basement of the house, and their present unit is leaving tomorrow.

Tuesday, 13th October

During breakfast the officers of the departing unit come in one by one and fervently thank the Hoares for their kindness, and express genuine sorrow to be going. Lady Hoare is much affected.

It is a beautiful morning and Sir Henry gets into his electric chair, and I accompany him to the lakes and the temples; or rather, I gallop at breakneck speed behind him. He is quite unaware that his chair goes the devil of a pace and I have the utmost difficulty in keeping up. As he presses the accelerator he asks me questions which demand answers and intelligent comments. He keeps saying 'Where are you? Why don't you say something?' When I do catch up I am so out of breath I can't get the words out. All he says (to himself) is, 'I don't understand what's come over the boy.' Mercifully when I was on the verge of total collapse we met Michael Rosse on the far side of the large lake. He had come from the Guards Brigade H.Q. near by. I am glad to have introduced him to the Hoares who will undoubtedly ask him to Stourhead again. Somehow I can't see Michael running after that chair.

Wednesday, 14th October

I motored with Captain Hill[1] to Polesden Lacey. The house was built by Cubitt in 1818 and looks from a distance across the valley much as it did in Neale's view of that date. The interior was, I imagine, entirely refitted by Mrs. Greville, in the expensive taste of an Edwardian millionairess. But it is not vulgar. It is filled with good things, and several museum pieces. The upstairs rooms are well appointed, in six or seven self-contained suites with bathrooms attached. There is a grass courtyard in the middle of the house.

Mrs. Greville has been buried in the rose garden to the west of the

[1] John Hill, agent to Sir John Dashwood at West Wycombe. He made many reports of prospective properties for the National Trust.

house, next to the dog cemetery in accordance with female country house owner tradition. The gardens are unostentatious and rather beautiful: the grounds very beautiful, with a splendid view across the vale from the south front to a wooded hill beyond. Queen Mary's Walk is a straight grass ride bordered with yew.

Sunday, 18th October

Last night I caught the 10.55 for Scotland. I did not sleep much because of the heat of my third-class carriage. It was not over-crowded. There were only two other bunks occupied. The train was an hour late reaching Stirling this morning. I made friends with a commercial traveller in my carriage by giving him some chocolate. In return I borrowed his soap. Then he managed to bribe a cup of tea for each of us in a first-class coach. There was no restaurant car. At Stirling I bought some bannocks and jam buns at a service canteen by buttoning up my old army mackintosh. Between Stirling and Oban I watched the brown burns dashing down the hill-sides; and from the train window inhaled the strong heathery, peaty smell. Of course it is pouring with rain. Aunt Dorothy met me at Connel Ferry. She is thinner since I last saw her in 1938, and she wheezes more, presumably because of her pipe. She smokes a ghastly tobacco called Afrikander Flake, which rasps the skin off one's throat. Ardachy, or Straw Castle as she calls it, was built by her before the war, literally out of deal lathes and cardboard. It is ugly outside and comfortable inside, for she has a cook, kitchen maid and parlourmaid (three sisters), a housekeeper and a housemaid, besides a chauffeur-handyman-gardener, and a farm worker, who is brother to the three sisters.

Tuesday, 20th October

This morning we motor over the mountains to a village by the sea. Aunt D. and Joan Hewitt[1] interview a land girl. I walk down the village street of single storey hovels, with one window on either side of a doorway. Very clean they look through the windows, but the accommodation must be very restricted, and the services presumably nil. Yet the inhabitants look well and robust. Aunt D., who defends everything Highland, says these hovels are surprisingly spacious,

[1] Dorothy Lees-Milne's friend who lived with her for over thirty years of her widowhood.

comfortable and warm inside. They are exactly what Walter Scott described in the Waverley novels, no more no less. I walk along the road and sit on a rock, the sun full out, with my feet just above the breakers. The gulls are screaming, and there are clearly defined views of distant islands and a jagged coastline. There is a delicious smell of salty, antiseptic seaweed. The place is remote and romantic, and melancholy. On the way back we have glimpses of mountain tops across fertile valleys, with corn and hay as yet unstooked.

In the afternoon Aunt D. sits on a panel in Oban judging 'call-up' cases, and listening to the pleas of her friends and neighbours to keep their servants. Meanwhile I walk round, or rather along the town, for it has no breadth and only has length, looking at the sea-planes land and rise, and the camouflaged boats bob up and down in the harbour. I approach the new Roman Catholic cathedral, of which only the east end is completed, the walls of the nave and west tower still standing roofless. The church is of granite and I pronounce it horrid, until I see on a notice board that Sir Giles Scott is the architect. Whereupon my interest is aroused. I look again, and find some merits in the design. I believe the thing may eventually have style, although the Gothic lancet windows are weak and conventional.

Friday, 23rd October

Today I climbed the highest of the two peaks overlooking Loch Etive from behind the house. It was a stormy day with only fair visibility yet I could see the Firth of Lorne beyond Oban, the isle of Lismore to the west, Ben More on Mull, the mountains of Morvern, and to the east Ben Cruachan and Loch Awe. I must actually have reached the summit, a thing one too seldom achieves. To the north there was nothing but desolate heathery bog, bare shoulders of rock and a purple sky curtain of storm and anger. Below me I saw distant deer, and above me a buzzard or two. Around me I heard the cackle of grouse. I was absolutely alone, enjoying uninterrupted views in every direction. There was not a human being within miles and miles and miles.

Sunday, 25th October

I went to see Jamesey who is ill in bed. We both agreed it was high time we got married. Jamesey has in mind a really rustic 'yeowoman'. But how, he asked plaintively, does one set about finding one? I could

114

only think of the old spinster with a patch over one eye at Earlswood Moat House. Dame Una interrupted our conversation by carrying into the room a silver crucifix given her by Lady Gregory.[1] Very ancient it was, and hollowed for the purpose of containing green leaves, arranged to sprout from the head, arms and feet of the cross, and represent the living Christ. She said it was Spanish.

Eddy was in Brooks's and I had tea with him. I congratulated him for having produced the reading of *Maud* by Laurence Olivier the other evening on the wireless, surely the best way, I said, of reviving interest in poetry. He said many such performances went on weekly, if only I took the trouble to listen-in.

Tuesday, 27th October

Lord Ilchester told me he was very cross with Esher and the S.P.A.B. for worrying him about making Holland House into an amenity centre after the war, and then never till this day telling him whether or not they wanted it. He complained that the S.P.A.B. in stating that £40,000 would suffice for rebuilding the house had badly queered his pitch with the War Damage people, for it was quite obvious to him that the actual figure ought to be in the region of £100,000. Now that the War Damage people knew about the lesser figure, he stood no chance of getting from them the full compensation.

Sir Courtauld-Thomson caught me again and made me have tea with him to tell me he had seen Lord Portal this afternoon. Lord Portal was more determined than ever to get Dorney Wood for the Cabinet's use. The Ministry of Works however want the full endowment of £200,000 now, and will not agree to the Trust having the £70,000 for the purchase of additional land. Matheson says this will make us review the whole proposition, which is accordingly less attractive to us than before.

Thursday, 29th October

I met Goodhart-Rendel[2] at his office in Crawford Street. The very next house to his has been bombed, and is sliced off. He is a captain in the

---

[1] Isabella Augusta Gregory (1852–1932). Irish playwright, literary hostess and patron, and friend of W. B. Yeats.

[2] Harry Goodhart-Rendel (1887–1959), architect. Gave Hatchlands, Surrey, to the National Trust, 1945.

Grenadiers, although over fifty, working at the Caterham depot, and simply loves it. He told me the order of his chief interests in life is: 1. the Roman Catholic Church, 2. the Brigade of Guards, and 3. Architecture. He walked restlessly up and down the room, talking about his men. He claimed that the type enlisting today is superior than ever before in physique and morale. He is anxious for the Trust to work out a modified scheme for taking over Hatchlands. The Trust must be satisfied with less endowment than they are asking for.

Mr. Frank Green's agent, James, has an office in John Street, Bedford Row. Its immediate neighbour has likewise been bombed to atoms. Without its support Mr. James fears his house may collapse without warning. He says Frank Green[1] changes his mind every day, but believes he really wishes to give us Culverthorpe, but not one square inch of garden; merely covenants and £10,000. I said firmly that these silly conditions were not acceptable.

I met Rick on the 3.40 for Aylsham as the train was leaving Liverpool Street Station. He had jumped through one door, I through another of the same corridor while the train was gathering speed. We collapsed in a heap of breathlessness, relief and helpless laughter. He was wearing a smart, rather flashy new suit that had belonged to a friend killed in the war. I was wearing for the first time Desmond Parsons's Irish suit, which Anne Rosse gave me. Both of us in dead men's clothes. From Aylsham station we walked to Blickling, he carrying my heavy bag. We stayed the night in Miss O'Sullivan's flat.

Friday, 30th October

We walked round the gardens and the lake, R. making countless good and not so good suggestions. We met the R.A.F. officer in charge, a Wing-Commander Fry, who is very proud of living in so great a house. He asked to be allowed to use the front door, but Birkbeck the agent and I refused, because it would necessitate the men using the hall and grand staircase. R. disagreed with us, saying that if we let him he would then be under an obligation and would co-operate with us in stopping R.A.F. vandalism in the house.

Miss James the housekeeper is in a woeful state because her dog was stolen on Monday by the R.A.F. and has not been seen since. In between her tears she told me he was the sweetest and cleverest being imaginable, and she loved him more than anyone in the world. To comfort

[1] Donor of Treasurer's House, York, to the Trust, 1930.

and distract her I led her on to her favourite subject, Blenheim. She told me how Gladys Duchess of Marlborough would have her spaniels in the staterooms in order to annoy the duke who was inconceivably fussy. He would spend hours examining the curtains looking for stains made by the dogs, and was very disappointed if he failed to find any. He would indicate to Miss James the exact spots on the carpet on which the front or back legs of certain tables were to stand. The duchess took drugs, and swore at the odd man for wheeling the coal into the cellar beneath her bedroom and waking her up with the noise. In her dressing-gown at the window she called him dreadful names. After an hour of these and similar tales, none of which I believe to be true, Miss James dried her tears and recovered her composure.

Willey the gardener explained to me how to cut back yews to make them 'break', which means allowing the green to sprout low down on the boles. He said, 'The crueller you are the better, so long as you give them air and light.'

Sunday, 1st November

I called for Anne Rosse at her uncle's house in Stafford Terrace, a house bought by her grandfather, Linley Sambourne, the *Punch* cartoonist of the 1880s. It is a period piece, untouched. It is choc-a-bloc with *art nouveau*. The Morris-papered walls are plastered with old photographic groups and Sambourne drawings, the frames touching each other, weird clocks galore, stained-glass windows, Victorian walking-sticks and parasols. Anne and I walked round the pretty back streets by Holland Park, and took a bus to the Ritz, where Michael joined us at 1 o'clock, and Oliver [Messel][1] at 2 o'clock. We talked over the luncheon table till 4. Oliver is a camouflage major in Norwich. He has discovered Ivory's[2] disused Assembly Rooms, made them into his headquarters, and is redecorating them.

Tuesday, 3rd November

Was met at Farnham [Surrey] by Mr. W. L. Wood, a newspaper proprietor, and wife, who motored me to their house. It was built by Wood in the colonial style, neo-Georgian with a portico of slender columns. Unfortunately in every room one hears what is going on in

[1] Oliver Messel, artist and stage designer. A brother of Lady Rosse.
[2] Thomas Ivory (1709–79), leading Norwich architect.

the next. When Mr. W. went to the loo I heard everything, but everything. We lunched at 12.30 off cold partridge, which I could not get off the bone, and tinned sausage. Mr. W. is a tough businessman sprung from I don't know where. He speaks softly and burrs his 'r's. He mounted me on a small black horse, I changing into my plus-fours brought for the purpose, and we rode to Frensham Common. It was a sunny, crisp, invigorating afternoon. He conducted me round the boundaries of the common to inspect a lot of 140 acres which the Robertson trustees have agreed to purchase for us. The lot covers a wide space of sandy heath and small Scotch firs, a natural lung in this horrid part of Surrey so near accursed Aldershot. We cantered along the grass. The Great and Little Ponds are drained of water so as not to make landmarks from the air. In the Great Pond thousands of birches have seeded themselves, and are already too tall to be uprooted. Mr. Wood knew Christopher Hobhouse[1] who wrote for his paper, the *Builder*, and had a great admiration for him. He thought Christopher the most brilliant writer of my generation.

Wednesday, 4th November

At 2.30 the Eshers, accompanied by Lady Eliot,[2] and I went round 16 Charles Street W.1. It is a palace. We all agreed it was unsuitable for offices, being far too rich and big. We saw the furniture stacked in the drawing-room, which I have got to sort through. Mrs. Greville's house steward had come from Polesden to be our guide. He was very drunk and lachrymose. Esher did not like this at all. I heard the man sobbing behind us as we went round, and felt sorry for him. He had been forty-two years with Mrs. Greville, to whom he was genuinely devoted. He was constantly intoxicated during her grand dinner parties. Once she scribbled him a note from her silver pad, 'You are drunk. Leave the room immediately.' He swayed down the table, and handed the note to Sir John Simon.

Saturday, 7th November

The servant situation at West Wycombe is becoming more and more impossible. All this week Helen has been hysterical, staying in bed,

[1] Christopher Hobhouse, author of a life of Charles James Fox. He was killed while serving in the Marines, 1941.

[2] Nellie, wife of Hon. Sir Montague Eliot, who succeeded in November 1942 as 8th Earl of St. Germans.

saying she is ill, but going out mysteriously to dine with the Americans and returning worse than before. The new butler has been frightfully rude to us National Trusts, and I was driven to call him an insolent scoundrel. Since then he has behaved himself better, but it is uncomfortable. He will not speak to me, and I feel the waves of his hatred.

Y. has been graded Class 4 by the army. He told them he was a homosexual and on that account they graded him so low. I was shocked because the reason seems a frivolous one. He might as well have said he preferred peppermints to chocolate biscuits. When Y. said, 'What earthly use would I be in the army?' I did think perhaps he would be no use. But what earthly use is he out of it?

In the dense blackout I walked, torchless, to dine with Margaret Jourdain and Ivy Compton-Burnett, who had also invited their great friend Soame Jenyns.[1] He is heavy, Jewish-looking (though he isn't a Jew), dark, sallow, has a seat in Cambridgeshire called Bottisham, and in peacetime works in the British Museum. We had an enjoyable evening. Miss C.-B. is not as good a conversationalist as Miss J., and is always listening to what the other is saying to her neighbour. It is very difficult to get them to talk together. Miss C.-B. says she cannot get on with her book; the war is drying her up. We agree that this war has produced no poetry or works of art. But she says perhaps it is too soon to judge; we must wait for the war to be over for the slow inspiration to eke its way out.

At Cheyne Walk I found Rick drinking tea and claret alternately out of tumblers. He gets very sleepy, he says, after one glass of the last since the crack on his head from a girder, and has to turn to tea to counteract the effects of the wine. I began the night on a small sofa. R. was in the big bed. I could not sleep a wink. First my toes were out at the end; then my head and chest out at the top, freezing. At 3 a.m. R. allowed me to join him in the big bed, and we talked. He said something; I said something; he said something; I was saying something, when all of a sudden I heard him snoring. I cannot for the life of me do this. I am a hopeless getter-to-sleep.

Sunday, 8th November

I took a 10 o'clock train to Luton, where a taxi met me and drove me

[1] Deputy Keeper of the Department of Oriental Antiquities at the British Museum.

to the agent's office at Luton Hoo, where I found Sir Harold and Lady Zia Wernher. They showed me maps of the estate and talked generally of their intentions to give the house, contents and some 1,000 acres. The National Trust must run the house as a museum, and they must be allowed to live in a part of it. The collections, most from the house and some from Bath House, Piccadilly, belonging to his mother, Lady Ludlow, are reputedly very fine indeed. Since they were stacked away in the chapel I was unable to see them.

The Wernhers are charming people. He is simple and forthcoming; she is pretty and sweet. She is a daughter of the Grand Duke Michael of Russia by his morganatic wife, Countess de Torby.

We got into a small car and were motored round the estate to Someries Farm and the old brick castle, a fifteenth-century ruin. We came back and walked through the walled garden, which is immense and contains an ocean of hothouses. We lunched in the agent's house where the Wernhers are living. We listened to the 1 o'clock news and were thrilled to hear that the Americans had invaded North Africa and Giraud had declared for the Allies in Algeria. Perhaps this is the turning point of the war in our favour, if only the campaign goes happily. Lady Zia said that although she was a Russian, she had never been in Russia. She speaks with a faint accent which is seductive. She said her father and mother had taken Kenwood, where she lived in the last war. The Wernhers bought some of the Chippendale furniture from Kenwood, and it is now at Luton Hoo. Lady Ludlow is still the actual tenant for life of Luton Hoo.

After luncheon he changed into uniform and I saw that he was a general, a staff officer with red tabs and a red band round his cap. We walked through the pleasure gardens, quite gone to seed, and over the house, which is now the Eastern Command headquarters. The house is terrible, outside as well as in. Built by Adam in the 1760s for Lord Bute, it was burnt down in 1840 and rebuilt by Smirke. It was deliberately gutted in 1903 and reconstituted for the Wernhers by Mewes & Davis, architects of the Ritz Hotel. The outside walls are still more or less Adam, but in 1903 a top storey with mansard roof was added. The roofline is very untidy, with odd chimneys and unsightly skylights. The interior, or as much as I could see of it, for it is boarded up to eye level, is opulent Edwardian and Frenchified. Walking down the cavernous basement passages is like being in a tube station. In one room below stairs I came upon my cousin, Joe Napier, now a colonel, billeted here.

After an early tea the three of us went to Luton station where we had to wait fifty minutes for the train to London. When the train came in it was crowded with people standing on top of each other in the corridors. Advised by a porter we all went to the rear of the train. Having boarded it we were greeted by a guard who conducted us into an empty, first-class Pullman saloon, with detached armchairs. We sat there like royalty, which one of us partly was.

Monday, 9th November

Esher met Miss Paterson and me at the drive gates punctually at 10. We had a slow drive to London because of the fog. Several times I nearly drove into the back of cars ahead of me. Finally Esher said, 'Now having averted three major catastrophes, we may arrive safely.' We discussed whether the Trust office and staff, including the typists, should move to Polesden Lacey. He said the English race would never reconcile itself to communal living. He thought this war had had a salutary effect in proving how odious communism would be to the English. Socialism had also been proved odious through the number of documents and forms we have had to sign in war-time. The English were all grumblers whatever people might say about Julius Caesar, 'and in any case he was nothing but an ice-creamer'. He had received a letter from the Margeries excusing themselves for working in Shanghai after the fall of France. The reason they gave was that unless they had done so, reprisals would have been taken against their relations. 'Now no Englishman,' Esher said, 'would have been actuated by that motive. On the contrary, an Englishman would take every opportunity to ensure that reprisals *were* taken against his relations.'

The General Purposes Committee considered at length whether the office should move to Polesden, or not. Finally it was decided that we should return to London. I like to think I was partly responsible for this decision, in stressing the disadvantages of communal living in the country and the difficulties of getting to and from the station. Esher, who was in the chair, winked at me.

Tuesday, 10th November

I met Benton Fletcher[1] at 3 Cheyne Walk. He thinks this house is a

[1] Major Benton Fletcher gave to the National Trust Old Devonshire House, W.C.1, and a collection of old musical instruments. The house was totally destroyed in the war. Today the instruments are installed in Fenton House, Hampstead.

suitable one for the Trust to buy with the War Damage monies in compensation for Old Devonshire House, which was destroyed by bombs last year. The house was last lived in by Prothero, Lord Ernle. The trustees are asking £5,000 for the freehold. Rick, who knows his Chelsea, says we should offer £3,000.

Mr. Russell, Mrs. Greville's solicitor, said that when he visited Buckingham Palace and handed his client's necklace to the Queen, she asked, 'Why do I have to pretend I know nothing about Mrs. Greville's will, when everyone I meet informs me that she has left her property to the National Trust?' Indeed the Queen spent her honeymoon at Polesden. I think this weighed with the executors, who have decided to make a public announcement straightaway.

Sir Courtauld took me aside to say he had received a letter from the Prime Minister, congratulating him on his gift of Dorney Wood, and intimating his great pleasure. I suppose Sir C. is now awaiting a further honour for his unparalleled munificence.

Thursday, 12th November

Helen has taken the news of our departure manfully. I feel sorry for her, as she will have to look for other lodgers. She knows she may do worse than have us. Yesterday the odious butler walked out of the house at 9.30 without a word of warning because Helen asked him, quite nicely, to fetch her some marmalade for breakfast.

Because of a slight fog the train chose to be three-quarters of an hour late on arrival at Paddington. This put me in a furious temper, and I rang up Sir Courtauld's secretary to say I could not keep my appointment. I had a snack at the station buffet and took a seat in the train for Newton Abbot.

I stay the night at Bradley Manor with Mrs. Woolner.[1] Her mother-in-law is living with her. Her husband in the R.N.V.R. is a grandson of Thomas Woolner the sculptor. At dinner I drank beer from a silver tankard inscribed 'To Thomas Woolner from Alfred and Emily Tennyson 1864.' Old Mrs. Woolner said her mother-in-law's sister married Holman Hunt, whose first wife was another sister. This Mrs. Woolner was so shocked over the deceased wife's sister business that she refused ever to speak to her sister again. Mrs. Woolner also told me that Tennyson used to ask her husband when he was a boy, 'Why

[1] Who as Miss Diana Firth gave Bradley Manor and 68 acres to the National Trust in 1938.

is your nose not as straight as your sister's?' He hated Tennyson in consequence ever after.

Diana Woolner's husband has been to Murmansk. Indeed to Russia on several convoys. He says the Russians shoot their own officers for the slightest breach of discipline, frequently unjustly and always without trial. He made friends with one naval officer who was to be shot at dawn for a most venial misdemeanour. He spent the previous evening with Woolner on board his destroyer, happily playing chess as though nothing were the matter. Next morning he was shot.

Friday, 13th November

A bomb falling near the house [Bradley Manor] this spring broke a number of windows, drawing out the leads, damaging the Blue Room ceiling, and dislodging many stone mullions and transomes. I had forgotten all the history of this house until I was reminded by reading the guide-book, every word of which I had written as recently as 1939. From time to time I discover total blanks in my memory since my accident in 1940.

In between changing trains in Exeter I walk to the cathedral. The west end is unharmed and the nave roof line is unbroken, but every window is blown out. This probably doesn't matter, but it gives the building a dead, skeletal look. A vast area to the west of the cathedral has been completely laid waste. I arrive at Montacute station at 9.15. Carrying a knapsack and two cumbersome files I walk to the King's Arms. I stay the night in this friendly, clean little inn. Mr. Yates,[1] the welcoming host, sits and talks to me over the fire, while I drink tea and munch a sandwich. This is the kind of rustic hospitality I like.

Saturday, 14th November

A cold white frost, and a most beautiful autumn morning. I am very content to be here. To warm myself I walk up the *Mons Acutus*, which is slippery with greasy mud. It is an ancient British earthwork with spiral terraces up it, and a 1760 tower at the top. The village below is wreathed in silver mist, and blue smoke from the chimneys is twirled straight in the crisp air. Then I meet Rawlence the agent and his absurd Sancho Panza, a risible, strutting sparrow, throwing a chest and

[1] Arthur Yates and Mrs. Yates subsequently became custodians of Montacute House for many years.

exclaiming, 'I, I, I have done so and so.' This is a warning how careful I must be not to become too proprietary in talking about the National Trust properties which I look after. The house [Montacute] is lovely, with the low sunlight on the orange Ham-stone walls and the crinkly glass windows. It is in very fair condition, thanks to Shoemark the village mason whose family has tended it for generations.

Sunday, 15th November

In Brooks's Lord Ilchester hailed me and we breakfasted together at the big table in front of the fire. He has a slow gurgling voice which rises into a whine. He is asking in the Lords whether the military should be allowed to walk into people's property and take over without previously serving requisition orders. I mentioned the case of the black unit doing this at Montacute. Lord Ilchester said that he had removed most of the good furniture from Holland House before it was destroyed, and only lost a few pictures which he valued. He had also moved the most valuable books from the library.

I had an impulse to telephone Mama this morning. I told her how much I had enjoyed my visit to Montacute, which was the most beautiful Elizabethan house in England. 'No,' she said, 'it is a perfectly beastly house. You can't see out of a single window.' 'But,' I said, 'I didn't know that you had ever been there.' 'On the contrary,' she said, 'I stayed there in 1892 with Robert who was a school friend of the Phelips boy. And I hated it.' I calculate that she must have been eight years old, when of course a small child would not be able to look out of those high windows.

The church bells have been ordered to ring this morning to celebrate the victory in Egypt, rather prematurely I think. However in Piccadilly I heard not a sound. After Mass Rick took me over 104 Cheyne Walk, having climbed a drainpipe and swung from a window ledge before my horrified eyes to break a way in as usual. He is determined that I shall live in it when we come back to London. After luncheon he and I talked to the Strongs in Mrs. Carlyle's kitchen. Mr. and Mrs. Strong were engaged in a hot discussion about the merits of J. S. Mill's correspondence.

I walked to 1 Hyde Park Gardens to tea with Sir Ian Hamilton. This house, which in 1910 was decorated by Roger Fry in sombre black and green for Aunt Jean, is redolent of memories of her and her lovely great luncheon parties. There used to be a perpetual smell of joss-sticks

124

burning in the hall. Sir Ian was in the dining-room which he now uses as a living-room. It is panelled and has Scotch ancestors on the walls above. He was lying on a sofa with a rug over his knees. Mrs. Leeper at the tea-table. He will be ninety in February, and is thinner and less frisky than formerly. In fact when I arrived he was quiet and listless. He appears to be asleep until something rouses his interest. Then he is full of fire. Mrs. Leeper talked to me about the Royal Academy plans for the rebuilding of London, and the war in North Africa. Suddenly Sir Ian woke up, and launched into a long, irrelevant story about his talking very confidentially in fluent but execrable French with Marshal Lyautey, who was stone deaf, at a Foreign Office reception, and realizing that the other guests were drinking in every word. He said he was in this house last year when a bomb destroyed the house opposite. He swears his house moved a foot out of place, hesitated for an awful second, and fell back into place. He can prove the truth of the statement by some marks made by a supporting girder in the basement. Sir Ian is always courteous and cheerful. He said that we were third cousins, once or twice, or thrice removed—I forget which—through the Menteiths of Cranley. I have always liked this old warrior, and I dearly loved Aunt Jean. When on leaving I shook his hand, with its boney protuberance from the wrist, he said, with much earnestness, 'Thank you, my dear boy.'

Monday, 16th November

Rick and John Russell organized a concert tonight at Whistler's House, 96 [Cheyne Walk], in which Eddy and young Benjamin Britten played on two pianos Schubert and Chopin, and a tenor, Peter Pears, sang extremely competently the Dichterliebe of Schumann as well as Seven Sonnets of Michelangelo, composed by Britten himself. Everyone said what a good concert this was. I am so ignorant I can only judge music emotionally, not intellectually. Ivy C.-B., who with M. Jourdain and John Pope-Hennessy dined with me beforehand at the Good Intent— Jamesey chucked this morning in favour of Lady Crewe[1]—said that at best music induces in her a nice, comfortable dreamy feeling. I said it is also conducive to thought. Jamesey is just frankly bored by it.

The concert was to raise funds to procure railings for the protection of Chelsea Old Church. Rick in his usual generous way had paid for

[1] Lady Margaret Primrose, a daughter of 5th Earl of Rosebery, K.G., Prime Minister, and widow of 1st and last Marquess of Crewe (d. 1945).

them in advance. Cecil Beaton on leaving thanked me profusely for the lovely party. I did not disabuse him by saying it was nothing to do with me. Actually I was in such pain with my leg during the concert that I could not sit. I stood outside the door of the ballroom with K. Clark, who I could see was cold and bored.

Wednesday, 18th November

At the S.P.A.B. meeting we discussed the Bath Assembly Rooms. The committee agreed, quite rightly in the circumstances, that the surviving walls, outside and within, should be preserved, that where partial interior decoration was left it should be repaired and reproduced, but that those rooms totally gutted without trace of decoration should be rebuilt with no attempt to replace original decorative treatment. I have a renewed respect for the S.P.A.B. They are a responsible body of, for the most part, experts, unlike the Georgians who are nearly all amateurs. Mrs. Esdaile, Marshall Sisson and Fyfe are intelligent and useful members. Esher was in good form. Miss Soppit said, 'We have not prepared the 1941 Report yet. Shall we print it with the 1942 one?' 'And publish both in 1945? I think that would be an excellent plan,' said Esher laconically.

Saturday, 21st November

I have got through a lot of difficult work this week and should be feeling pleased with myself. Instead I have such a consuming sense of guilt, about nothing particular that I can recall, accompanied by an uneasy queasiness in the stomach, that I can only attribute it to mental instability.

Sunday, 22nd November

Immediately after breakfast in Cheyne Walk, which was horrid, cold weak coffee as usual, and cold meat which I can't face at this hour of day, Rick and I went once more to 104. The owner has taken every stick of furniture out of it, leaving nothing but the curtains in what will be my bedroom. This means that, if I take it, I shall have to furnish it entirely. As I have no capital at all, I cannot raise £20, far less £50 to buy equipment. This saddens me for I do believe the house is just what I want. From the sitting-room window I watched the low orange sun make through the fog a bleeding daub on the river.

126

Jamesey and I walked through Camden Hill to his new flat. We looked at some fascinating and some extraordinary houses, notably Aubrey House, a Queen Anne country house stranded in this nine-teenth-century urban area, and next door to it, 'Tower Crecy', the most astonishing, thin, gaunt monster of a house imaginable. It is thoroughly Pre-Raphaelite, all turrets, like the late lamented Lululaund of Herkomer. Jamesey's flat is rich and rare, spotlessly new and clean, but I do not covet it.

Had tea with Catherine Fordham — now Kennedy — in 98 Cheyne Walk. She said that if she had had to wait another two days she would never have married at all. Now it is over she is pleased. He is older than her, with five wild children, is a general, the D.M.O., in fact a very important soldier who planned the North African campaign. I said to Catherine surely it was surprising that at such a time he could have thoughts of matrimony. She said that, although the campaign had not come off, all the planning was over and done with weeks ago. He had nothing else to do but wait, and propose to her. He was so relieved by the campaign's success, that he instantly became ten years younger.

Wednesday, 25th November

In the Travellers' Club Harold was dressed in tails and white waistcoat, the first time I had seen anyone so dressed since the war began. He said he had been told to put on these clothes by the Camroses, with whom he was to dine, and suspected the presence of royalty, the King of Greece most probably. Harold was looking sleek, smarmed and bald; and was in fact feeling very shaken and stiff, poor thing, having been run down by a taxi on his way to Buckingham Palace to see a diary of Nigel's in the hands of a brother Grenadier officer on guard there. Another taxi driver picked him up, put him into his cab and asked where he should take him. Harold said, determinedly but rather un-convincingly, 'Buckingham Palace.' 'No, no, sir! Come, come! St. George's Hospital or the Westminster?' was the reply. But Harold insisted, not however without being taken to St. George's first.

Harold talked of Mrs. Greville, a common, waspish woman who got where she did through persistence and money. She was her father's illegitimate child, her mother being unknown. She married the reputable, dull Captain Ronnie Greville, and jumped off from this safe spring-board. She built herself a fictitious reputation for cleverness,

E* 127

and was not even witty. But she had the ambition to cultivate ambassadors and entertain them at Polesden Lacey, so that in her constant travels she could demand return favours in special trains and red carpets, much to the chagrin of foreign officials.

Jamesey said he would dine with me at Brooks's, for he had no money at all. Actually he is far richer than I am. I told him I had already invited John Gielgud to supper, if he were free. Nevertheless Jamesey insisted on eating immediately for he was ravenous. So I ordered dinner and we began on pheasant. Then a message came that John Gielgud would have supper with me at 9.15 at the Ivy. It was then 8.15 and we were already surfeited. But we finished our dinner, and James decided he would come to the Ivy too. I made him promise me he would behave, even if he disliked John. We walked to the Ivy in the blackout and James told me Harold had come upon a passage in Thraliana in which Mrs. Thrale lamented the fashionable vice among young men, especially prevalent in Scotland. This she attributed to the kilt. She said Sir Horace Mann and Mrs. Damer were her informants. Raymond Mortimer said afterwards that Signor Piozzi may have been the root of Mrs. Thrale's suspicions.

Jamesey immensely liked John Gielgud who is charming, but inattentive. In conversation sophisticated remarks patter off him like undirected raindrops. He kept nodding to left and right to his friends coming and going. He is about to fly in a bomber to Gibraltar for a four weeks' performance of sketches. He says if there is no rival show of legs, the troops will come. He was very scandalous about M.B., who decoyed a young man into his Eaton Square house, and made him strip M.B. and beat him. The young man laid on with such violence that M.B. screamed in agony, and the butler appeared. When confronted with the scene all the butler remarked was, 'I thought you rang, sir.'

John said that in pre-war days he was able to keep all the suits ordered for him on the stage, and so had a large, free wardrobe. Nowadays the suits are severely rationed.

When I entered Brooks's for the night I thought there was a piece of the railings missing in front of the club.

Thursday, 26th November

On leaving the club at 8.45 I saw workmen tearing out a large chunk of the William IV railings which flank the doorway. I was livid with rage, and told the porter to allow no more to go. At Waterloo Station I sent the club secretary a furious telegram: another to Lord Ilchester, and another to the Professor [Richardson].

I walked from Dinton station to Little Clarendon. This dear little Tudor house was given to the Trust in 1940. Mrs. Engleheart the donor, opened the door. She was dressed in a mauve moreen conventual habit down to the ankles. On her feet were black sand-shoes. A silver girdle round her waist. On her head a mauve bonnet with pearl beads on the crown. She is eighty-seven and lives with her gentle, down-trodden spinster daughter. I like her, although she cannot be described as a dear old lady. She has imposed in the deed of gift stringent conditions that we shall never put in electric light, radiators or the telephone. She is a fanatical Papist, and has a chapel in the garden made of bits and pieces of rubbishy antiques including, as a facing to the altar, the cantilever springs from the Penruddock family coach.

Mrs. Engleheart told me that her great-grandmother, who lived to be ninety-seven, brought her up as a little girl near Birmingham. I think the name may have been Viscountess Southwell. This great-grandmother had been a friend of Dr. Johnson, and Mrs. E. showed me a Chinese porcelain teapot with a silver spout which had belonged to him. In fact these particulars tumbled out because in looking at her china cupboard I admired this piece. She remarked, 'That is the doctor's teapot which he gave to Granny.' So I asked, 'Which doctor?'

These poor old people have no indoor or outdoor servant.

Friday, 27th November

I walked from Sole Street station to Owletts [Cobham, Kent]. Daphne Humphreys welcomed me. She is now married to Sir Herbert Baker's third son. We strolled round the chalk pit, looking at the spindleberries. One forsythia was actually in bloom. Sir Herbert,[1] who has had a stroke, is eighty, kind, Christian-like, and cultivated. He was reading French poetry when I arrived. He insists on accompanying one, dragging his legs in a manner which pains one as it must pain him. But he will not give in. We lunched and discussed which pieces of furniture ought to stay permanently in the house. Lady Baker is no less delightful than her husband, who is also her cousin. She was an Edmeades of

[1] Sir Herbert Baker (1862–1946), architect. Joined Milner's 'Kindergarten', 1902. Collaborated with Sir Edwin Lutyens as architect for New Delhi from 1912.

Nurstead Court, two miles away. They call themselves with justifiable pride, yeomen of Kent; but they are more than that. The Bakers have lived at Owletts since 1780. Both are of stalwart stock, and their integrity is written in their faces. We talked of Christopher Wren, and Lady Baker said to her husband, 'I wonder if future generations will attribute all decent buildings of these times to Lutyens or Baker?' Daphne, who accompanied me back to the station, said that Sir Herbert bore no resentment against Lutyens, and even gave the casting vote in favour of his election to the presidency of the Royal Academy.

Sir Herbert is devoted to South Africa and told me he wanted all the contents in the house associated with that dominion to be regarded as his memorial. Among them are the Dutch chests with brass hinges and the oriental porcelain he bought out there. But the whole of Owletts indeed is as much a memorial to him as it is of its seventeeth-century builders. Besides, he has contributed several additions, like the clock in the drawing-room. Baker was Cecil Rhodes's specially chosen architect. I feel that in spite of his detractors—and he is not popular today—there is something great about him when he is creative, and not being simply imitative. I admire his South Africa House. I prefer it to most of the trash around it.

I went to Cumberland Lodge for the night. Lady Shaftesbury, belonging to the 'sweet' type of patrician, and a clipper of 'g's, is staying. Magdalen too is all 'sweetness', combined with real goodness. Boydie is sour, and I feel sure dislikes his father. Lord FitzAlan was in bed, having had a fall. He was cross because the doctors had forbidden him going to London more than twice a week. He complained that he was more busy than ever with his House of Lords committees. I said, 'I believe, sir, that you just go to bed whenever you hear I am coming to stay.' He said, 'It is you who keep away when you hear that I am up and about.' He told me that Smuts's presence in Westminster Hall was impressive, though he, Lord F., heard not a word he said. But he fails to understand why Smuts talks about the great fight continuing into 1944, for he believes that, if we drive Rommel out of North Africa, Hitler is already beat. He regards the turn of the tide in Russia as a major defeat of the Germans. Boydie said over port that his father was habitually optimistic owing to his great age; and that all old people underestimated Hitler's reserves.

Alathea came for dinner. Yesterday she was at the Buckingham Palace party given for the Americans. She had to stand for two hours for there was nowhere to sit. Princess Elizabeth complained to her that she hadn't a minute to spare for her real friends. Alathea says she is good at trying to find words for strangers, but it is a great strain for her. Not so for Princess Margaret Rose who burbles away naturally and easily.

Wednesday, 2nd December

I met the builder at 104 Cheyne Walk who thinks he may be able to do the necessary work in time, i.e. by mid-January, but I am still rather worried by having no furniture, not to mention no money for the expense of moving in.

This morning I had a letter from Lord Ilchester thanking me for having drawn his attention to the railings at Brooks's. He at once took the matter up with Lord Portal at the Ministry of Works. Apparently it was just a stupid mistake, and the club secretary, poor old fool, and the Ministry appeal panel were to blame. Ilchester assured me that the pieces of railing taken away would be replaced. Professor Richardson also wrote to me to the same effect. If these railings really are saved it will be owing to one of those rare chance interventions, my happening to stay the night at Brooks's while the demolition men were beginning their beastly work.

I met Sir Courtauld-Thomson in Jermyn Street. He took me aside into a hat shop to tell me he is lunching tomorrow with the Prime Minister, and is presenting him with a copy of the deed of transfer of Dorney Wood. I can scarcely believe the Prime Minister will be very thrilled by this token. I am sure Sir C. is hoping for a peerage. We shall see.

Thursday, 3rd December

A cold, raw, grey December day on Frensham Common. I was begged to forestall the felling of some scruffy Scots firs on a little property which does not even adjoin ours, by accepting covenants over the land they stand on. Urged, cajoled, threatened, bullied, I was inconclusive and, weak ass that I am, failed to tell these people outright that their covenants were not acceptable. Oh, to be like a sledgehammer instead of a wet dish cloth!

Friday, 4th December

Helen had General Acres to dinner tonight. He has been promoted from the American Bomber Command to what amounts to being Commander-in-Chief of the whole American Air Force in Britain and Europe. It is hard to understand, for he is quite dumb in company and, Helen says, scarcely more talkative when alone with her. Yet on looking at him closely tonight I thought, 'You are cleverer than you seem. You put women on pedestals, and humble yourself in their eyes.' He thinks Helen the most brilliant conversationalist he has ever met. His father was a rancher in the West, and he had to educate himself. He has piloted every American machine that has been produced, and the other day returned from the U.S.A. in a new machine which goes 700 miles an hour. It is scarcely credible. It is a secret that the U.S. are producing these machines in large numbers. No wonder the runways are being lengthened so that England is becoming one mass of concrete.

Sunday, 6th December

Helen entertained to luncheon ten shooting guests, including Prince Radziwill who sat next to me. She thinks he is divine, but in reality he is a very ordinary man with a moustache. Eddy and I slunk off to walk in the woods and talk. Half-way up the lane his nose bled, and he had to sit on the bank while it poured like a fountain. He was quite unconcerned for it does this daily, and spoke about Paul Latham[1] all the while. He nourishes a sort of masochistic affection for Paul, who treats him as a fractious child treats an over-loving, over-solicitous great-aunt. Talking of age Eddy said that old women were pleasanter than old men because they resigned themselves more readily to their condition, and were, on the whole, content to enjoy vicariously the happiness and success of their children; whereas old men tended to remain competitive long after they could be of any use to the community. They would not resign themselves to the shelf, but must always be interfering in concerns for which they were no longer qualified. Lytton Strachey was the first person to point this out to Eddy. I think it is true. In any case men are naturally jealous of other men, particularly old men of young men.

Mama wrote yesterday that Simon [Lees-Milne], my nephew, is desperately ill with meningitis in a London hospital. Only last weekend he was at Wickhamford in the best of health. On Thursday he was stricken. Helen and Eddy say there is never a chance of a child recovering from meningitis without being mentally defective. I wonder if

[1] Sir Paul Latham, 2nd Bart (1905–55), M.P. 1931–41.

this is so.[1] The news has depressed me greatly, more so than I would have thought possible, for I hardly know the child. I conclude that perhaps blood is thicker than water, notwithstanding all my protestations to the contrary.

Tuesday, 8th December

I walked to West Wycombe station to catch the early train. The mornings now are pitch dark at 8 and barely light at 9. I find it impossible to wake without a knock at the door. How dependent one's body is upon the course of the sun. I watched it rise over High Wycombe. Like a magician's wand, the rays roused the houses from decent, grey, shrouded haystacks into what they really are, hideous, pretentious little dwellings of the most commonplace architecture.

In London my first appointment was in Garrard's St. James's Street office, with Horne and Sir John Oatley to discuss the report they have made on Knole, before typing it out for the Trust and Lord Sackville. Sir John Oatley is considered the cream of the estate agent's profession. He is a highly respectable old gentleman of about seventy, very clean-shaven, beautifully trimmed moustache, snow-white starched collar and cuffs, pin-stripe suit without a rumple, and, over highly polished black shoes, brown spats. His rôle is that of confidential grandfather to every member of the nobility and gentry who owns more than 5,000 acres in Kent and Surrey, and more than 25,000 acres in Northumberland and the Welsh Marches.

I walked to the Cumberland Hotel at Marble Arch to meet one of the Trust's tenants. The Cumberland is just the sort of place she would choose. She was looking particularly common in an enormous shovel hat, erect from her neck like a Queen Anne lady's headdress. She had come to London to tell me she wished to break her lease. From a very dirty metal pot she poured out pitch black Indian tea, and from somewhere under that ghastly hat and a peroxide wig a catalogue of domestic woes. When she confided in me her dislike of her husband I became wary, and switched off my moderate allowance of sympathy.

In Heywood's shop Anne [Hill] promised me the loan of a sofa and Nancy [Rodd] of two chairs for my house.

In the Hyde Park Hotel Elaine [L.-M.] told me that the L.C.C. hospital will only vouchsafe her the minimum information about Simon's condition. They treat her as though she were an imbecile,

[1] Fortunately it was not so in this case.

instead of the child's mother. She is not allowed to see him because when she leaves he cries for hours, and this is the worst possible thing for someone suffering from cerebral disturbance. She only knows that he has not got meningitis, but is half-paralysed. I counselled her to get our doctor to inform Simon's hospital of the family trouble. I told her that our cousin Billy Northey drove his car into a tree and killed himself, supposedly because of a fit.

Tuesday, 15th December

Benton Fletcher wishes himself and me to be co-trustees of a fund, deriving from rents of two houses in which he has a life interest, for the benefit of the new Cheyne Walk house we are buying. As soon as the war is over his collection of musical instruments from bombed Old Devonshire House will be installed in this house.

Tancred Borenius[1] told me he knew Polesden Lacey very well and would give any advice or help I might need. He said some of the pictures were good, the china was first-rate, and the whole collection a most interesting one.

I dined at the Ritz with Geoffrey Houghton-Brown[2] and Morogh Bernard. Morogh told a true story about a Belgian friend of his who with a rich aunt escaped in a closed car when the Germans invaded Belgium. The aunt, who was very delicate, died in the car. The niece could not stop to bury her for obvious reasons. For three days she continued driving with the aunt's body propped in the back seat. On the fourth day this state of things became insupportable, because it was hot summer weather. So the niece put her aunt on the roof of the car wrapped in some valuable rugs. At last she was able to stop at a café, and get out for a meal. When she returned to the car the rugs had been stolen, together with the aunt, whose remains she never saw again. Now it appears that, since the aunt's death cannot be legally certified, the niece must wait thirty years before she can inherit her money.

I stayed the night in Geoffrey's flat in Pall Mall on a sheetless bed, surrounded by pots, pans, and stacks of furniture waiting for the removal men to call the following morning at 8.30.

[1] Tancred Borenius (1885–1948), lecturer and writer on art. Editor, *Burlington Magazine*, 1940–45.
[2] Connoisseur and old friend of J. L.-M.

All the servants have gone from Polesden Lacey except the housemaid, whom I have re-engaged. I met there Mr. Abbey of Christie's who has completed the inventories of all the contents save the pictures, which Sir Alec Martin[1] is listing tomorrow. I went round the rooms with Abbey who pronounced that there is hardly a piece of furniture of museum worth, the bulk of it being made up, or deliberate copies. We ate sandwiches and drank tea in the servants' hall after this depressing perambulation. I am disappointed by his verdict.

I found Di [Murray] in Cheyne Walk in deep gloom of spirit. When people are mentally ill for no apparent cause, I find it difficult to sympathize and impossible not to be irritated.

Thursday, 17th December

I went very early to Heywood Hill's shop to buy Christmas cards; and happened to arrive just as poor Heywood was about to go off to the army, for he has at last been called up. Anne very miserable and unnaturally cheerful. She is to have a baby in May. Heywood slunk off sadly and infinitely quietly, as is his wont, Anne trying to be brave. I meant to appear unconscious of the true situation, and chatted away brutally; then left as soon as possible.

Wednesday, 23rd December

I met Mr. Abbey from Christie's and his secretary at 16 Charles Street. He galloped round this house less thoroughly than Polesden for the simple reason that he thinks there is nothing in the furniture line worth keeping for show purposes. On the other hand he thinks some of the silver is valuable, notably a few James II porringers, Queen Anne salvers and Georgian teapots. He classifies a piece with lightning rapidity. He picks up a salver, blows on its underneath, rubs the moisture off the hall mark, and makes a pronouncement immediately. He has discovered a number of distinct forgeries among the silver. There were two large porcelain jars he had not seen before. He gave a quick glance at one, tapped it, and without hesitation dictated to his secretary, 'Nankin, blue, lambrequin border at base, date so-and-so,

[1] Sir Alec Martin (1884–1972), Managing Director of Christie's and Hon. Sec. of National Art Collections Fund.

value £40 each.' He valued a dinner service without looking at more than one plate, without investigating whether the service was complete, or even counting the number of pieces.

Sir Roy Robinson[1] sat himself down next to me at luncheon. He is a large, blustering, cruel-looking, unsure-of-himself man. He complained that people when making their wills and intending to leave woodlands to the Forestry Commission would not consult him. He wanted to know what we were going to do with the Blickling and Polesden woods. Bearing in mind our recent differences with the Forestry Commission I was as non-committal as could be termed polite.

Thursday, 24th December

I went home for Christmas, or rather I stayed with Midi in the village, having half my meals with her and half with the family. Midi's younger child Veronica is undeniably beautiful with copper-coloured hair and a fair skin, but she tries to be funny, and is strikingly unfunny. Bamber[2] is a sensitive, delicate and adventuresome little boy.

Deenie has come down from Stowe for Christmas. She is very miserable because one of her two great friends is dying, and she regrettably made a deathbed promise that she would have the surviving friend to live with her for the rest of her days, a rash thing to do. And so I told her.

Mama told me how last week she was in the room while Papa and Colonel Riley were planning a Home Guard exercise to take place the following day. Rather brutally they intended to humiliate another officer for stupidity, saying to each other, 'William, the damned fool, will never be able to capture the aerodrome. If he were the slightest use, of course he would, etc.' They then discussed how it ought to be done, tracing on a map the complicated route he should take, mentioning the names of bridges, roads, villages and the map numbers. Mama all the while was pretending to read *The Times*, but was actually jotting down on a pad all they said. When they left the house she rang up the damned fool William, and reported to him word for word what they had said, giving the exact map references. The result was that much to their surprise and disgust William captured the aerodrome

[1] Afterwards Lord Robinson (1883–1952), forester from Australia, chairman of Forestry Commission, 1932–52.

[2] Bamber Gascoigne, television star and author.

with flying colours. When I told Midi this she said, 'Your mother told me in confidence that whenever she wants to get out of the Red Cross functions she puts her thermometer on the hot-water bottle, and shows it to your father, who positively forbids her to leave her bed. Your mother, to make her feigned illness more convincing expostulates with your father just a little, but not too much, knowing that he will not give his consent.'

Tuesday, 29th December

I went to Boarstall Tower which 'the anonymous benefactor', Mr. Cook, is presenting to the Trust. It is the Tudor gatehouse to a large house of the Aubrey-Fletcher family, which was destroyed at the end of the eighteenth century after the owner's son and heir met a premature death there. [A. D.] Peters the literary agent is the tenant. On the second floor is one superb room, the length and breadth of the building with, at either end, huge bay windows from floor to ceiling. You freeze in it in winter, and boil **in** it in summer. I shall recommend it.

Wednesday, 30th December

In the office this afternoon the telephone bell rang, and Eardley said to me, 'You are wanted. The name is Stuart Preston[1] or something like that.' I was amazed. Stuart flew from America yesterday. He is a G.I. The last time I saw him was at dinner with Harold in the House of Commons in the summer of 1938. I remember Harold saying, 'The next time we see Stuart over here, he will be in uniform.'

Thursday, 31st December

I was sent to Harrods agency to try and reduce the price the vendor is asking for 3 Cheyne Walk. I am a perfectly hopeless bargainer. The agents held out for £4,000. Tentatively and apologetically I asked whether they would not reduce it to £3,500. No, they said, of course they wouldn't. I gave in without a struggle and agreed to their £4,000, which I consider a reasonable figure. I would rather go without a thing

[1] Stuart Preston came to England in the van of the American troops. His military duties were at the U.S.A. headquarters in London. In 1944 he went overseas with the invasion forces. Meanwhile he was much fêted in London social and literary circles owing to his charm and intelligence.

than haggle over it. But the National Trust will not be of this opinion, and I shall be in disgrace. However I feel sure Benton Fletcher, who is mad keen for us to buy the house, and who quite likes me, will forgive me.

I 'saw' or rather 'slept' — and not alone — the New Year in. Could there possibly be a happier augury for 1943? I think not.

I walked to Brooks's and had breakfast with Simon Harcourt-Smith. The War Office had told him that the Germans stood to lose 1,000,000 men by the time Rostov was reached, that is to say in total since the Russian offensive began last November. He took me to look at 3 Tenterden Street off Hanover Square, now divided into several apartments for Jewish costumiers and tailors. It is a wonderful eighteenth-century house with a perfect façade and thick, contemporary iron railings along the pavement. It has a mitred stair rail of mahogany over twisted iron balusters, rococo plaster ceilings, good wainscoting and arcaded doorways. It is remarkably unspoilt, not even damaged by raids and retains several original glass panes in the windows. Simon claims that it is the old town house of the Harcourt family.[1]

I left him for 16 Charles Street, where I went over the house inventory in hand, marking what to keep and what not. Stuart called for me at 1.30 and took me to lunch at the Berkeley. Luncheon cost 17/- for two, without drinks. It consisted of indifferent thick soup made of God knows what, minced chicken hash and no pudding. Really scandalous. I returned to Charles Street and was joined by Miss Paterson, who found all sorts of valuable household things like soap, mops, brooms, etc., impossible to buy nowadays even at exorbitant prices. We put these aside with a view to buying them for the new house, if allowed to do so. I dined at Brooks's with Nigel Birch[2] who talked affectionately of Tom Mitford, and Randolph whose marriage is, he says, breaking up. But then Randolph only married to have a son. And the young Winston is now born.

Saturday, 2nd January

Trenchard Cox[3] lunched at Brooks's. A very affable man whose chief purpose in life seems to be charity to his neighbours. He has just been appointed private secretary to Sir A. Maxwell, the Permanent Secretary at the Home Office. It is a good appointment but involves work from 9 till 8 every day, including Saturdays. We walked to Charles Street. He looked over the furniture and agreed with Mr. Abbey that it was not of very high standard. In normal times Trenchard Cox is custodian

[1] Needless to say it was demolished after the war.
[2] Now Lord Rhyl, Conservative politician, who has held several ministerial posts.
[3] Now Sir Trenchard Cox, Director of Victoria and Albert Museum 1956–66.

of the French furniture at the Wallace Collection. Stuart joined us at 2.45. He and I left to catch a train to High Wycombe. We chased it down the platform and the guard allowed us to jump into the van just in time. In the train he talked with rapture and awe of his dinner last night with the Duff Coopers. He finds her wondrous, incredibly flippant, brilliant and witty, but cruel and un-middle-class. He kept on repeating the last phrase, with wide open eyes. 'But of course,' was all I could find to say, 'what else do you expect?' He says that in his billets in North Audley Street he sleeps on straw with one blanket.

Tuesday, 5th January

Woke up to find snow and a tightening of the chest, the beginning of a cold. Breakfasted early and caught a bus to Cookham, and on to Netley Park. This is a Surrey property of which I expected greater things than were apparent under the snow. A bad 1840 house with great plate-glass windows and ugly grey stucco front. I looked at the downstairs rooms, of which the licentious soldiery have made an awful mess, smashing the pair of gilt looking-glasses in the drawing-room. But then they should have been boarded up with the chimney-pieces over which they hang. They are Louis Philippe, I guess, with oval medallions containing portraits of a lady in the crests.

I got back to West Wycombe at 8 feeling tired. Yet I sat up in the office till 11 waiting for Q. who never telephoned. Went to bed torturing myself unnecessarily.

Friday, 8th January

My temperature being sub-normal I decided to risk pleurisy, pneumonia, death, and go to London to catch a glimpse of Q. even if I had to come straight back again. Waiting for the bus in the half light and the frost my body felt sweaty hot, and my hands and feet like icicles. The extremes of temperature simultaneously in one body seem to me most unnatural and odd. In Charles Street I gave the old caretaker, Mrs. Reid, a pork pie as a present. It was by way of throwing a sop to Cerberus. For when Q. breezed in she was quite polite to her. I find the attitude of humble women to well-dressed women invariably the same, suspicious and resentful. And when Q. breezed out after five minutes of ecstasy, Mrs. Reid, though cordial, looked triumphant. Then Harold [Nicolson] called to leave a note for Stuart. He was bright and shabby, so Mrs. Reid beamed upon him. Harold strode up and down the stone hall nostalgically but unregretfully recalling the awful parties he had attended in this house. In between the interruptions I managed to work away at my listing. Again the doorbell rang. Mrs. Reid bustled eagerly from basement to ground floor. Stuart walked in, and because he is under thirty Mrs. Reid beamed upon him. Over a huge fire in the dining-room Stuart and I crouched under the steel scaffolding and between the stacks of French furniture. I ate sandwiches and Stuart a plateful of ready-cooked American field rations of meat minced up with beans from a tin which Mrs. Reid heated for him. Disgusting it looked too. Both of us drank whisky from a flask. I continued to work alone in this eerie house, and left after dark, purloining like a thief in the night a broom, a brush and a cake of scrubbing soap.

I dined with Q. at Prunier's off homard à l'americaine and a glass of champagne each. I was obliged to stay at Duke's Hotel, St. James's Street.

Saturday, 9th January

Cough very thick in the morning, otherwise surprisingly well. Health is largely determined by one's state of happiness or the reverse.

Frank Partridge [the dealer], whom I called on, told me the collections at Luton Hoo and in Bath House were incomparable, notably the French furniture, the pictures and the English porcelain.

At 104 Cheyne Walk I found Miss Paterson and the new char, Mrs. Beckwith, a dear, gentle little mouse from Battersea, sweeping and washing floors busily. Jamesey called and took me to lunch at the Good Intent. He is very happy at the moment. He talked of Stuart whom he had met last night dining with Harold. He thinks him personable, but in that Pope-Hennessy way is terrifyingly analytical. Asks me if he is sincere. Suspects insincerity. I don't yet know, I tell him. We return to the house and this time I really get down to sweeping and clearing away the mess of two years' accumulation of air-raid detritus. Jamesey very immaculate with a calf-bound book under one arm follows me around, asking querulously if it is really necessary for me to sweep. He says other peoples' ploys of this kind are a great bore. This makes me laugh at him. He soon slopes off to call on Logan Pearsall Smith.[1] When he

[1] Logan Pearsall Smith (1865–1946), man of letters. Of American Quaker origin.

has gone Miss P., Mrs. Beckwith and I drink tea in front of a huge fire in my room, sitting on the bed, the only piece of furniture that has yet arrived.

After dinner I went to 4 Kings Bench Walk to stay the night at Harold's. Jamesey was going to warn him to expect me there. He and Harold went to an American party tonight. Harold came in at 10.30 and we talked till after midnight. He makes me talk freely as though I am cleverer than I am, and feel happier than I am. He is still optimistic about the outcome of the war. He said the Poles' estimate of losses was considered the most accurate. They declare that the Russians, whom of course they hate, have lost 4,000,000 men and the Germans 2,500,000. The Czechoslovakian Prime Minister, with whom Harold lunched yesterday, had that morning been interviewing two Czech youths just arrived in England after walking across Germany. They reported that every German they met spoke of defeat as the inevitable outcome for them.

Monday, 11th January

Miss Paterson and I motored up to London for the meetings. The Polesden Lacey reports were considered at great length by the General Purposes Committee. They said the combination of reports on agriculture and art by [Hubert] Smith, the new Chief Agent, and myself, with a foreword by the Secretary, was just what they had hoped for. They agreed to let me do what I thought best with the contents subject to Clifford Smith[1] and Kenneth Clark endorsing my opinion. Sir Edgar Bonham-Carter urged, sensibly I thought, that we keep Polesden looking like an Edwardian lady's country house, and not a museum.

Tuesday, 12th January

By the early train to London again in order to meet Kenneth Clark at Charles Street. Found Stuart there for he had rung me up the previous evening after dining with Jamesey. Together we sorted out the pictures for K. Clark to look at. Stuart left and K. Clark arrived. He was extremely helpful and took much trouble examining all the pictures, of which he was to my contentment even more critical than Christie's, and recommended keeping even less than they did. More-

[1] H. Clifford Smith (1876–1960), Keeper of Department of Woodwork at the Victoria and Albert Museum before the war.

144

over he offered to motor down to Polesden with me one day and look through the pictures there.

I joined Stuart at the Connaught Hotel but since we could not get a table we lunched at Brooks's. Stuart had spent the weekend at Panshanger. The only other guest was Lord Hugh Cecil.[1] He and the Desboroughs spoke about Lord Rosebery and Queen Victoria not as legendary figures, but as friends whom they had all known. Lady Desborough is in fact a step-granddaughter of Lord Palmerston and a great-granddaughter of Byron's Lady Melbourne. Stuart slept in a room the walls of which were hung with the heraldic achievements of a Lord Cowper, an eighteenth-century ancestor who was a Prince of the Roman Empire.

Thursday, 14th January

Today we leave West Wycombe for good, to return to our London office and life. Whiteley's only sent one van, and that an hour and a half late, instead of the two ordered. I drove Miss Paterson and Miss Ballachey in the National Trust car stacked with our own belongings. On the way we picked up my dachshund Pompey. He was sick, once over Miss Paterson's second-best coat and again out of the open window into a London street. Dreadful confusion on arrival at the office, but worse when Miss Paterson and I reached 104 Cheyne Walk after dark. The charwoman had not even lit a fire for us. There was no electric light because the company said the house was too damp to test the wiring. No stick of furniture yet save one bed each. The Ascot heater not working, and so no hot water. We had an uncomfortable night, Pompey sleeping and falling off a chair beside me.

Saturday, 16th January

Some furniture arrived this morning. Miss P. and I worked like Trojans. I had to help haul my large sofa through the window on the first floor, since it had stuck on the staircase. After tea I changed and went to Ian Hamilton's ninetieth birthday party. He had invited ninety friends, mostly relations, and all the children from the neighbouring streets. He gave them a conjuring entertainment and a Punch and Judy show, with one marionette arrayed as Hitler. Mrs. Churchill

[1] Later Lord Quickswood (1869–1956), fifth son of 3rd Marquess of Salisbury, the Prime Minister. Provost of Eton 1936.

was leaving the door as I arrived. I talked to Shane Leslie about his boy Jack, now a prisoner of war since Boulogne. He often hears from him and says Jack laughed when the Germans manacled him. Dined with the Pope-Hennessys, Dame Una talking of Shane Leslie's new edition of Cardinal Wiseman's love letters to Lady Herbert of Lea.

Sunday, 17th January

Rick turned up last night a Coldstream guardsman, looking the picture of health, but in actual fact depressed and overcome by the whole experience. He said he could not cope and was so dispirited, with so little to say, and that said so haltingly that I, friend as I am, was really bored. For the first time since I have known him I made an excuse to leave, and slunk home to bed.

The siren went during dinner at Brooks's, and the noise of our gunfire was worse than I have ever known it. During the night there was a second raid. Miss P. was rather frightened by the din, so we sat under the stairs in our dressing-gowns. Pompey was quite unmoved. I did not like to ask Miss P. if she regretted our having left the country for this sort of thing.

Monday, 18th January

Horne and I, and the clerk to Mrs. Greville's solicitors went to consult counsel, a Mr. Raymond Needham, at his chambers in the Temple about a financial point to be forwarded to the Capital Issues Committee, relating to some £500,000 stock. It was interesting how very lucidly and confidently the clerk unravelled and presented the complicated story. I mentioned this afterwards to Horne, who said this is what often happens: intelligent solicitors' clerks become first-class at their jobs, yet because of their cockney voices get no further up the scale and never become attorneys. It seems all wrong to me. Needham was like a wise old owl listening behind thick horn-rimmed spectacles, interjecting a word only occasionally, yet grasping the issues quietly and faultlessly, and finally pronouncing a definite opinion.

Tuesday, 19th January

Lunched at the Ivy with W. L. Wood to discuss Frensham Common. I could barely hear a word he mumbled through his closed yellow teeth. He gave me a delicious meal of braised beef and French salad, coffee mousse and a sweet white liqueur. I then went for an interview with Sir William Leitch at the Ministry of Works, and Ussher of the Treasury, about the large legacy of £200,000 which Sir Courtauld is leaving for Dorney Wood.

Wednesday, 20th January

In the morning I met Clifford Smith at Charles Street. I am hoping he will confirm the decisions I have come to in the choice of contents to be retained. At 2.30 to Miss Davy to discuss Cliveden accounts. It appears Lord Astor is so ill that he cannot attend to details. And because he is a Christian Scientist no one may refer to his bad health.

Went to tea with Jamesey in his flat to meet Rose Macaulay and Lady Crewe. Lady C. was there when I arrived, wrapped in expensive furs and wearing black gloves. She talked spicily to Jamesey in whispered asides, and they giggled a lot. This behaviour did not make a comfortable trio. Then she talked to us both about Polesden Lacey. 'Whatever you do, you will have to rip off the yellow buttons in the drawing-rooms,' she counselled me. She told how Mrs. Greville's mother was the wife of the day-porter at Mr. M'Ewan's brewery. McEwan 'for convenience' put him on night duty. I brought some of my photographs of Manoeline architecture to show Rose Macaulay, who is shortly going to Portugal to write a book for the Ministry of Information. My first impression was of a very thin, desiccated figure in a masculine tam-o'-shanter, briskly entering the room. James says she is like Voltaire to look at. Actually her profile is less sharp than her full face, and is handsome. She talks too fast and too much.

Saturday, 23rd January

Lunched with Margaret Jourdain and Ivy Compton-Burnett to meet Elizabeth Bowen. When she first came into the room I thought she was ugly with a prominent nose and a drop on the end of it. Then I decided she was handsome, but not beautiful. She has a long face. A forward tuft of hair dances above a bandana tied round the forehead. When she smiles her charm is apparent. She speaks well and rapidly but speech is suddenly interrupted by an occasional stammer, not enough to embarrass one because she has the mastery of it. I liked her. We talked of the recent bombing. The two 'brown girls' as Helen

147

calls them, admitted that they were terrified last Sunday night. Indeed the four of us confessed we were. I. C.-B. is apt to be shy during a meal. During coffee she expands.

My house is settling down. The room with three large and long windows on the front faces the river and the big barge moored alongside. A fourth window at the west end faces Lots power station and the bend in the river opposite Battersea and the next bridge upstream. The windows being so very dirty, since the cleaners have not yet come, make it all but impossible to see the views, but I know they are there. My glazed curtains have white sheaves of flowers on a cherry ground, and are torn and shabby. The floor is parquet. In one corner beside an Adam hob-grate is the Empire bureau with fall flap on which I write this diary. Other pieces are my unsightly bed with hideous servants' pink cover; an upright winged armchair in crimson damask; a silk covered sofa of a different crimson; a mahogany half-circular fronted commode; an anthracite tove always burning in the other fireplace; Persian rugs; a large painted tin tray of Margate, *circa* 1850 over one chimneypiece. The room is thoroughly unpretentious and on the whole pretty.

Sunday, 24th January

Breakfasting at Brooks's I sat with Lord Spencer who told me with disgust that during a seven-day absence from London 'they' took away the contemporary gates from Spencer House for scrap. Attended High Mass at the little Sardinian chapel in Warwick Street. It is far and away my favourite worshipping place in London. The candlelight flickered across the silver hearts which line the walls of the presbytery while the transalpine chants made me long for Italy and for peace and goodwill among nations.

Monday, 25th January

Went to Warfield House, Sir George Leon's near Bracknell, for luncheon, and stayed till 4. He considers making over his house and 400 acres, consisting of four small farms with pedigree herds. Rather an absurd, opinionated little man, but public-spirited and pathetically patriotic like many rich Jews on this side of the Channel. We parted fast friends. The red brick house is Queen Anne. He has had it colour-washed, and the thin window sashes and even the reveals painted dark blue. The interior was decorated sumptuously by Lenygons before the

148

war. There are fawn pile carpets in every room and passage. All the wainscoting and the grand stair flight have been pickled. His furniture is first-rate, chiefly late seventeenth- and early eighteenth-century walnut. He showed me a suite of Charles II armchairs from Holme Lacey with particularly delicate stretchers. His pictures are immaculately cleaned and varnished, and include Poussins, Richard Wilsons, Cuyps. A typical, safe, rich, decent man's collection.

Met Jamesey at Brooks's and he conducted me to Argyll House. Lady Crewe was curtseying to Hapsburg Archdukes. Straightaway Jamesey got off with Lady Cunard,[1] and was delighted with her and the party. I disliked her and it as I knew I should. Stuart drank too much and we had great difficulty in getting him to leave. James and I had some anxious moments with him in the bus. In the restaurant he ate no dinner and talked of lords and ladies in a loud American voice.

Wednesday, 27th January

Went by train to Farningham Road where I was met by Sir Stephen Tallents[2] in tweed breeches, a blue polo sweater and no hat. A jolly, extrovert, pipe-sucking man, clever, well-read yet uncultivated. He accompanied me on foot to his house, St. John's Jerusalem, which is a pretty place, with an early monastic chapel attached to an early eighteenth-century house. It is surrounded by watercress beds and willow plantations. Lady Tallents is big, handsome, outspoken and rather eccentric. She is very musical and sings. I liked this place and considered it worthy.

Thursday, 28th January

Dined with Oliver Hill the architect, at his house in Cliveden Place. It is at the west end of the row, an eighteenth-century house near Sloane Square. One end is cut back at an acute angle to allow a stream to flow beside it. Oliver Hill has decorated the rooms in his own inimitable, modernistic way which I admire. His eating-room walls are lined with a kind of grey granite, incised with life-size graffiti of nudes by Eric Gill. With a strong light thrown across the walls the graffiti stand out impressively. Hill has just bought from a house in Shropshire

[1] Emerald, widow of Sir Bache Cunard, 3rd Bart., whom she married 1895. Well known hostess. She died 1948.
[2] Sir Stephen Tallents (1884–1958), civil servant and writer.

149

some English seventeenth-century tapestries, probably Mortlake, of idyllic Hampton Court scenes. He much admires our Mortlake tapestry which he borrowed from Wickhamford for the exhibition in Whistler's House in 1940. He is a tall, shaggy, rough, ruthless creature, very deaf and untidy. He usually has saliva dribble on his chin, and he wears dark blue woollen shirts with frayed collars, and a flopping, striped knitted tie. He told the other guests that Mama has a most uncanny power over birds; that during her three days' stay in Cheyne Walk for the exhibition the Chelsea birds found her out, and flocked to her bedroom window.

Saturday, 30th January

Stuart's portable alarum clock went off at 6.30 a.m. with the most tremendous din. This dreadful clock h~s for him some esoteric significance. Whenever he comes to stay the first thing he does is to produce it from a voluminous pocket and place it carefully on a table, like setting up a tent. The last move is to pick it up, fold it away, like drawing up the tent pegs. There is something atavistic in the procedure. Perhaps he had Bedouin forebears.

Margaret Jourdain and Ivy C.-B. came to tea. I had forgotten at what time to expect them or if I had even specified a time. To my surprise and concern they arrived on the dot of 4. They are slightly prim and correct, and it evidently distressed them that I had to descend to the kitchen, make and fetch the tea, and lay the table in their presence. I was made to feel that I was not behaving quite as I should. As it was, I did not like to spend time making toast. It was a horrid tea in consequence, and this they clearly minded, without saying so. To make matters worse John Russell, whom I had bidden to meet them, did not turn up till after 5, having been to a concert. However they stayed till after 6. Ivy C.-B., talking of the ineffectual results of the Germans' last raid on London when they hit a school and killed thirty children, observed, 'It isn't as though they were even impeding our war effort. On the contrary, they are really helping it by making the milk ration go further.'

Jamesey took me to dine at the Royal Court hotel, where we drank sweet Sauterne. He stayed the night on my lielow, but slept very little on account of the loud ticking and striking of my clock, he maintained. I maintained that had he not spurned the spare bed he would have slept soundly.

Took the 1.30 to Cullompton in Devon to stay two nights at Brad-field with Mrs. Adams, who was Lottie Coats, sister of the present Glentanar and the Duchess of Wellington. She was formerly Mrs. Walrond and her son is Lord Waleran. The Walronds have owned Bradfield since 1100. Her father bought it from this impoverished family and put it in trust. She is the present life tenant, the next her son and then the children of the duchess. I find country peoples' houses bitterly cold. Here one green log faintly glimmers in a small coal grate. Adams, the present husband, is a jovial retired naval commander who cracks bawdy jests and whose every adjective is 'bloody'. Yet he is a decent country gent, like my father. He listens to every news bulletin on the wireless right to the end of the postscript.

Mrs. Adams talked a great deal about her family; how her younger son died a few months ago of drink, aged thirty-four, and his wife two months before him, of dropsy. Commander Adams told me she too drank. Mrs. Adams worries about her sister at Stratfield Saye, where there is no electric light and no central heating. The little duchess, Maudie, lives in her bedroom, and freezes. The Queen rang up the duchess a year ago to ask if it were true that the treasures in Apsley House had not been evacuated. The duchess admitted that it was true. 'Well then, I am coming round at 11 with a van to take them to Frogmore,' the Queen said. And punctually she arrived with the King. With pencil and paper she made lists and decided what should be moved and what left behind. 'You mustn't be sentimental, Duchess. Only the valuable pictures can go,' she said. Mrs. Adams who is simple and sweet, said to me in her broad Scotch (or is it Glasgow?) accent, 'I quite realized when I married into the Walrond family that they were the squirearchy, whereas I was only a tradesman's daughter. Our ethical standards were entirely dissimilar. I had to adapt myself to the family I had married into.'

Tuesday, 2nd February

Spent the day walking round the estate, the garden and the house, now a military convalescent home. The outside of Bradfield was almost totally rebuilt in 1854. A coarse local stone was substituted for cob in reconstructing the mullioned windows and gables. The inside has likewise suffered, though not so generally. The restorer had the wit not

F

to tamper unduly with the remarkably fine great hall with its Henry
VIII medallion busts in the panelling, the Gothic foliage frieze, Jacobean screen, and the tempera painting of Gog and Magog. The
Spanish Room with grotesque interior porch and painted overmantel is
equally remarkable, all in a barbaric way. I do not however much like
the house, or property as a whole.

Wednesday, 3rd February

I had a horrible day with Colonel Pemberton at Pyrland Hall near
Taunton. He is a fiendish old imbecile with a grotesque white moustache. When I first saw him he was pirouetting on his toes in the road.
He has an inordinate opinion of himself and his own judgment. He is
absolutely convinced that Pyrland is the finest house in Somerset and
he is doing the Trust a great service in bequeathing it. The truth is the
property does not comprise land of outstanding natural beauty and is
of insignificant size; moreover the house, though large, and basically
eighteenth century, has been thoroughly Victorianized as to windows
and rendering. The army occupies it at present. It has a nice Georgian
staircase and some plaster cornices and mahogany doors on the curve.
I was drawn into several acrimonious arguments with the old man,
whom I cordially disliked, for he insisted upon contradicting whatever
I said. He gave me an exiguous lunch of bread and cheese, both hard as
wood, a baked potato in its skin, dry as sawdust, and watery apple pie
with Bird's custard. Ugh! He expected me to return and waste the
following day in discussion. But I had already made up my mind after
the first half-hour of the visit. I could not have borne him or Pyrland
an hour longer. Having hated me like poison he was nevertheless
furious when I left at 4. I conclude that he has to have a victim on
whom he can vent his spleen. I got back to London in time to have a
late supper of oysters and stout with Gabriel Herbert.

Friday, 5th February

Lady Colefax's luncheon party; but she had bronchitis and stayed in
bed. Norah Lindsay acted hostess in her place. She was wearing a flat,
black hat like a pancake on the side of her head, pulled down over one
eye. It was adorned with cherry-coloured buttons. Her white frilled
blouse had more cherry buttons. She is kittenish, stupid–clever, and an
amusing talker. On her left was Osbert Peake, now a Minister of some

sort, a boring, stuffy man. Jamesey was on my right and in the circumstances we had nothing, but nothing to say to one another. On my left was Laurie Johnston,[1] who had just seen my father at Hidcote. A man called Palewski,[2] who is General de Gaulle's *chef du cabinet*, and rather spotty, talked about North Africa. He has just returned from Casablanca where he attended the Churchill-Roosevelt meeting. He said Roosevelt was in high spirits; he had to be carried in a chair from the aeroplane for he cannot walk at all and can barely stand unaided. After luncheon, which was delicious, Laurie Johnston took me aside to ask if the National Trust would take over Hidcote garden without endowment after the war, when he intended to live in the South of France for good. He is a dull little man, and just as I remember him when I was a child. Mother-ridden. Mrs. Winthrop, swathed in grey satin from neck to ankle, would never let him out of her sight. Jamesey calls him a Henry Sturgiss American.

Sunday, 7th February

Midi, Stuart and I went to Windsor by train. We walked to Eton and looked for our various boys in their houses. Then Stuart and I lunched with the Provost, Lord Quickswood. There were just the three of us. I was surprised to find Lord Q. such an old man. He was shy at first, though full of solicitude for Stuart, the American soldier ally, who seems to be treated by all society as a lion. But then Stuart is attentive to the old and throws off anecdotes and literary quotations like pearls before swine. Lord Q. warmed after a time, but has little charm, and is impersonal. An old-fashioned luncheon of roast turkey, brown potatoes and sprouts, 'shape', that ghastly wobbly pudding and bottled blackberries, accompanied by beer followed by sherry. Lord Q. showed us all the portraits in the Provost's Lodge from the Gheeraerts of Lord Essex to the Romneys and Beecheys of old boys. He also took us over Lower School, and Upper School, showing us the bombed bit. The Headmaster's room has quite gone, all but the roadside wall. There is a deep crater where it was. Stuart fascinated by it all, and particularly by Lord Quickswood's use of 'ain't', his top hat and white bands. Stuart asked if we might see the College Library. Lord Q. thought for a

---

[1] Major Lawrence Johnston, creator of Hidcote Manor garden, Glos., which he gave in 1948 to the National Trust largely through the persuasion of Lady Colefax.
[2] Now President of the Constitutional Council of France.

moment, and said apologetically, 'I much fear I cannot do that. My man is out this afternoon, and I do not know where to switch on the lights.'

Tea at the Cockpit. Stuart took out Lady Desborough's grandson, and I Francis Dashwood who is in Pop. After College Chapel Stuart and I called on Mrs. Montgomery[1] who lives in a hideous corner house facing the entrance to Windsor Castle. She is the eighty-year-old daughter of Sir Henry Ponsonby. She has evidently had a stroke and it is not easy to understand what she says. She is wizened, sharp and brimful of talk. She repeated to Stuart the most flattering things told her about him by Logan Pearsall Smith, who is a close friend. She spoke of Queen Victoria who was her godmother and whom she disliked. She said that during dinners at the castle no one was allowed to speak, and if they had to ask for something, not above a whisper. Dinners were interminable and dreadful. The Queen would address her family in German. The familiar phrase, '*Das ist schrecklich!*' haunts her. She once witnessed the Queen greeting Mr. Gladstone, who had been summoned to dine. Gladstone was nervous about what his reception would be, and fumbled with his walking-stick. He was then over eighty. But contrary to expectation, when the Queen appeared she went straight up to him, leaning on a stick herself, and said, 'Mr. Gladstone, you and I have known days when neither of us was lame,' and laughed very sympathetically.

Monday, 8th February

I sat down on a sofa in Brooks's to read the evening paper. A form next to me leant over from the shadow and said, 'I was right. The man simply loathes comfort, or any semblance of it.' It was Esher. 'Who? When?' I asked. He was referring to Matheson who, he said, deliberately selected the most uncomfortable chair in a room, and perched on it in the most uncomfortable way. We talked about the Country Houses Committee, and I asked if Michael Rosse might be elected to it. He agreed.

I dined at the Travellers' with Harold, James and Stuart. Harold pulled me up for using the word 'relative', which he said was bedint. Jamesey agreed. Now I come to think of it, it is. Harold and Stuart talked of North Africa and the war, which made Jamesey sulk. He com-

[1] Alberta Victoria Ponsonby, married 1891 Major-Gen. W. E. Montgomery who died 1927. She died 1945.

154

plained he could not bear any mention of the war, and 'wanted literature from Harold only'. After dinner over port Jamesey said to me that Stuart irritated him with his permanent smile of appreciation. Stuart, with whom I walked away at 9.30, said that Jamesey irritated him with his *petit maître* manner, his finickiness, his Miss Mitford, tidy little appearance. Of course they will be dining together tomorrow night, and were probably dining last night, and making similar criticisms of me.

Thursday, 11th February

Matheson and I had an interview with Sir Robert Wood, Secretary to the Board of Education, to discuss the Board's co-operation with the Trust in the use of country houses after the war. He was fairly helpful and promised to put me in touch with various educational departments.

I arrived in the full swing of Cecil Beaton's party in Pelham Place. Cecil's house is sophistically decorated. It is nineties-ish, with red flock walls and varnished aspidistras in tall pots, and tight, little smart leather chairs. He was saying about his secretary 'When I go away I leave her, not on heat, but on board wages, I mean.' While talking to Alice Harding I felt something boring, boring into my spine, which means that one is being talked about maliciously. True enough, on turning round I saw Eddy and Nancy sitting on a low sofa dissecting each guest one by one and hooting with laughter. I joined them. Nancy was telling how Lady Leconfield[1] had been certified for descending in the lift at Claridge's stark naked. The little lift boy was sharply reprimanded by the hall porter. In self-defence he protested that he could not see above the lady's knees, she was so tall.

Friday, 12th February

I had an interview with Sir John Maude at the Ministry of Health. It was unprofitable. He bluntly said that old houses were totally unfitted for medical purposes.

Saturday, 13th February

Did not go to the office this morning but at midday met Gerry Villiers at 16 Charles Street, and tried in vain to find a stair carpet for him to

[1] Violet, wife of 3rd Lord Leconfield, who d.s.p. 1952.

buy. All we did find were some candle bulbs which he took away without buying. He begged me to get Professor Richardson the job of designing and making Mrs. Greville's tombstone, for he is the contractor who provides Portland stone for all the professor's works of this kind. He was almost appealing. I said it was not within my power to commission the professor to do anything of the sort, although I guessed the executors would commission him.

Anne Hill came to tea. We were alone and ate toast and golden syrup. She is to have a baby in May and is now bigger than Midi. She says the child already jumps about in her womb so that the bedclothes literally heave at nights. Nancy is the greatest help to her in the bookshop. As we talked I finished scraping off the anti-bomb stuff from my west window. Now I can enjoy the full view up the river of Lot's power station. Everyone says it is the best view in London.

Mrs. Montgomery told James she supposed I was too young to be in the army. 'On the contrary,' said James, 'he is too old.'

Monday, 15th February

All day at Polesden going round the house with Christie's inventory. It is strange how happy I am at Polesden. Chips Channon[1] asked me to look for and bring back to him a blood-stone, which was his last present to Mrs. Greville. But I can't, I can't, even if I find it.

Wednesday, 17th February

A tiresome and unprofitable meeting about the English Town Exhibition all morning. At 12.45 I lunched with Michael Peto at the Guards Club. He was amused and amazed that I had never been inside the building before, and kept repeating breezily, 'It is very brave of you to admit it openly,' as though I had something to conceal and be ashamed of. He is liaison officer between the American H.Q. and the War Office. He said the Americans in Tunisia could not encounter a more terrifying baptism of fire than Rommel's Panzer divisions were giving them.

Thursday, 18th February

Today I bought a new eye-glass on a black string. It is the greatest

[1] Sir Henry Channon (1897–1958), M.P. and diarist.

help in reading menus and bus numbers, instead of fumbling for spectacles.

At 6 o'clock I went to St. George's Hospital where Stuart has been removed, for he is suffering from jaundice. He is happy there because he is in the centre of London and can see Apsley House from his window. He is quite a different colour, no longer grey, but saffron. He pulled up the bedclothes and showed me his stomach which is bright lemon. I delivered chocolates, stamps and writing paper.

Jamesey talked about his rich, eccentric, plethoric admirer with whom he stays in Scotland. He assures me no demands whatever are made; but active adoration from a respectful distance keeps him warm, and is what he likes.

Friday, 19th February

Puss Milnes-Gaskell rang me up at breakfast and I lunched with her in the Ladies' Carlton Club. How tiny she is! She has come out of waiting at Badminton. I said I was reading the Henry Ponsonby book and enjoying it. She said, 'They', meaning Queen Mary *en principe*, did not like it at all. Their indignation was aroused against Sir Henry for having betrayed a private secretary's confidence in recording in letters to his wife matters of such a personal nature; not so much against Lady Ponsonby who after all is responsible for publication of these documents. Stuart says he regards the book as a last fling of the old-fashioned Whiggery against the Monarchy.

Saturday, 20th February

Went to see the Sergeant[1] [Stuart] in St. George's Hospital at 3 o'clock. Found there Stephen Spender who stayed talking for some time. He was in London fireman's uniform, wearing a blue fireman's overcoat. He is extremely handsome still, with an open radiant face framed in fuzzy, wind-blown yet close-cut hair which in its stellar way reminds me of Einstein's. In fact his looks are Teutonic and his mother was a German. Is he as innocent and guileless as he appears? He is very polite, with a schoolboy's awkward good manners. I hardly know him. I suppose Stuart murmured something, for he rose from a chair, shook

[1] Stuart Preston was known to his English friends as the Sergeant, because he was a sergeant in the U.S. army. But woe betide the friend whom Stuart overheard using this term of endearment.

157

hands nervously and said, 'Oh, yes, Jim.' He is shy and childlike which is endearing. Eddy says he can be a great bore for he is unrealistic and often silly, like most idealists. This I can well believe. I asked him if he saw anything of Henry Yorke,[1] who is also a fireman. He said Yes. Henry has written a new novel attacking the lower orders which Spender of course finds shocking. Yet as Eddy again says, Henry at least knows them, having lived among them; whereas Stephen has merely slept with them, which is not the same as knowing them uncarnally, and so romanticizes them. Indeed he got on to the sex lives of the lower orders this afternoon. He says they are on the whole remarkably strait-laced and puritanical, except the taxi drivers, who are the bohemians of the lower classes. Being constantly on the move, roaming around, they are on the fringe of the lives of poor and rich alike, especially of the Ritz rich. Their lives are so full of the promise of romance and actually so frustrated. After he left, Stuart said how successful the encounter had been. He immensely admires Spender. Funny creature Stuart, with his boundless capacity for admiration, his extravagant interest in people, his keen awareness of environment and absorption in class distinctions, at least in the multivariant intellectual and social distinctions of English life. He is as sensitive to our traditions as Henry James. Then I watched him eat his tea, so grossly, or do I mean youthfully? He consumed during this meal the whole of a pound pot of jam someone brought him yesterday. I was aghast and wondered whether in pre-war days I was ever so lavish.

Midi, Keith and Eddy came to tea. Eddy said, 'You do *not* take sugar with your tea. You take medicine.' And I said, 'You take liberties.' But unfortunately this retort was not my own.

Jamesey on the telephone tonight said he did not admire Stephen Spender. He contradicted his first observation that Stephen was disingenuous, saying that perhaps he was ingenuous; and if so, then he was stupid. That he wrote silly prose and his poetry was incomprehensible. He was like Wordsworth whom James detests. This resemblance I do not see.

Sunday, 21st February

I walked with Pompey from Chelsea, across the park to Paddington. From Windsor station we walked, Pompey off his lead, good as gold, down the Long Walk, past the Copper Horse to Cumberland Lodge;

[1] Henry Yorke (1905–74), wrote novels under the pen name Henry Green.

(and in the afternoon back to Windsor). I was five minutes late for luncheon and they had begun eating. They being only Lord FitzAlan, Magdalen and Mrs. Wyndham[1] (Methuselah's wife), sweet, fragile and shaky. Lord FitzAlan was worried by the rumour that the Pope might be leaving Rome for Brazil. I said it was the cheap Protestant press that was fabricating the rumour. We looked through the Catholic papers and, sure enough, they made no reference to it at all. It is sad how the Protestant papers must invent the most ridiculous canards to discredit the Pope these days. Lord F. was also worried about Tunisia. He thinks our delay in attacking will enable the Germans to muster reinforcements to outnumber us. Stuart expressed unfeigned delight in the American reverses, thinking them the best thing that could happen, 'for we are a conceited, self-satisfied race,' he said humbly.

I had tea with Mrs. Montgomery in Windsor. It was, I believe, a success. We found we liked and disliked the same people and the same books. She was thrilled that I knew Ivy Compton-Burnett, whom she considers our greatest novelist. She has lent me one of her books that I have not yet read, as a hostage she explained, so that I should have to come back and return it to her. Alan Pryce-Jones is her cousin. She loves Jamesey very much and the Sergeant [Stuart Preston] not so very much. She absolutely loathes Queen Victoria and Evelyn Waugh. She cannot feel dispassionately about anyone. We touched on Raymond, Eddy, Basil Dufferin. As their names cropped up, 'Now we have another,' she cried eagerly. 'We will put him *here*,' indicating a place at the large empty tea-table, 'and will come back to him when we have disposed of X. We will give him ten minutes,' or 'quite twenty minutes' as the case might be. When I left she referred to me as being 'quite one of us'. 'I loathe low-brows,' were her parting words. What will she think of me when she finds me out?

Monday, 22nd February

Cecil [Beaton] dined with me. I was rather alarmed having him alone. For one so sophisticated he is shy. And his polished courtesy makes me shy at first. He is very observant, misses nothing, the speck of potato on one's chin, the veins in one's nose, the unplucked hair sprouting from the ear. Yet how sensitive and understanding he is! After ten minutes I succumb to his charm, and am at ease. For there is nothing one cannot say to him. At least I think there is nothing. Talking of the Kents whom

[1] Gladys, later Lady Leconfield, wife of 5th Lord Leconfield.

he knew well, he said the Duke refused to take the war more seriously than a tiresome interruption of his life, and was never moved with compassion for the R.A.F. This irritated Cecil. So did the Duke's pernicketiness and perpetual grumbling. But he had innate good taste, without knowledge of the arts. We talked till 11.20 and went our several ways. I drank too much this evening. Pompey was sick on my bed during the night.

Tuesday, 23rd February

At 2.30 a Colonel Adams, solicitor to John Christie, called to discuss the possibility of Glyndebourne being handed over.

In Heywood's shop I asked Anne to lunch with me on Friday, in order to plead with her that they raise Nancy's salary. They only give her £3 10s. 0d. a week.

Was miserable all night trying to make up my mind whether to break with Q. or not, having received a letter from her this afternoon ending, 'I see a gulf yawning between us.' Now the dreadful thing is that it will continue to yawn, and I shall not make up my mind.

Wednesday, 24th February

Had an interview with the Royal Society and Professor Richardson about Newton's birthplace [Woolsthorpe Manor] in Lincolnshire. The Royal Society regards the little house as of the very highest importance from the historical point of view, the formative years, the vision of the falling apple, etc. To them Newton is what Shakespeare is 'to us', as Mrs. Montgomery would say.

Friday, 26th February

Called at the bedside at 6. Stephen Spender came with some books but did not stop longer than to say that he had dined with the Princesse de Polignac[1] last night. James, who was present, asked Stephen if it were true that she was the origin of Proust's Madame Verdurin. Stephen did not seem to think so, but said she knew Proust very well and her stories about him were fascinating. Proust used to take a taxi for a hundred yards and tip the cabman 100 francs for the pleasure of feeling himself a 'grand seigneur'. This practice got him into trouble.

[1] Princesse Edmond de Polignac, born Winifred Singer. Friend and patron of artists, musicians and writers. Died 1943.

Walked to tea with Anne Hill in Little Venice. She is truly one of the world's worth-while women, so intelligent, male-minded, and deliciously humorous. She is "a dark mare" and worth a million more than the glittering women, such as Nancy. I tackled her about their underpaying Nancy, which she admitted. She did not resent my interference but explained laughingly that whereas Nancy got paid £3 10s. od. she only got £2 10s. od.; that the shop barely paid its way. She accompanied me on foot across the Park, and left me at Hyde Park Corner.

Stuart was sitting in bed eating a lobster. No wonder he was in bad form, and feeling languid. He complained that Stephen Spender had stayed too long and tired him out with talking, talking. He believed he came so often, sometimes twice a day, in order to talk about himself, his poetic perplexities, his wish to write better, his teeming ideas and inability to express them right (so unlike Tennyson and Swinburne, he said), the usual anxieties of a poet. But I am sure Stuart is very proud of being the recipient of these confidences.

He told me, also with pride, that Mrs. Corrigan has sent him eggs and provisions. Referring to Raymond's *Channel Packet* she asked Chips, 'What is this book everyone is talking about, called *Chanelle Jacket?*' She spoke quite seriously about Richard Gare de Lyon. Chips told Stuart this morning that there are two things the Englishman doesn't forgive—ill manners, and a person striving to move in a class to which he does not properly belong. Rather acidly I told Stuart of Robert Byron's remark to Chips at the time of Munich, 'The trouble with you, Chips, is that you put your adopted class before your adopted country.' Robert was proud of this remark and repeated it to me.

Dined with Catherine Fordham and her new husband, General Kennedy, a nice, quiet man with no humour whatever. Catherine supplies these deficiencies. After dinner he expanded and talked about the war. He is sure the British soldier is not made of the same mettle as the German. He spoke of the Russians as our enemy no. 1 and said that we must hope for their utter exhaustion; and that they were hoping the same of us. I told him Tony Beaumont's story of the German prisoner whom he recently interrogated. When asked, 'What do the Germans truly think of your Italian allies?' he replied, 'The same as the Russians think of the English.' Kennedy was at Casablanca with the

161

Prime Minister and had many stories about him. Mr. Churchill was found by his valet sitting on his hot-water bottle in the aeroplane. The valet said, 'This is not a good idea, sir.' 'It is not an idea. It is a coincidence,' was the reply. To get to Casablanca they left secretly at 2 a.m., arriving at 10 a.m. for a late breakfast. Randolph greeted his father on the tarmac. 'Well, this is a surprise for you, Randolph.' 'Not at all,' said Randolph, 'a woman in Algiers told me a week ago.'

Monday, 1st March

On the train from Waterloo Clifford Smith kept reiterating how he did not wish to ask the Trust for too high a fee for his advice, yet could not afford to accept too low a fee—the same old story and very tiresome. I could not listen and just said, 'Yes, yes,' hoping thereby that he would take the hint, and shut up. We went slowly round Polesden Lacey together. The old boy is going to be quite a help in the selecting and discarding of contents. He is really very sweet and kind, though the most crashing bore. After a picnic in the servants' hall I gave him the slip, and wandered round the garden in the glorious sunshine, and picked violets out of the frames for Q. After delivering these on my return to London, I went to the hospital.

The whole of London congregates round the Sergeant's bed. Like Louis XIV he holds levées. Instead of meeting now in Heywood Hill's shop, the intelligentsia and society congregate in public ward no. 3 of St. George's Hospital. When I arrived Stephen Spender, looking worn out by his fireman's duties, was sprawled on the end of the bed. Raymond came for a brief visit. Lady Cunard called at the moment when the entire ward were stripped to the waist and washing. She pronounced the procedure barbaric. Then a member of Stuart's unit came to announce baldly that he must expect to be in the front line when the invasion starts. S., quite unconcerned, said he could not possibly be killed. I wonder, does every soldier feel as confident?

By dint of bussing, walking and bussing again miles in the blackout, I finally reached Osbert Lancaster's flat. Only myself for dinner, deliciously cooked by Karen—chicken and rum jelly. Karen very affectionate and sweet. I admire her total indifference to the world's opinion. Whereas Osbert is incorrigibly social, she is a natural recluse. On my return I found a charming note from Q. thanking me for the violets and foreseeing the gulf narrowing.

Caught the 9.47 with Clifford Smith and Kenneth Clark for Polesden again. The former is at his worst on occasions such as this, when he has to hold his own. It was quite obviously K. Clark's day, but old Cliffy bundled me into a carriage corner, wedged me there and aired his views upon irrelevant matters in Christies' inventory. K. retired disdainfully to a distant corner, declined to speak and read Maurice Bowra's book.

We only had one hour at Polesden but K. was the greatest help. He looked at all the pictures and his general opinion of them was favourable. He pronounced a few small Germans to be trash and recommended selling two van der Vliet portraits, and a bad Cuyp. He said the David was a fake. On Bookham platform he told me that to accomplish anything today a man must be resolute and ruthless, and must act and think afterwards. He impresses me as being extremely intelligent and capable, very ambitious and energetic. He has the missionary drive, just as he has the tight, resilient build and physique of George Lloyd. He dresses like a dapper footman on his half-day off. He is immaculate, spruce and correct in blue topcoat, gloves and blue Homburg hat. He talked about the National Trust and disapproved of 'your Mr. Matheson' for not having sufficient 'standing'. He offers personally to hang the pictures for me at Polesden.

After luncheon at Brooks's I drank coffee with John Christie who talked about Glyndebourne. He seemed rather mad and was very excitable. He was so angry with the Government for their lack of enthusiasm over his plans to promote opera that he was barely articulate. After 6 I called at the hospital. While Harold was talking to Stuart, Eddy commented on the latter's hands. He asked, could I not tell by his hands how ill he was? Honestly I could not.

Eddy gave me a drink in Chester Square and lent me three pictures for my house, a large Graham Sutherland, a smaller Samuel Prout and a Bonington drawing. These I took away.

Wednesday, 3rd March

An air-raid this evening in retaliation for our having bombed Berlin. The guns made a terrible noise. Miss Paterson and I crouched together, she knitting furiously, I reading with grim concentration. We were both so horribly frightened that we drank glasses of neat whisky.

Got through a hard day's work at Polesden with Clifford. We decided finally what to keep and what to dispose of. We also moved all the pictures up from the cellar and stacked them in the blue cloakroom.

I rose very early and boiled myself an egg. Then caught the 8.20 from Liverpool Street to Cambridge. Professor Richardson drove me, the Secretary of the Royal Society and a builder, in his old-fashioned motor into Lincolnshire. I felt very tired all day and dozed in the car, ruminating upon Q.'s remark last night, 'I want to hold you for ever', but read in the train Cecil Beaton's 'Libyan Diary' in *Horizon* and finished *Wives and Men*. Thought I must be beginning influenza. A cold day, so I wore my fur-lined coat, but the sun shining brightly at Woolsthorpe I took it off while we lunched under a haystack.

Newton's house[1] in which he was born in 1642 is about twenty years older. It is Cotswoldy, with good steep pitched roof, stone corniced chimneys and mullioned windows. It has four large bedrooms, one of which was partitioned off about 1666 with panelling of that date so as to form a study for Newton. Upstairs the L-shaped room is said to be the one whence Newton watched the apple fall. The original tree's descendant, now very aged, stands on the site of its forebear in the little apple orchard in front of the house. The secretary is going to find out what species of apple it is.[2] Tenant farmers have lived for 200 years in the house. The present ones are only leaving because all the surrounding land has been exploited commercially for the limestone, and is now arid, blasted heath and hummocks of infertile slack. It is a scandal that good agricultural land is allowed to be so treated by commercial firms and left thoroughly wasted and useless. The little manor house has light, but no sanitation. There are earth closets in the garden.

I lunched with the Kennedys, whose bed arrived yesterday for my spare room. It is of inordinate length.

[1] Woolsthorpe Manor, Lincs., was given to the Trust in 1943 through the Royal Society and the Pilgrim Trust.

[2] The authorities at Kew Gardens disclosed that it was a very old, if not otherwise extinct species, called the *Flower of Kent.*

I went to St. George's at 3 and found Stephen Spender talking to Stuart. He rose and left as I approached. After a few minutes Lady Cunard came with Lord Queensberry who is a Governor of the hospital. He is the boxer marquess, a youngish forty-five, with a deep resonant voice. Lady Cunard wore a pale fur toque to match her fur coat. She is small and incredibly vivacious and about seventy. She has a white powdered, twisted little face and deeply mascaraed eyes. She frolicked in like a gusty breeze, talking volubly, and quite unconscious of the impression she was making upon the other patients, who being rankers must be astounded by the Sergeant's host of society friends. She kissed Stuart in an animated and natural manner. She pressed Lord Queensberry into reciting two Shakespeare sonnets, which he did in a low and rich tone, but with bitterness and hatred in his voice, which was not becoming. Lady Cunard applauded each sonnet too loudly. She was polite and attentive to me, and wanted to have the National Trust explained to her. Before she left she invited me to luncheon tomorrow, which I declined, and to dinner on Monday before a concert, which I accepted. I doubted whether at heart Stuart approved, and I feel sure Jamesey, who is at present in bed with a high temperature, will not.

Monday, 8th March

I arrived at the Dorchester at 8 and was wafted in the lift to an upper floor, then directed down airless, daylightless passages to Emerald Cunard's apartments. Her sitting-room is sympathetically furnished with French things. Already assembled were Lady Moore,[1] Garrett Moore's lovely wife, and Lady Lamington,[2] a pretty woman. Garrett Moore[3] followed me. I have known him more or less, less rather than more since Eton days. He is tall, thin, willowy, sharp-featured, distinguished and patrician. A poetic and romantic-looking man if ever there was one. Lady Cunard darted like a bird of paradise into the room at 8.25; and we dined off expensive, pretentious food which lacked the necessary refinements of good cooking. Our hostess kept complaining how bad the Dorchester food was, and how at this stage of the war the country should have learnt to have adequate butter and milk distribution. I sat on her left, Lady Moore on my left. The latter is animated

[1] Joan Moore, the pianist, now Countess of Drogheda.
[2] Riette, wife of 3rd Lord Lamington. She died 1968.
[3] Now Earl of Drogheda, K.G.

and bewitching. Her coif à la Queen Alexandra was most becoming. Lady C. was a little *distraite* throughout, I thought; and conversation was not sparkling in spite of a promising beginning.

At 10 we went below to a concert given for Sibyl Colefax's benefit by the Griller Quartet and Denis Matthews at the piano. Unmusical though I am, I enjoyed it immensely. Lady Cunard introduced me to all and sundry, some of them my friends of a lifetime, as though I were a visitor from Mars. And so I suppose I am to her. I walked all the way home from the Dorchester, cogitating the evening's experience, and thinking myself a fool for being so buttoned up, and suspicious – of what? Some friendly and decorative and sophisticated people in a circle to which I do not belong.

Tuesday, 9th March

At 6 to St. George's, arriving simultaneously with Logan Pearsall Smith. I wanted to retire but Stuart earnestly begged me to stay. Pearsall Smith is an old, frail man, of heavy, ungainly build. He may be a bore for he tells long stories 'at' one, in a laborious, monotonous tone, laughing all the while and salivating a good deal. But he was quite funny with his story of a practical joke he played on Virginia Woolf in pretending to be the outraged person whose name she had in *Jacob's Room* 'taken in vain' from a tombstone in Scarborough churchyard. This delightful blackmailing story was interrupted by tiresome Lady H—[1] arriving. Again Stuart implored me not to leave, so I did my best by talking to her in order to allow him to have some conversation with the old man. When he had left I helped get rid of Lady H—. Stuart got back into bed, looking tired indeed. He promptly began eating a lobster. Whereupon Harold arrived. I got up to go, not without promising to return tomorrow, for there was apparently something very important S. had to tell me alone. But S. never is alone; and doubtless won't be tomorrow.

Wednesday, 10th March

I picked up the Eshers in the National Trust car and motored them from the Lansdowne Club to Polesden Lacey. Lady E. sat in front with me, Lord E. behind. He behaved like a schoolboy, calling out for me to stop at intervals, so that he could buy cakes, she rebuking him.

[1] Name forgotten before it could be recorded.

Referring to the appalling cold of West Wycombe in winter and Helen's apparent indifference to it he remarked 'People are never cold in their own houses. They derive warmth from satisfaction with the economies they are making.'

At Polesden they went round every room, and looked into every corner, cupboard and drawer. They commented on every object, liked the outside of the house and the grounds, and distant view. Esher said he had no quarrel to make with my plans and schemes. Yet he teased me unmercifully; also joked about Matheson's dislike of comfort and terror of beauty.

I dropped the Eshers at Paddington station, and went to see Jamesey. He was lying in bed with the curtains drawn. Under the shaded lamp his pallid face looked like old ivory. With his glowing coal eyes and glossy hair he resembles a Florentine prince. Then I called on the Sergeant and gave him Lady Esher's violets with her love. He was better, but there was no opportunity to hear those important words, whatever they may be. I give up. Dined at the Travellers' with Harold. Raymond [Mortimer] and Roger Senhouse present. Since Harold and Raymond talked politics together throughout the meal I was entertained by Roger. He has a moth-eaten, shabby appearance. He is, I fancy, a virtuous man with only a light regard for the truth. When the two R.'s left, Harold assured me how responsibly he took his onerous duties as a governor of the B.B.C. He feared he was losing Jamesey's confidence. I reassured him on this point.

Thursday, 11th March

A gruesome luncheon at the Bagatelle with Mrs. Bruce Ismay[1] and three other old hens, one of whom has some needlework she wants to lend to the Trust. It comes from Stoke Edith in Herefordshire.

Went to St. George's for the last time because Stuart leaves tomorrow. Lady Desborough[2] had just paid him a visit like a queen, a chauffeur following her with a shawl. Mrs. Montgomery had written to her about me and described me as an Eton boy. She honestly believes I am still there!

[1] Widow of the chairman of the White Star Line. Bruce Ismay (1862–1937) was on board the *Titanic*, but did not 'go down' with her in 1912 as some ill-disposed people at the time thought he should have done.
[2] E. A. P. Fane ('Etty') married 1887 1st and last Lord Desborough. One of the souls and mother of Julian Grenfell, the soldier poet, killed 1915.

Was unwell during the night, so had breakfast in bed where I remained all morning. Anne Rosse telephoned and came to see me for ten minutes. It was a lovely morning with the sun streaming through my windows. She was enchanted with the view of the river and the mud flats, for the tide was low. Miss P., like the saint she is, came back at midday to give me some soup. Pompey is ill too, and shows no sign of improvement, which is a worry.

Saturday, 13th March

I lunched with Anne Rosse and Bridget Parsons.[1] Afterwards we taxied to the Dorchester and waited in Lady Cunard's suite. She waltzed in on her small, beautiful little legs (the Sergeant says I must notice her feet, the most beautiful in the world), looking frail and ill as the old do who are made up to the eyes. Hers had mysterious drops exuding from the corners. She pulled down all the blinds, saying, 'I hate the sun. I hate the elements. We must get away from nature, or we shall get no-where.' We drove to see Carlyle's House in Cheyne Row. I was rather embarrassed by Anne saying, 'Only you would bring her to see a catacomb with nothing in it.' Indeed I had forgotten how little there was to see nowadays, everything of interest being packed away, and the windows of the principal downstairs rooms boarded up. The visit was not a success, and Lady C. returned to the Dorchester almost at once. Anne and Bridget and I walked here for tea.

Monday, 15th March

After breakfast I carried out what I had resolved. That is to say I took Pompey's basket, hid it away, burned his two bones, his cotton reel, his blanket and cushion in the incinerator in the yard. I threw his chain as far as I could into the river. I got a taxi, and told the driver to take me to the vet. I held the little dog on my knees without looking at him, without thank God, seeing his eyes. I told the vet to destroy him, and walked out, and away. All this I did without a qualm, for his cough was getting worse, and his fits persisted. For five or ten minutes I felt almost jubilant. Had I not done the right thing? Would someone ever do the same service to me? In walking rapidly along the embankment I felt, at

[1] Lady Bridget Parsons (1907–72), sister of Lord Rosse.

first with surprise, then shame, the tears coursing down my cheeks. By the time I reached the door I felt nothing but unmitigated grief. I had been no better than a murderer.

Miss Paterson was terribly upset when she came back from the week-end. I know she holds me responsible for the dastardly deed. But she is so good, she does not say so.

I dined with Puss Gaskell at the Berkeley. Douglas Woodruff[1] and his wife, formerly an Acton, to both of whom I felt antagonistic and was provocative, Carmen Wiggin and Hubert Howard, were there. Mrs. Woodruff told me that Alec Dru and Evelyn Waugh were her two best men friends. The first I could accept. The second finished me. I said that Evelyn represented the English Catholicism which was anathema to me. It was the very reverse of Roman Catholicism. It was sectarian, superior, exclusive and smug. Besides, Evelyn was the nastiest tempered man in England, Catholic or Protestant, and not an acceptable advertisement of the Christian faith. I said his review of Raymond's book was personal vituperation. Having delivered myself of these ill-mannered phrases, I felt better and enjoyed the dinner party. I talked to Puss about Queen Mary's gifts to Mrs. Greville. She promised to find out from Queen Mary which they exactly were. I shall thus be able to identify them. She said there was nothing the Queen would like more than to visit Polesden and 'play around'. Thank God, she can't.

Tuesday, 16th March

I took two of the Polesden pictures to Drown's, one to have the fungus which has assaulted it cleaned off, the other, the David, to be examined by him. Drown positively declares that it is genuine, contrary to K. Clark's opinion. I lunched at the Travellers' with Johnny Dashwood, who grumbled a good deal about Helen and her desire for a house in London, which he says he cannot possibly afford. Instead he wishes she would take a small flat and a job in London, and leave him to live at West Wycombe with a housekeeper, the prettier the better. He said that to raise the necessary endowment for West Wycombe the Trust could sell thirty acres of outlying parkland at £800 per acre.

Dined with Sibyl Colefax (we are on Christian name terms now) at the Allies Club. Roger Senhouse and an American woman, a Mrs. Stephens from the embassy, were the other guests. Sibyl read us Nigel

[1] Editor *The Tablet* 1936–67. Married 1933 Hon. M. I. Acton.

Nicolson's last letter to her from Tunisia. I am bound to admit it certainly was a good letter. When I told Jamesey afterwards, he said Nigel is sure to be killed so that we must endure the chagrin of hearing him described as a Julian Grenfell. We had the best dinner at this club in years, real pot au feu, ragoût and a lowly Algerian wine, which nevertheless had that heavenly, nostalgic twang of the Mediterranean.

Thursday, 18th March

Wrote my name in the Cardinal's book at Archbishop's House as Dame Una enjoined me to do at yesterday's S.P.A.B. meeting. Very few names seemed to be written, and mine was the third today. I noticed Dame Una's and John's, and General de Gaulle's.

At 2 o'clock to Martin's Bank at which were present Colonel Robin Buxton, Lord Sackville,[1] his solicitor, and Lord Willingdon[2] — the first and last Knole trustees. They had been lunching well, and I was given a glass of port. We discussed Knole. Lord Sackville could not have been more friendly or anxious to co-operate. I can't think why Eddy does not like him more. He is gentle and sympathetic and always treats me with paternal affection because I am a friend of Eddy. We left it that I was to send him Garrard the estate agent's figures for his comments, whereafter the trustees would decide how much endowment they could and would provide — the capital suggested is enough to yield £3,000 p.a. I am not sure how pleased the Trust will be with me for disclosing these figures, but I believe we must always be absolutely frank with decent donors like Lord Sackville. My sympathies are always with them. In fact my loyalties are first to the houses, second to the donors, and third to the National Trust. I put the Trust last because it is neither a work of art nor a human being but an abstract thing, a convenience.

Friday, 19th March

Gordon Russell[3] called on me in the office. He began talking about alabaster, saying he knew I was interested in it. Surprised I said, 'Yes, and why?' He had visited the monuments in Wickhamford church and enquired why they were so clean. 'Because,' the answer came, 'Master

[1] Major-Gen. 4th Lord Sackville (1870–1962).
[2] Present Marquess of Willingdon.
[3] Now Sir Gordon Russell, then member of the Board of Trade Design Panel.

Jim washes them.' The object of his visit was to express a fear lest the National Trust, in becoming a very large landowner, might dwell too much on preservation, and sterilize too much of the country. The Trust ought to become more positive in its outlook, ought to develop along contemporary lines. It ought not to employ exclusively archaic-minded architects, but avant-garde architects. Above all, it must not conceal, say, modern necessary things like petrol pumps under olde-worlde thatched roofs, etc. I said I agreed with much of this, but pleaded that we were solely a preservation body and had to care for our own properties, which did not for the most part comprise petrol stations and gasometers. The C.P.R.E. was the body which he should stimulate. He said no one knew anything about the C.P.R.E. I begged him to stimulate it. He is a shy craftsman, and as such has my sympathies. He has been made chairman of the Committee of Craftsmen and Designers of the new Utility Committee.

This afternoon I took the tube to Richmond, and thence a bus to Petersham. I walked down the long drive to Ham House. The grounds are indescribably overgrown and unkempt. I passed long ranges of semi-derelict greenhouses. The garden is pitted with bomb craters around the house, from which a few windows have been blown out and the busts from the niches torn away. I walked round the house, which appeared thoroughly deserted, searching for an entrance. The garden and front doors looked as though they had not been used for decades. So I returned to the back door and pulled a bell. Several seconds later a feeble rusty tinkling echoed from distant subterranean regions. While waiting I recalled the grand ball given for Nefertiti Bethell which I attended in this house some ten years or more ago. The door was roughly jerked open, the bottom grating against the stone floor. The noise was accompanied by heavy breathing from within. An elderly man of sixty stood before me. He had red hair and a red face, carrot and port wine. He wore a tail coat and a starched shirt front which had come adrift from the waistcoat. 'The old alcoholic family butler', I said to myself. He was not affable at first. Without asking my name, or business, he said, 'Follow me.' Slowly he led me down a dark passage. His legs must be webbed for he moved in painful jerks. At last he stopped outside a door, and knocked nervously. An ancient voice cried, 'Come in!' The seedy butler then said to me, 'Daddy is expecting you,' and left me. I realized that he was the bachelor son of Sir Lyonel Tollemache,[1] aged eighty-nine. As I entered the ancient voice said,

[1] Sir Lyonel Tollemache, 4th Bart. (1854–1952).

'You can leave us alone, boy!' For a moment I did not understand that Sir Lyonel was addressing his already departed son.

Sir Lyonel was sitting in an upright chair. He was dressed, unlike his son, immaculately in a grey suit, beautifully pressed, and wore a stock tie with large pearl pin. I think he had spats over black polished shoes. A very decorative figure, and very courteous. He asked me several questions about the National Trust's scheme for preserving country houses, adding that he had not made up his mind what he ought to do. After several minutes, he rang the bell and handed me over to the son who answered it.

The son showed me hurriedly, I mean as hurriedly as he could walk, round the house, which is melancholy in the extreme. All the rooms are dirty and dusty. The furniture and pictures have been moved to the country for safety. There is no doubt whatever that even without the contents this house is worthy of acceptance because of the superlative interior treatment, the panelling, the exquisite parquetry floors, the extraordinary chimneypieces, the great staircase of pierced balusters, the velvet hangings, etc. It is a wonderful seventeenth-century house, and from the south windows the garden layout of symmetrical beds, stone gate plinths and ironwork is superb.

The son was full of complaints. Once we were away from the father, whom he clearly holds in mortal dread, he became confidential. He said the family were worth £2,000,000 and did not receive as much as 6d. from each £; that they had two gardeners instead of twelve, no indoor servants except a cook (and himself). He told me he was distracted by looking after the Ham property and the Lincolnshire estate. At times he felt suicidal. I looked straight at him, and knew that the poor man meant it. When I waved goodbye the faintest flicker of a smile crossed his bucolic face, and a tiny tear was on his cheek.

Slept in the office on a camp bed, Eardley on another. We gossiped ourselves to sleep.

Saturday, 20th March

Went to Windsor in the afternoon to see Mrs. Montgomery, 'Mrs. Betty' I am now to call her. Met her on the doorstep, and we pottered across to St. George's Chapel. She is very bent and walks with difficulty. It was impossible to ask her questions about the chapel because she talked ceaselessly of other things. She said she was one of the original 'Souls'. Jean Hamilton was a great friend and so brave about her cancer which she referred to by the dreaded name. Mrs. Betty wanted me to bring Raymond to see her, but I don't think he would come. I like her coined words, 'pointful' and 'dank' being most frequently used. 'Carp' is another. And her proverb, 'A bird in the hand is worth a feather in the cap.'

Dined with Q. at the Mirabelle. She offered me a £1 towards the evening expenses, which I accepted without demur. I do hope and believe she meant me to. I told her I hated the Mirabelle. Got home at 11.30 and sat over the fire for hours. Felt overcome with loneliness. It was too late to ring up Q. I have nothing to reproach her for, yet I keep thinking, 'Would I, if I were she, gratuitously go off to . . . for ten days leaving Jim behind in London?' Obviously, yes, I ought to in the circumstances. But would I, that's the point? I am such a fool in these respects. She is obviously right. She has duties. Every day I have a letter, sometimes a postcard too. There can be no mistaking their underlying meaning — which is now, and not for ever.

At home after work I sat reading *Asylum Pieces* by one, Anna Kavan — experiences of a woman about to become mad and finally shut up in an asylum. I became hideously and terrifyingly depressed by these stories and was obliged to drink neat whisky. At the Dorchester Eddy Sackville-West told me he felt horribly unwell and did not know how he was going to get through dinner. He sat on Emerald Cunard's left, and was brilliant and amusing. On his left Stephen Spender's wife, with ringlets down her neck. Me so wedged between her and Stephen Spender that I could only raise my fork to my mouth when neither of them was doing the same thing. Conversation is always general at this table. Lady C. gets cross if two guests try to talk to each other. She is a watchful hostess, and whenever there is a pause in the scrum throws in a ball, usually of a most unexpected sort. I stayed till 11.

Chips [Channon] walked with me across the park. He tried to pump me about the Sergeant, so that I wondered at first whether he were in love with him. He asked me whether Stuart was really rich, or really very poor. Everyone was asking, for S. is extremely mean with money if he is not poor. I honestly did not know. Was S. an imposter, he wondered? I said such an idea had not occurred to me. I thought an imposter was a person masquerading as someone who he wasn't. But I volunteered to observe it was rather a pity that S. was undiscriminating

173

in his choice of friends. Chips did not agree, and asked me to explain what friends I had in mind. I could not do so for fear of being rude. He said, No, in that respect S. had not erred. He cared for distinguished people like Lady Desborough and myself. I could not help laughing. Then he said I looked years younger and handsomer than Stephen. I said Stephen was a very handsome man. I had never been that. More awkward laughter. When we parted in Pont Street, he said, 'Do not worry yourself about the Sergeant. He is being well looked after by X.B. He won't come to any harm.' I said, 'I don't believe it. Besides, I am not his keeper.'

Tuesday, 23rd March

This conclusion was confirmed by what Stuart told me at dinner to-night. He said it took him some time to realize that X.B. was madly in love with him in the same teasing sort of way that Robert Byron once was with me. When he was obliged to tell X.B., who is one of Chips's best friends, that he could not return his affection, he received, much to his astonishment, a tremendous scolding from Chips. Chips was plaintive. He had meant to do S. a good turn by introducing him to a rich man who would ply him with champagne and load him with jewels. But, said S., 'I can buy my own champagne, and I don't like jewels. Thank you all the same.' Oh, the cynicism, the worldliness of these people!

Wednesday, 24th March

I go to Polesden with Margaret Jourdain who thinks but little of the contents, apart from the pictures. Mrs. Bruce Ismay and Mrs. Foley came over for the day. Boring old women. I am sure M. J. bothers with them only because they are rich, for she is far too intelligent for them. They are sugar, and she is salt. I picked violets and daffodils and dropped them on Emerald Cunard at the Dorchester. Then to see Jamesey, who was sitting up in bed correcting proofs. Jamesey said Emerald Cunard does not know me yet. This is true. She thinks I am very fond of him, Jamesey. Yes, but how fond does she think I am, I asked? Little escapes her, he says, but sometimes she gets hold of the wrong end of the stick. Logan Pearsall Smith has written to him: 'Who is this Jimmy L.-M.? Mrs. Betty writes that he is delightful, although Master P.-H. comes first.'

When I told Eddy today that I was going this afternoon to stay at Gunby Hall, in Lincolnshire, with Field-Marshal Sir Archibald Montgomery-Massingberd,[1] he could not believe his ears. Could there possibly be such a man? Indeed the field-marshal received me in his study. He is tall, large, a little ponderous, handsome and impressive; yet very gentle and kind. Lady Massingberd is slim, grey, jolly and also kind. They are Peter Montgomery's uncle and aunt on both his father and mother's sides of the family and are very fond of him. But because he has not yet married they are leaving him out of any subsequent settlement of Gunby which they may make. The house is 1700, symmetrical, of secondary size, and of deep-plum brick with stone dressings. Every room and passage within has simple contemporary panelling. It was built by the Massingberds and is full of their portraits, including two Reynoldses. Now the Air Ministry is threatening to fell all the trees in the park and demolish the house, both in direct line of a runway which they have constructed without previously ascertaining the proximity of these obstacles. If the threats can be averted with our help, the Montgomery-Massingberds are ready to make the property over to the Trust straight away. They are such dear people that even if the house were worthless I would walk to the ends of the earth to help them.

A plain dinner with only water to drink. Wine and spirits are put away for patriotic motives. Hot water cut off for the same reason. Otherwise the house full of servants, including a butler and pantry boy and four gardeners. Of course they revel in their imposed suffering. I wish I did.

Friday, 26th March

The Field-Marshal was incapacitated by sciatica this morning so Lady Massingberd took me round the house and gardens, both of which I pronounced to be of national importance. Then I wandered round the grounds by myself. It is curious how the moment I leave London I feel ill and dispirited.

The Field-Marshal told me last night that of all the politicians he had dealings with Neville Chamberlain was the most abjectly ignorant of military matters. He smiled sweetly when Sir Archibald as G.O.C.

[1] The Field-Marshal (1871–1947) was C.I.G.S. 1933–36. Lady (Diana) Montgomery-Massingberd died 1963.

endeavoured to explain some simple manœuvre, but did not know the difference between a division and a company, and made no effort to learn.

Nancy came round at 3.30 and found me painting the stairs. I took her to Carlyle's House, after which we returned here and made toast. Eddy and Dame Una Pope-Hennessy joined us—a most enjoyable tea. The Dame looking like a priestess, sat on an upright chair so as to see out of the window. She said the Cardinal's Requiem Mass was wonderfully moving. It went like clockwork as though it had been rehearsed. All the bishops and abbots in the kingdom were present; also the Papal Delegate and the Archbishop of New York. She said I was a fool not to have asked for a ticket. She feels sure Bishop Mathew will be the next Archbishop of Westminster. I do hope so, for he is a brilliant and witty, if worldly man, and has been courageous in the air-raids.

John Russell came and talked after dinner. He has a new job in the Admiralty and is well paid. He left his article on Henry James's house at Rye for me to read. He is ambitious to become a recognized man of letters. At 2 o'clock in the morning I was woken by the telephone. It was Stuart to tell me he had been dining with Emerald Cunard, Rex Whistler and Duff Cooper, and they had talked of love and kissing on the mouth, one of Emerald's new pet subjects. He was in ecstasy over the evening. Petulantly I asked why this astounding piece of information could not have been withheld until later in the morning.

Was called by telephone at 5.30, cooked my breakfast and by 6.15 was off. Met Hubert Smith at Watford and drove with him straight to Burton Agnes in the East Riding. Here we were taken round by young [Marcus] Wickham-Boynton on leave from the army. He and his mother are undecided what to do. He struck me as obstinate, if not owlishly stupid. Burton Agnes is still well kept up and not requisitioned. It is superbly beautiful. Walls of rose red brick. The hall screen and chimneypiece are stupendous. So are the painted panelling of the drawing-room, the japanned room and the staircase with arcading. When I was here in 1936 the house was dilapidated and spooky. Mrs. Wickham-Boynton, before showing me round, said one room was haunted, and it was not a room you would expect to be haunted. I was asked to guess which it was. When we came back to our starting point I told her which I thought the haunted room to be. I was right. There is a screaming skull immured in this house. When it was removed ghostly noises and manifestations of a terrifying kind took place. But with the recent tarting up of this house I suspect that the spirits have been driven away.

When I stayed—also in 1936—at Bradshaw Hall near Bolton there were two skulls mounted on silver seventeenth-century stems. They were religiously kept upon a Family Bible. Col. Hardcastle, the owner, told me that one day his housemaid in dusting broke a skull off its stem. He took both skull and stem to the local jewellers to be mended. But that night and the following such a caterwauling ensued from the skull left behind in the house that he and the servants were terrified. Col. Hardcastle had to retrieve the broken skull and stem, and beg the jeweller to come and mend them in the room to which they belonged. He never had any further trouble. One of the skulls was supposed to be Bradshaw the regicide's, and the other his wife's.

I have little hope of negotiations over Burton Agnes coming to a conclusion. The owners are at least candid about their motives. Smith and I stayed at a squalid local inn, with filthy food. I could hardly bring myself to get into bed lest the blankets touched my face.

Tuesday, 30th March

Very cold up here and windy. A grey, melancholy day. We drove by Goole and south of the Humber through stark fenland and potato-growing fields that stretch wearily into infinity. At Norton Place we motored round the boundaries of the estate. Smith's opinion was that this was good second-class agricultural land, and the farm buildings were in no bad state of repair. I find it very tiresome that acceptance of a beautiful house by Carr of York has to depend upon such irrelevancies. We continued to Stragglethorpe Hall, now a nursery school. We were conducted round by the owners, Colonel and Mrs. Jack Leslie. It is a mid-sixteenth-century half-timbered house on a stone base. A misleading, fakey sort of house, yet not unpleasing. The owners want it to be used after the war by disabled servicemen.

Wednesday, 31st March

Went to see Jamesey who is better. He said Clarissa was enchanted with her tea with me on Sunday. I was naturally pleased but said that I never would have guessed it at the time. We asked each other: why does one see in every affair a picture of oneself enjoying the same ecstasy, the same unalterable relationship right into old age? For one knows perfectly well that such a state of things cannot last longer than a matter of months, possibly only weeks.

Thursday, 1st April

To Knole in the afternoon, where I talked to Lord Sackville and his agent for one hour and a half. Discussions began stickily but ended hopefully. I stayed to tea, Lady Sackville[1] dispensing. She is a singularly brash and ignorant woman, whereas he is the exact opposite, well-bred and educated. He told me Eddy's mother[2] and grandfather were both bleeders like Eddy.

Friday, 2nd April

Johnny Dashwood lunched with me at Brooks's. An expensive guest for he had a gin and tonic, a whisky and soda and a bumper brandy. We talked of West Wycombe affairs. At 2.30 the town clerk of Liverpool and two other worthies came to see me about Speke Hall. They are resentful of the Trust having been left the Hall and consider Liverpool corporation the proper body to hold it, since they are older than the National Trust by 700 years. It seems to me a curious reason to put forward.

I took the 4 o'clock train to Preston. Stuart came with me to Euston, the faithful creature, and walked up and down the platform until the train left. At the Park Hotel, Preston, they would not give me dinner because I arrived after 9 o'clock, and only some dry cheese sandwiches, without margarine, and tea to drink, for 4/6.

Saturday, 3rd April

At 9.30 Bruce Thompson[3] arrived, then Sir William Ashcroft who

[1] Anne, widow of Stephen S. Bigelow of Boston, married 1924 4th Lord Sackville as his second wife.
[2] The first Lady Sackville was Maude Cecila Bell (d. 1920).
[3] Then the National Trust's representative in the Lake District, having been on the head office staff until shortly before the war.

motored us to Rufford Old Hall. There we were met by Mr. Brown, Lord Hesketh's know-all solicitor, the Treasurer of the Local Committee and Philip Ashcroft, who has arranged the rural implements in the small museum. All such meetings are most formal in the north, I notice. We went round house and garden, both of which I know well, on a conducted tour, headed by Sir William. The sole outcome of this visit was that my recommendation to remove the ivy from the red brick 1660 wing was adopted.

Sir William, who is Sheriff-elect, entertained Bruce and me to luncheon in the County Hall; then took us to see a ghastly exhibition of local artists' pictures in the Town Hall. Bruce and I took a taxi to Samlesbury Hall to meet its trustees, an astonishing bunch of Lancashire businessmen with red faces, protuberant paunches, execrable taste and strong accents. They conducted us round with much solemnity. They are contemplating handing the place over to us. The Hall has been gravely tampered with, externally and internally. Its 'speres' and movable screen have been cut up to make a bogus minstrels' gallery. There is much mock magpie work. House and ugly outbuildings are crammed with a vast collection, formed by the late Mr. Lewis, chief of the trustees, of Italian and Continental cabinets, some perhaps good, and the majority devastatingly ornate. All unsuitable in this black-and-white setting. The trustees entertained us to a vast, substantial but delicious tea at 3.30. I caught the 5.25 from Preston, reaching Euston at midnight tired and hungry, having eaten a few sandwiches on the train.

Sunday, 4th April

Robert Lutyens told me that the quality of the Adam furniture at Osterley was indifferent – a surprising statement. In rebuilding Middleton [Park, Oxon] for Grandy Jersey[1] before the war he found him an obstinate client. Virginia too was difficult because she insisted on having a cocktail bar and other Hollywood features introduced. The house was built to hold forty people, including servants, at weekends. He said the old Middleton house was of no interest. Nevertheless he preserved the portico. He said the new Waterloo Bridge was bad because it looked as though it could not stand up to the weight of present-day traffic. An engineer's ingenuity did not necessarily make good architecture.

[1] The present Earl of Jersey.

The Sergeant must be a very simple man. He said he had been obliged to tell X.B. that he could not see him again. His conduct was spoiling a beautiful friendship, etc. X.B. was suicidal, and quivered so on receiving this broadside that he could not hold his glass, and had to put it on a table. S. has come to hate him as far as he can hate anybody. He said, 'Do you know, he tried to embrace me in Chips's house, and Rex Whistler walked into the room.' He was very indignant at being exposed to such a false situation. I said, 'Couldn't you have laughed it off without being unkind?' 'Laugh?' he said, 'Laugh? But it is no laughing matter.' I said, 'But it seems to me it is.' Then he said a Cabinet Minister was mad about X.B. 'Marvellous!' I said. 'Not at all. X.B. won't look at him.' I see no way out of the tangle.

Tuesday, 6th April

Went this evening with Q. to the ballet — *Sylphide*, *Quest* and *Façade*. *Quest* a new ballet, with music by William Walton and décor by John Piper. Interesting and colourful, but I shall have to see it several times before I understand it.

Thursday, 8th April

Yesterday I was quite ill, and had to stay in bed. Terrible headache, and turned my head first to one side of the pillow, then the other, like the pendulum of a clock, seeking and never finding relief. Not since my hospital days have I been unable to read, when ill. And what did I think about? Nothing whatever. The mind can be a total blank and blackness, conscious only of that relentless, regular throb.

This evening I dragged myself out of bed, bathed, shaved, and took a taxi to dine with the Osbert Lancasters. Contrary to expectation I enjoyed myself. So often when one has a temperature and is feeling like death, one can be gay, and scintillate, knowing that when the festivity is over, one will collapse again.

Friday, 9th April

Although on fire-watching duty I dined at the Dorchester, prepared to dash off if the siren went. I sat on Emerald's left, Cecil [Beaton] on my left, Lady Pamela Berry, Peter Quennell, Garrett [Moore]. I drank everything offered me to keep myself going. Emerald said Stuart was in love with Alice Harding, that he was a virgin, that he told Duff Cooper and Rex Whistler he understood kissing on the cheek to be more passionate than on the mouth. All sorts of nonsense sparkled off her like miniature fireworks. Emerald gets gay on one sip of cherry brandy and pours forth stories helter-skelter, wholly unpremeditated, in an abandoned, halting, enquiring manner that appears to be ingenuous, and is deliberate. Her charm can be devastating. Left for the office just before midnight.

Saturday, 10th April

Unless I write in my diary the events of the past day that evening, or at latest the next morning, there is little point in keeping one. Is there anyway? A catalogue of names, places and engagements is stale and unprofitable. That is what a diary tends to become after a time. And I cannot stop. I would like this diary to entertain two or three generations ahead when I am under the sod. I cannot really believe that I ever shall be dead. The prospect is too squalid to dwell upon. It is impossible to think that I and those I love, and our loves can be snuffed out like a streak of wind over a wave. Surely some lingering vibration must be left behind, for ever?

The Sergeant said I credited no one with sensibility but myself — quite true; that I believed the world to revolve round me — quite true (who doesn't?); that I supposed only *I* understood the meaning of love, and the mysteries of the universe, etc. — quite true. What about him, for instance? Well, the truth certainly is that he does lack sensibility, and has no inkling of the meaning of love or the mysteries. He is a feather on the stream of life. Feathers can be decorative but they are easily blown about. But he is a very clever feather all the same. He also quivers with sensitivity, if not sensibility.

Poor thing, he has had a row this morning with Chips, who advised him to get a transfer out of London, anywhere so long as he leaves the capital. And the reason? He is unwittingly destroying X.B. who is suffering from a breakdown, being odious to his old mother, cruel to his young wife, and about to commit suicide or else murder the Sergeant. It makes me indignant with the egoism of these people. How dare they behave like this? I told S. he had made a mistake in seeing

X.B. again. He admits it, but says his intentions were strictly 'honourable'. They were idiotic. At all events he is moving his belongings from Chips's house and will not see him again.

Nancy came to tea. Quite alone with her I am not at ease, and never have been. I think she recognizes this, for just as she was standing on the doorstep about to leave Cecil [Beaton] turned up. She stayed for another hour and left ultimately with him. I was not in good form, and feared I was going to have jaundice. I went up to a glass and said, 'My God, how yellow I look!' Nancy said Nonsense, so did Cecil, so did Anne Rosse whom I saw later. I felt almost disappointed.

Sunday, 11th April

I was about to enter my bath when Emerald telephoned. She talked for thirty-five minutes while I was in a state of semi-nudity, about books, French politics in the thirties and forties of the last century, about Guizot and Madame de Lieven, about Whig hostesses and there being no great ladies today. 'What about Lady Desborough?' I asked, shivering. Emerald said her food was too bad for her to qualify, and she was too little of a snob. In her day, Emerald went on – while my right foot which had touched the water, dripped – every country house had powdered footmen. Even so, such an establishment was cheaper to run than two rooms at the Dorchester today. She talked of Jean Hamilton. Her two best friends were Lady Desborough and Norah Lindsay – 'Are you sneezing, dear?' – Her house was hideous. She herself was sweet, but her skin was too delicate. Had I read Santayana? 'Yes, I thought him a worse charlatan than Charles Morgan.' At last she rang off. I got to Mass in Cheyne Row, and was absolutely sure I was going to have a severe chill.

I decided during Mass that I really must not saddle myself with the nicest people who bore me. I promptly invited one to lunch with me at the Queen's Restaurant. She insisted upon coming back to 104 and staying to tea. She complained about her horrid daughter who, to spite her, had married a Hungarian-Jew refugee, who is a communist, and not even a gentleman, my dear.

At 11, Stuart telephoned from the Savoy where he was having supper, to tell me he had walked today from Fairlawne to Sissinghurst, and there met Vita for the first time. He thought her beautiful, but was disappointed that she was not as Spanish, masculine and hirsute as he had pictured her.

I left the office early to greet Magdalen FitzAlan-Howard who came to tea. I don't suppose an uncharitable or horrid thought has ever passed through her head. Sitting close beside her over the 'Earl Grey' I wondered whether all that goodness was aware of the badness inside my head, only three feet from hers. I hoped not — any more than a soul is aware of the guts, intestine, viscera (or whatever the disgusting things are called) inside the most beautiful body of the twin soul held within its arms. Lord FitzAlan called for Magdalen and insisted upon climbing my narrow stairs which, now painted, are pitch black and dark for a blind nonagenarian, and admired my room and view.

James dined with me at the Café Royal, having come from Lady Crewe's literary party. He said she was unusually gauche and awkward. Chips was there, asking, 'Where are the poets? Is Lady Colefax a poet?' James was horrified by the X.B. story and the cynical rôle played by Chips. When I wanted to confide in him some of my problems he instantly became bored and inattentive. I ought to have learnt by now never to ask for sympathy from a friend. James rapidly changed the subject and once again said, with sparkling eyes, how much he was longing to sleep with a woman, and Cecil [Beaton] told him how easy it was. If Stuart thinks I am egocentric, James is far worse. He not only knows, but proclaims that he is the centre of the universe.

Wednesday, 14th April

At 1.30 I take a train for Dulverton [in Somerset]. I still feel ill, and my cold will not go. My nose blows catarrhal gobs like leather oysters. I am feverish, and can neither smell nor taste. Cigarettes disgust me; and yet I am in a smoking carriage. The day is sunny and warm, and the railway cuttings are a mass of primroses. The leaves of the trees are yellow-green and turn upwards. Summer is here.

At Dulverton I prepare to walk to Pixton [Park], but Mary Herbert[1] meets me down the road in an old car. Pixton is like an Irish house, large, shabby, chaotic and comfortable. Laura Waugh[2] and Bridget Grant[3] come in late for supper from farming. They are both cold and

---

[1] Widow of Hon. Aubrey Herbert (*d.* 1923) and daughter of 4th Viscount de Vesci. She died 1972.

[2] Her daughter (*d.* 1973), wife of Evelyn Waugh.

[3] Another daughter, wife of Major E. Grant who died 1947.

distant. Mary, a magnificent, imperious stag by Landseer, perhaps an eagle, is masterful and very clever. She is full of opinions and Catholic prejudices. She said Lady Salisbury told her that Lord FitzAlan had risen to his great heights of wisdom and saintliness through conscientious persistence. As a young colonel of a regiment he was ordinary, and not particularly saintly. His brother, the Duke of Norfolk, made him go into the House of Commons. From that moment he cultivated his natural intelligence. Aubrey Herbert valued his counsel highly. Mary thinks the Vatican has consulted him on the appointment of the new Archbishop of Westminster. For he is the leading lay Catholic in this country. She thinks Magdalen ran away with somebody before the last war, was hauled back by the family and held in disgrace for ages. I question the truth of this.

Thursday, 15th April

I took a taxi to Ashwick to see Mr. Frank Green about Culverthorpe which belongs to him. Nothing much came of the interview beyond threats. The old tyrant lay in a large four-poster, wearing a striped dressing-gown and a woollen nightcap with a bobble on the end of a string. The bobble bounced up and down his nose as he spoke. His face is that of a rugged, wicked John Bull. It is an eighteenth-century, Rowlandsonish face. He dismissed the subject of Culverthorpe, which was the purpose of my visit, and concentrated on the Treasurer's House, York. Was he to understand that someone had dared, had dared to shift the furniture in one of the rooms? Did I not realize that he had put little studs in the floors to mark the precise spot on which every single piece of furniture in the house was to stand? I did. Then no piece of furniture was ever to be shifted therefrom. He looked me full between the eyes in an accusatory manner. I flinched under the awful gaze. 'There!' he cried out, '*you* are guilty. I knew it,' and the bobble on the string flew around his cheeks and on to his mouth. In a rage he blew it up again. In actual fact I was not guilty. I hadn't been to the house for ages. 'Mark my words,' he went on, 'I am an old man. I may not have very long to live. But I warn you that, if ever you so much as move one chair leg again, I will haunt you till your dying day.' And he wagged a skinny finger under my face. I slunk off, chastened, with my tail between my legs.

The taxi driver who was waiting for me said, 'You look as though you had seen a ghost, sir.' 'I have,' I said. I dismissed the taxi and walked back the remaining miles. A hot, Mediterranean day. I was struck by the beauty of the deep wooded valleys, each with a rushing stream at its foot. The cherry blossom was full out. The magnolia tree at Pixton looked like a giant Christmas cake, covered with solid pink and white icing sugar.

Friday, 16th April

Back in London I lunched with John Russell at the Russell Hotel to meet Professor Geoffrey and Mrs. Webb.[1] He is a bearded figure in a black suit, she, plain, unwomanly, bespectacled, blue-stocking. Both so earnest and middle-class in their humourless outlook. Ten years ago I should have wanted to make fast friends with them. Today I cannot be bothered because I am just a little too much of a snob.

Saturday, 17th April

Joined the Sergeant at his American canteen where I sat with him while he ate his final luncheon. Such a good meal it was, too, for one shilling. I remarked how tidy and clean these G.I.s looked compared to British rankers. S. said the regulars were fed and looked after better than our regulars. I took some of his clothes and books to keep at Cheyne Walk while he is away.

Jamesey came for the night, arriving at 11.45 when I was asleep on the sofa with the *Guermantes Way* open on my lap. He was in a state of hysterical bewilderment. He had been dining with M.A.B. who told him he was 'beautiful as the dawn', and gave him a strong drug. He suspected she wanted to seduce him, and was repelled but fascinated. He fears the next time he will be lured into her bed. 'But isn't that just what you are wanting?' I asked. 'Don't be so disgusting,' was the retort. M.A.B. told him some terrifying things: how Lady Crewe in spite of her indolence intrigues like a mole; by sheer determination she undermined the Alington marriage because Napier Alington, a hundred years her junior, with whom she was madly in love, married without telling her.

Sunday, 18th April

James and I breakfasted at Brooks's, then went to Warwick Street where

[1] Geoffrey Webb was secretary of the Historic Monuments Commission. M. I. Webb was author of *Michael Rysbrack, Sculptor*, 1954.

I wanted to get a palm. But they only had one communal bit of box for all to kiss. We walked to Waterloo Station, met John Pope-Hennessy and took a train for Polesden Lacey. John spent the afternoon assiduously viewing the pictures while James and I ran around the bedrooms, gossiping and giggling, he purloining a black coal-scuttle glove and some india rubbers. Then we lay on the grass in the sun, he imparting further astonishing things which M.A.B. had regaled him with as they went over Argyll House by candlelight. Lady Crewe believes no relationship, no emotion, no motive to be straightforward, and suspects everything and everyone. This is truly Proustian. She is very attached to, and attracted by Jamesey. I looked at him carefully this afternoon, and I see that he is beautiful with his amber complexion, coal-scuttle eyes and black wavy hair, even if one discounts his fascinating mind.

To Lady Cunard's box at the Phoenix. After the concert Bridget [Parsons] dined with me at the Turkish restaurant. She is ravishingly beautiful with her long, arrogant neck, golden hair, fair complexion and sulky mouth. This evening she was pathetically sweet, I say 'pathetically' because her nature is not sweet but sour. And there is poignancy in watching her trying to overcome her nature.

Tuesday, 20th April

A letter from Stuart, saying that all his letters will be censored. This puts a restraint upon correspondence. What hell life is today! There is Stuart, intellectual and sensitive, treated like a Spartan slave, and made to undergo a Commando course, for which he is totally unfitted, among plebeian thugs, yet submissive, uncomplaining.

This evening I had a talk with Harold while he was bathing and changing. He said we must bear in mind that the values and standards of Chips and his world were not ours, and we must not be shocked by them, or corrupted by them, but outwardly amused, if inwardly censorious. Chips was not a bad man, but his loyalties were often mistaken. He would go to any lengths in the interests of his chosen friends, even to that of absolutely doing down some innocent individual. In other words, I said, he would commit evil for the betterment of evil. Harold said, 'Well, you could put it like that if you were the headmaster of a boys' preparatory school.'

I took him to dine at Brooks's. He purred with approval of the silver plate and the excellent service; and our bottle of Burgundy. He complained that his enemies criticized him for being National Labour when they saw how much he enjoyed the delicacies of life. They called him inconsistent. He said, 'True, I do not care for the society of the lower classes. I have no desire to live with them, or be like them. I hate them. I do want them to become like me.' He said Lady Gerald Wellesley[1] was determined to sue somebody for saying she was drunk during the Poetry Reading at the Aeolian Hall, and preventing her from reciting on the platform. Indeed Vita [Sackville-West] to prevent this contingency accompanied her to the Hall, and like a saint never let her out of her sight, except when she went to the loo. This however she did five times within three-quarters of an hour, coming out each time less sober than when she went in. At last Vita said, 'But, Dotty, you can't possibly want to go again!' She sat down on the Bond Street pavement screaming, and tapping with her stick, because by herculean methods they had mercifully prevented her from being presented to the Queen. She threw Harold's arm off her shoulder, shouting, 'Take your bloody arm away!' Harold fears she may decide to sue him. 'You see,' he said ruefully, 'it is always the innocent who get punished.'

Good Friday, 23rd April

I worked in the office all morning. In the afternoon took the train to Yarmouth, to stay over Easter with the Kennets. Kathleen and Lord K. alone. He was more agreeable and attentive than I have ever known him, so that I liked him more than I had previously thought possible. He showed me his precious books — *The Book of Hours*, medieval, with brilliant hand-coloured miniatures — and read Tennyson and Traherne to us in a toneless, melancholy and low voice. Throughout this visit I felt distinctly unwell, with intolerable toothache. Desperately kind Kathleen tried to find a dentist for me, without avail. Is this general unwellness and tiredness (I went to bed at 9.30 and had breakfast in bed every day) due to the sudden onslaught of vigorous eastern air after the quiet, insalubrious air of London? A hurricane was blowing every day. One afternoon Kathleen and I punted on the lake. On Sunday we motored to tea at Somerleyton, a hideous red brick edifice of 1860. Hideous indeed, but fascinating and more than just a Jacobean pastiche. Well-kept garden, and well-ordered estate. Somerleyton now a naval hospital, but the Somerleytons living in a part of it. Lord Somerleyton rugged, and at first surly, but in conducting me through the Maze, warmed. He suffers from that typical English public schoolboy

[1] Dorothy Wellesley, later Duchess of Wellington and poet, died 1956.

affliction—shyness. She kindly gave me Veganin to alleviate my toothache. On Sunday night Peter Scott broadcast the postscript to the 9 o'clock news, to which we listened reverently. It was good—how splendid of him to be able to do it!—and Kathleen of course delighted and proud.

Monday, 26th April

I left Fritton for Blickling. On the way lunched with Oliver Messel in Norwich. Oliver as a Captain in khaki seems a contradiction of nature. He took me to the Assembly Rooms. He has made his men repair ravages and paint the walls of the rooms an appropriate Messelish pink. The 1750 interior decoration of panelled swags and plaster ceilings is very elegant. The proportions of the rooms are finer than those of the Bath Assembly Rooms. It is splendid what Oliver has done.

At Blickling after tea I walked through the park, map in hand, past the folly tower to Itteringham, which is at the far end of the estate. I fought my way against, or was driven by, a tearing, blinding, deafening hurricane. I hardly knew where I was going until I found myself deposited beside the lake at Wolterton, in full view of the imposing, red brick house. The park is flat and meagre. Lady Walpole lives with a brigade of Guards in the house. On my return through the park I came upon a wretched rabbit in a snare, and could not kill it. I walked past feeling ashamed, sad and physically sick.

Miss James the housekeeper told me over a cup of tea that at Blenheim up to 1939 precedence in the servants' hall was rigidly observed. The visiting valets and maids were, as I already knew, called after their masters and mistresses, *viz*. Mr. Marlborough and Mrs. Bibesco; and, which I did not know, the valet of the eldest son of the house always sat on the housekeeper's right, taking precedence even over the valet of the most distinguished guest, whether Archbishop, Prime Minister or Prince of Wales.

Tuesday, 27th April

Birkbeck and two architects from the Ministry of Works and I examined the condition of the house. After tea in the officers' mess Birkbeck and I looked at the recently burnt-out part of Hercules Plantation. We found another fire burning and put it out by stamping, beating. I was sadly deficient in this respect, alas, Birkbeck doing most
188

of the work effectively. The exertion gave me sciatica. When the fire was put out I came upon a scorched wooden board on the ground, raised it and lo! it was a trap-door over a Home Guard bomb dump, from which smoke was pouring. I looked down into the pit bravely, but refused to descend to see what the smoke issued from. Stayed this night with the Birkbecks, nice, cosy, easy people.

Wednesday, 28th April

In an ambling country train from Aylsham to Dereham [in Norfolk] I did not read, and sat looking out of the window. First, I counted the telegraph posts. When I got to ninety-nine I thought this was a silly waste of time. I looked at the wild flowers on the embankments. The physical effort of pinning the eye on an object from the moving carriage, and swivelling the body round soon made me giddy. I desisted. Instead I looked at the faded photograph under the luggage rack of children paddling on Yarmouth sands. The vision palled. My thoughts turned to love. It seemed to me incredible that any human being could not fall in love with woman and man, and, furthermore be in love with both simultaneously. It was just not true that one could not be in love with more than one person at a time. To go further, there was absolutely no reason why one could not be in love with a horse or a dog. If one were—and I never have been—should one be ashamed? In other words, was I wicked to allow such throughts and questionings to pass through my mind? The Church would say Yes. Then the Church ought to revise its precepts. All I do know is that 'in love' is damned and devilish, can only bring unhappiness and must be eradicated root and branch. Therefore one is left with unadultcrated jolly old lust exclusively. And a good thing it is too. If only, however, one had complete mastery of one's emotions! At this moment there was a jolt, the train which had stopped, started, gathered speed, and flashed past the noticeboard with Dereham written in large letters. I had failed to get out. Oh Lord! No doubt the Church would say this was a judgment for harbouring impure thoughts.

At the next station I descended, telephoned to the previous station to apologize for not having got out, and for a taxi. I motored miles, and at great expense, instead of motoring a short distance for nothing. Arrived at Elsing Hall late. It js a 1470 house built in square knapped flints; and has square gables typical of these parts with heraldic finials and twisted chimney-stacks. It has been unfortunately restored in the 1850s. Nearly all the mullion windows have been re-paned with plate glass. A moat completely surrounds the house. There is an open roofed hall, and an intact 1470 chapel. Mrs. Thackeray and her sister Miss Clarendon Hyde are the owners, and the last of their line since the reign of Egbert. The line was Browne, their mother being the Browne heiress. The Brownes held the place for two hundred years, inheriting from the Hastings, through the de Warennes, the first of whom married a daughter of William the Conqueror. At any rate their neighbour Lord Hastings, having lately celebrated on a grand scale the Astleys' ownership of Melton Constable in direct descent of eight hundred years, was very put out when the Browne representa-tives, not to be outdone, followed suit by celebrating their inheritance of humble Elsing in direct descent of one thousand years.

The present owners are impoverished. They have one indoor servant only. The house is incredibly shabby, dirty and primitive. The porch room ceiling fell when Norwich was bombed and the débris has been left on the tables and chairs. I noticed an early Georgian dolls' house, complete with contemporary furniture, and suggested to the old ladies that they should cherish it. They were amazed by the suggestion. The walled garden is an absolute wilderness. It is pathetic how within three years country people, who are unable to travel, become blind to the squalor to which they have been reduced. In spite of the terrible *délabrement* among which they live, these ladies with their long Plan-tagenet pedigree, their courtesy and ease of manner, were enchanting.

On my return to London I dined with Geoffrey Houghton-Brown to meet Colin Agnew. He bought three-quarters of Mrs. Greville's pictures for Polesden. He said she was a true friend, but a terrible enemy (like others in her world I can think of).

Thursday, 29th April

Lunched with Lady Harris, who is very amusing, and very deaf. She speaks in a honeyed voice, slowly and distinctly, with raised eye-brows, and makes outrageous remarks with no emphasis. Osbert [Lancaster] was bright gold like a guinea with jaundice, but feeling well, which annoyed Eddy who was present and bright green, and feeling ill us usual. Osbert turned to his mother-in-law and shouted in her ear, 'My pee was paler this morning.' In the evening I went with Johnny Churchill to Auberon Herbert's coming-of-age party. I drank rum and ate mincepies with the Herbert girls.

Friday, 30th April

Eardley and I motored to Betchworth [Surrey] to see Broome Park. The house is not important, being a muddle of Georgian periods over-Victorianized. The grey drawing-room alone is unspoilt. It has a 1750 rococo ceiling and walls with plaster swags in panels, retaining the original paint. But the gardens are like Stourhead in miniature and were laid out about the same date. There are three lakes, a sun temple, and a Gothic hermitage, both *circa* 1750 and exceedingly good. The lakes are bordered with primulas.

Saturday, 1st May

I went from Westwood where I stayed last night to Kingston House, Bradford-on-Avon, was shown round by the agent, and talked with young Mr. Moulton who with his brother and sister owns the place. It is a textbook example of the Jacobean style, yet with a somewhat tight, fussy Victorian air about it. Ted told me it was refaced from top to bottom in 1850 or thereabouts. A full-scale replica of it was exhibited at the Paris Exhibition of 1900 as an example at that date of the ideal English country house. Inside it is rather over-restored, although there are some fine panelled rooms and several interesting contemporary fireplaces on a monstrous scale. Undoubtedly it is an important house, and with its lantern windows and terrace balustrading of intricate carved stone, recalls Montacute.

Sunday, 2nd May

I left Westwood early and got to Swindon at 10.30 where to my surprise I found Stuart at the station before I expected him. On stepping out of the carriage, I saw a tall, smiling figure wearing a long gas cape on the platform. We took a taxi bound for Marlborough and were put out two miles this side of that town because we had reached the ten-mile radius limit from Swindon allowed the taxi driver. We walked the rest of the distance and lunched in Marlborough. Stuart is still distressed about the X.B. incident and worried about what Chips might yet do to him. He is over-sensitive and hates making enemies. Having a very charitable and sunny disposition he is hurt and surprised when he meets evil in others. After lunching at a Polly's Pantry we walked two miles down the Bath road to visit Miss Ethel Sands[1]

[1] An intellectual, Europeanized American artist.

and Miss Hudson who are living in a small, late Georgian rectory at Fyfield. Miss Sands opened the door. She looks like the typical American spinster one meets in a seedy *pensione* in Florence. She has a round smiling face and a gash of prominent teeth. She is rather like an ugly horse, yet her mother was a famous beauty, as indeed we witnessed from the drawings of her by Sargent. Miss Hudson is older and resembles old Lady FitzAlan. We did not like her so much. Stuart said they belonged to the '*haute Lesbie*', and theirs was a romance of years. They looked to him like two old men wearing wigs. Stuart began by talking to Miss Sands, so I had Miss Hudson. My attention was distracted from her by what the other two were saying. Miss Hudson is a Catholic but passionately anti-clerical and anti-Vatican. She attributes blame to the Church in Spain, Ireland, Poland and in fact everywhere; notwithstanding she is most devout. Ethel Sands showed us her modern pictures, including Sargents and Sickerts of herself and Nan Hudson. They gave us toasted buns and chocolate cakes for tea. After tea I talked to Ethel Sands, and Stuart to Miss Hudson, to whom he paid not the slightest attention, while politely answering Yes and No, and listening to our conversation about Proust and Lady Bessborough. In talking to Miss Sands you realize how very astute she is behind her simple manner and nervous giggle.

Wednesday, 5th May

Lunched at Sibyl Colefax's canteen with Nancy [Mitford] and Bridget [Parsons]. Nancy brought me Edith Sitwell's *Poet's Notebook*. Bridget rather catty about her nearest and dearest. Nancy whispered that she believed Peter Derwent had proposed to Bridget and had been rejected. Instead of being flattered Bridget seems to be affronted by each proposal of marriage she receives. Strange.

James, who was to stay with me after M.A.B.'s party, never arrived or telephoned; so by 1 a.m. I presumed he was not coming and went to bed. At 3.15 I was awakened by a violent pealing of bells. I was angry and disagreeable. Jamesey pretended to be aggrieved, which made me angrier. He said his behaviour was turning the other cheek. I said it was cheek all right.

Thursday, 6th May

At 5 o'clock I was given gas and had a molar tooth extracted. I was
192

quite frightened beforehand. I did not like the preliminaries, although the anaesthetist was kind and gentle. The gas did not smell disagreeable, and within a minute I was off. There was no escape, yet I sought it. I gasped for fresh air and had to take deep breaths; and they involved more gas. The battle was fruitless. I imagine drowning is like this: a terrible stifling, but soon over. I woke up abruptly with a tug. I suppose the tug was the tooth coming out. Time becomes quite mad in the circumstances. I thought, 'Now I have to face my tooth coming out,' and was worried. It had already come out. I looked at my watch. It was only ten minutes past five. Ten minutes only, which had seemed an age of unconsciousness. The gap in my mouth bled but I did not feel too unwell. I asked the dentist what he did to bring me round. He said he merely took away the mask and within 1½ minutes I was round. I did not realize that all this time of the operation I was inhaling the gas. My jaw may ache, they say, for ten days. Stuart says he loves gas. It is a vice with him and he welcomes any opportunity to have it. The experience makes one understand how close life is to death, and indeed wonder which is the more real, consciousness or unconsciousness.

Friday, 7th May

Accompanied Johnnie and Mary Churchill to Congreve's *Love for Love* with John Gielgud and Yvonne Arnaud; superbly done and the scenery by Rex Whistler. Johnnie is not the least grown up, and lives in a delightful fantasy nonsense world. He talks *eggy-peggy*[1] as we used to do when we were at the Priest's together, aged eighteen.

Sunday, 9th May

In a bitter cold, piercing wind I walked round the Manor garden at Wickhamford. The lawns are now unmown and the grass is a foot high. The beds are overgrown. Yet the garden is surprisingly beautiful still. Midi thinks more beautiful than when it was kept up. Before catching my train I went to Benediction in Evesham. I was unaccountably moved by the procession of the children, all so clean and *endimanchés*, little girls in white veils, little boys with Mary blue sashes, all singing lustily without a trace of self-consciousness. Would I like to be the father of the little dears? The answer is an emphatic No.

[1] A child's language which consists of putting *egg* after the first letter of every syllable. Invented to confuse and annoy grown-ups.

To Mark Watson's[1] new flat in Park Lane looking down upon the green bosom of the park trees. He has an orange tree in a tub, bearing fruit and blossom. The strong, exotic smell made me long for Spain or Portugal. Old Tancred Borenius rushed up to me, saying breathlessly, 'You are the one person I wanted to see about an article I am writing for the Burlington on historic houses.' Raby of the Ministry of Works had told him he must consult me on several points. He did not put a single point to me; but talked volubly of Mrs. Greville's shortcomings, I am heartily tired of that deceased lady.

Tuesday, 11th May

Had several drinks of very neat whisky with Jamesey in his dolls' house flat. Then the objective of the visit, M.A.B. arrived. She is dark, thin, with most beautiful legs; and has a dead white, slightly horsey face. She was dressed in black, very smart; had exotic scent, plenty of gold bangles and bracelets, and a suspicion of a blue bow somewhere at the back of her hair. She moved delicately as though she might dope, with the dope fiend's caution. She drank a lot, and seemed to admire James a lot. She was very entertaining in a dead-pan way which was disarming. Talked of Welbeck, Wilton and other habitual haunts, her relations, friends, enemies, anything that came into her head, without forethought. She was good company, and very sophisticated. I liked her up to a point.

Thursday, 13th May

Philip Farrer lunched with me at Brooks's. He is a mystery man. I cannot make out what the purpose of his life is. He must be verging on sixty and is handsome in a military way. He was an intimate friend of and admired above all men, George Lloyd, whose political opinions he shared to the full. I first met him in my Lloyd days when he was Lord Salisbury's secretary. He admitted today that in the Spanish Civil War he went to Spain as a spy. He reveres the Duke of Alba, and cordially dislikes Lord Cherwell,[2] the 'Prof'.

[1] Hon. Mark Watson, 4th son of 1st Lord Manton. R.A.F.V.R. 1940–5.
[2] Professor F. A. Lindemann, 1st and last Lord Cherwell (1886–1957). Physical scientist. Personal Assistant to the Prime Minister.

I went to a party at Sibyl Colefax's. Harold and Desmond [Shawe-Taylor][1] were elated by the African victory. I sat for a long time on a sofa with old Princesse Edmond de Polignac. She had ensconced herself for the evening in one place, spread and immobile, with a hat on, rather like a large Buddha. There is something godlike about her, and she is very Faubourg Saint-Germain. I wanted but did not like to talk to her about Proust. Her sentences are interspersed with French expressions. She seemed not particularly interested in her surroundings. She kept asking me in an indifferent manner who so-and-so was who had come up to talk to her; and when I replied that I had absolutely no idea, chortled as though taking me into her confidence. But this illusion was spoilt somewhat by her asking me my name (and not registering when I gave it, for it conveyed nothing to her) on the plea that if she wrote to the Chavchavadzes she would want to say she had met me. Then she said she never wrote to the Chavchavadzes.

Friday, 14th May

Lunched today with Captain Berington of Little Malvern Court, a pathetic little dark man who has recently inherited the property. For centuries it has been in his family and the Blessed Sacrament has been in the house since the Reformation without a break.

Saturday, 15th May

While lunching in Rick's café next door Ethel Walker sat herself down at my table. For months I have watched her pass my windows in a lost, painful stagger, with her fat old dog on a chain. She is an ancient woman with a face striated like the valleys of the moon, a face balanced on an overweighted sack. Her voice is like the thunder of waters from a subterranean cavern. She told me she had just completed her master-piece of two small children, very naughty, bad sitters. Miss Walker grumbled at the food and ate the lot.

I took the train to Windsor to have tea with Mrs. Betty [Montgomery]. I enjoyed the visit. She lent me several books, including *Au Bal avec Marcel Proust* by Marthe Bibesco. Mrs. Montgomery never met Proust. But he sent her his photograph which she showed me. It is of a sleek young waiter wearing a gardenia. Mrs. Betty is irritated that Proust has 'come into fashion'. Even this fact 'can't make me drop

[1] Desmond Shawe-Taylor, musical critic.

him'. We 'put him on the block' for quite twenty minutes, and we pinned beside him Lord Alfred Douglas, who as a young man, Mrs. Betty said, was no Adonis but spotty and without colour. She once met Oscar Wilde who afterwards said of her to Lady Oxford, 'She is so deliciously morbid.' She claims that she is a 'Catholic atheist', and that Jamesey and I are the only other members of this sect. She said to me without forethought, 'Just hand me my spectacles, dear James II,' and when I left, 'Tell Jamesey he is still James I.'

Monday, 17th May

I lunched with Sibyl alone at her canteen in Belgrave Square. On this sort of occasion she is simple and totally unpretentious. She never tries to be the great lady. She told me how poor she had been all her life. It had not mattered because, apart from entertaining her friends, all her recreations and tastes had been inexpensive ones, like bicycling in her early days, and reading. She said that I must go and see Logan Pearsall Smith who wished to meet me; and that with Mrs. Betty I was rapidly becoming James I. I said that if I told Jamesey this he would pay her a flying visit, and I would be James II again in a flash. I went to Jamesey at 6 o'clock and nobly pressed him to go to Windsor. Clarissa and Harold were present. Harold said the description he gives in his new book[1] of the meeting with James Joyce in Paris was the occasion when I accompanied him.

Tuesday, 18th May

As Dame Una's guest I heard Father D'Arcy address the Wiseman Society on Portugal and Spain where he has just been. Before the lecture I had a long talk with Rose Macaulay, back from Portugal collecting material for her book on Anglo-Portuguese relations. James and I agreed afterwards that she must be an unhappy woman. She has that dried-up look of the unenjoyed. Father D'Arcy told me that Georges Cattaui has become a priest in Switzerland.

After dinner I went, at Jamesey's request, to M.A.B.'s flat. Although it was a hot night, the curtains were drawn, and the two were crouching before a red anthracite fire. M.A.B., tiny, and huddled up, much the worse for whiskies, mumbling in her attractive, but incoherent manner, and hiccoughing. She intersperses every sentence with

[1] *The Desire to please.*

'darling' and 'sweetheart'. Her language is stagey and twentyish. Speaking of some family she said, 'They're nuts like us', and to Jamesey, 'I can't read a book with woodcuts in it. Woodcuts are such a bore. Wouf!' James, with whom I walked to Sloane Square, told me he was encouraging her to write her experiences. 'Tales of an old world mistress,' was her reply to this suggestion. She said she had been the Prince of Wales's mistress. His hair, she said, was the most attractive part of him. She also had an affair with Lord Dudley[1] at the same time. Once she was flown in the Prince's aeroplane to stay with Lord Dudley on the Riviera. She was given a bedroom sandwiched between Lord Dudley's and the Prince's. Both kept wandering into hers all night so that there was a great mix-up. 'Finally the woman with molars came along.' When Jamesey confided in her that some of his friends were homosexual she replied, 'Darling, now I'm going to say something that will make you cross. I never felt that way when I was young.' When he told her that his dislike of Sibyl was inexplicable, she said, 'It's chemistry, my dear.'

Wednesday, 19th May

A very hot day at Cliveden. The site over the river is, as John Evelyn observed in the seventeenth century, superb. The house too is well worthy of the Trust. It illustrates the very end of the Palladian tradition. Barry conceived it with a real regard for architectural principles. It is heavy and majestical outside. The interior, altered by the architect J. L. Pearson in the nineties, has very little distinction. The Astors were away and I went inside. The famous Orkney tapestries have been taken down. The pictures, including the Reynoldses are hanging, for the greater part of the house is still in use by the family. The splendid gardens are unkempt.

Anne Rosse dined with me. Having seen her home I walked to the Dorchester to get a taxi. After waiting an age I saw Lady Crewe and Lady Victor Paget get into one, so I asked if I might accompany them, and take the taxi on. They said yes, but the cab driver was furious because I had not asked him. We mollified him. In the taxi we talked of happiness, and Lady Victor said she had not had fifty-two days' happiness in her life. Lady Crewe said she knew at the time when she was happy. Lady Victor said to her, 'That is because you have been loved.' Lady Crewe retorted partly under her breath, for she did not

[1] 3rd Earl of Dudley (1894–1969).

want me to hear, 'It's not true. I've *not* been loved.' Her tone was one of indignant rebuttal.

Thursday, 20th May

I left the house at 7.30 and took the tube to Hendon station where Forsyth picked me up. We motored to Six Mile Bottom station where we met Professor Trevelyan who had come by train from Cambridge. We motored him to Blickling. I felt tired and needlessly depressed. Forsyth is a good old man but so respectable, so conventional and so dull. Goodness is by no means enough. G. M. Trevelyan, that distinguished historian and Master of Trinity, is dry as a stick and totally lacking gaiety and humour. He is very uncouth in his dress and person, and has long, untrimmed hair down the back of his neck. I was sitting behind him and as we approached Blickling he took out his false teeth and cleaned them with his handkerchief. I remember watching old Lord Dysart do this in the lavatory at Brooks's. He was very blind and was scrubbing his set with one of the hairbrushes.

Trevelyan enjoyed the day and adjudicated upon the colour with which to paint the cottages on the estate to, I believe, everyone's satisfaction. Miss James was delighted to see me and, when we left, Willey the gardener handed me some flowers. 'You seem very popular here,' the professor barked. I think he said it approvingly, but he is dour.

Saturday, 22nd May

In the morning I saw Lady Berwick who talked about the future of Attingham and asked me to stay. Then I passed Q. in St. James's Street. She was accompanied by a friend. With the touch of her hand all my misgivings evaporated and I was happy.

I had tea with Y. who is hoping for another child having averted a miscarriage. She was lying on a sofa after injections. I stayed with her till after 7. She told me how before she was married she had to have an abortion. She went early one morning to a squalid villa in the suburbs of London dressed in her drabbest clothes. She had the operation on an old deal kitchen table, and was sure the instruments were not properly sterilized. She was determined not to give her name for fear of blackmail. She paid £75 in banknotes and walked away, bleeding profusely and feeling wretchedly ill and absolutely unfit for any effort.

There were no taxis in that part of London and she had to take a tram and then a bus. Her loneliness and misery were worse than her physical suffering. Women's tribulations could not be borne by most men.

I dined with Marie Belloc Lowndes in her charming small house in Barton Street. Just ourselves. She gave me an orange cocktail, iced, from a jug, and quaffed her glass like a medicine. She was wearing a flowing, flowered dress over her enormous wide frame down to her ankles. Her dinner was the best I have had since the war began—gulls' eggs (two each), fried salmon with rich sauce, poussin with red wine, a pudding, coffee, African brandy. How does she manage it? She talks volubly with a French intonation, rolls her 'r's, is excellent company, extremely knowledgeable on most subjects and very gossipy. There is no writer on the Continent whom she does not seem to know. She is certain that the Prince Consort was a Jew. She said Magdalen FitzAlan-Howard was shrewd and her stupidity assumed, the better to sweeten relations with her mother; that Lady FitzAlan was a clever, though difficult mother. This is a sad thing to have heard.

Mrs. Belloc Lowndes has insatiable curiosity about people. She began dinner with, 'I am told there is a most charming, handsome and clever American over here, a Mr. Sergeant. I am sure you must know him. Do tell me all about him.' Oh Lord, I thought, the same old subject. 'To begin with,' I said, 'he is called Mr. Preston. He happens to be a sergeant in the American forces. So his friends refer to him as *The* Sergeant. It is true he is everything you say.' 'Oh, I would so much like to meet him. Will you introduce him to me.' 'Of course,' I said. 'That is easily arranged. He would simply love to know you. You will like each other immensely.' At that moment the telephone rang. To my intense surprise Chips Channon (how does he know the engagements of his acquaintances?) was on the line to tell me that Stuart's young brother, a G.I. was in London at a loose end, looking for Stuart. Where was Stuart? I said I thought he was staying the night in the country. What was to be done with the brother? He was now at Chips's house. Chips could not possibly give him a bed for the night. Not in that enormous house in Belgrave Square? I thought that strange. So I said I would willingly put him up. I would call for him at 10.30. 'No, no,' said my hostess, 'send him r'round here at once. What is he like?' 'What is he like?' I asked Chips. 'Fascinating. The living spit of Stuart,' Chips said.

Marie Belloc Lowndes was full of excitement. She is always eager to make new friends, to be kind to the young and to show goodwill

199

towards our American allies. In ten minutes time the doorbell rang. I opened the door. Without saying a word a short, sallow, oleaginous youth, wearing large square spectacles, stood on the mat, shaking my hand like a pump handle. He was surprisingly uncouth, answered 'yah' to our enquiries whether he had got the right number of the street door, and whistled when he was not grunting. My hostess's face fell a foot, and she threw me a beseeching glance which clearly meant, 'Surely there must be some mistake.'

Sunday, 23rd May

I took the young yahoo—who turned out to be a gentle, diffident, rather pathetic yahoo—to the station, and spent the rest of the morning reading Gerard Manley Hopkins. I lunched at the Ritz with Diana Worthington and Sir Timothy Eden. Diana and I walked all the way to Cheyne Walk, she flitting like a will-o'-the-wisp beside me, and laughing. She is either down in the dumps or pie in the sky. Today she was in the sky. Quite a jolly tea party assembled, some by invitation. Some were just strays. Besides Diana there were Ivy Compton-Burnett, Margaret Jourdain, Dame Una, Roger Senhouse, Mark Watson. Roger, thinking to flatter Miss C.-B., endorsed Raymond's tribute to her in *Horizon*, wherein he says she is the nearest approach to Henry James among novelists of our generation. Miss C.-B. said sharply that she could not read Henry James. Roger said afterwards that no one talked more tattling nonsense, but he succeeded in getting her down to bedrock. I didn't hear how he succeeded, for she hates talking about literature and wards off any reference to her own novels, parrying it by referring to Margaret Jourdain's books. At times when she goes on and on like a clockwork toy about nothing in particular I do wonder if she could be a bore. But her own starchiness is so like that of most of her characters that I am always fascinated listening to and watching her.

Mark Watson brought a drawing of himself by Augustus John. He had fetched it this afternoon. Though a good likeness it was not a good drawing. He said John had been drawing him for over a year and was not yet satisfied with the result.

Wednesday, 26th May

I spent all yesterday in the train from Euston to Windermere. This morning Bruce Thompson motored me through heavy rain across the moors, to Kendal and Appleby. The intermittent sun and great plumes of black cloud made a sublime scene sweeping and chasing each other across the moors. Yet, cockney that I have become, I find the mountains lonely and depressing. We stopped on the side of the road before Appleby at a wood where Mary Thompson [Bruce's wife] and some land girls were measuring trees for the Ministry of Supply. All the trees are being taken from this part of the world. We lit a bonfire and ate luncheon. We moved on to Temple Sowerby, the McGrigor-Philips's house. Mrs. McGrigor-Philips is a tall, ungainly, exceedingly coy woman, and a low-brow writer under the pen-name of Dorothy Una Ratcliffe. He a grubby, red-visaged, hirsute old teddy bear. They laid down a lot of nonsensical conditions in making over the house, intending to provide the minimum endowment although she is a millionairess, having inherited an enormous fortune from her uncle, Lord Brotherton. Bruce Thompson was infinitely patient and polite, and only occasionally betrayed what he was thinking by pursing his lips. The house, which I once saw in 1938, is of tawny orange sandstone, a beautiful texture, yet in photographs looks dull. Although the core of the house is Jacobean, what one now sees is eighteenth century: Venetian windows and a staircase ceiling, *circa* 1740 of rich Italian plasterwork. Temple Sowerby is at present occupied by the Railway Wagon Repairers and their families. The Philipses retain one small wing and a caravan for a bedroom. The walk above the flowing burn at the rear of the house is very romantic. From the front are distant views across green pastures of the mountains in the Lake District. It is a lovely setting.

Friday, 28th May

Dined at Dame Una's house with her and James. She said Mrs. Belloc Lowndes was by far the most mischievous woman she knew. She, the Dame, was devoted to her but since her rule in life was never to be indiscreet, a restriction was thereby put upon their confidences. James and I, after draining the whisky in his flat, began walking to Chelsea. After nearly an hour we realized we had been walking in the opposite direction and were quite lost. This was brought about by earnest talk of our various perplexities. I had warned James that he ought to be more reticent with his women friends who were incorrigible gossips; that by confiding everything in them he risked betraying his men friends, and there was a freemasonry among men friends which he ought not to abuse. He said I was Machiavellian. I said tartly that I hoped my character might improve with age. He doubted it. He assured me he could not possibly have a friend without being honest to him or her. I could not agree with this policy and said surely it was better to withhold the truth, and not to spill it before everyone who took one's fancy. One must have loyalties, and they necessitated reticence. But no. He immediately disclosed how M.A.B. had passionately kissed him in a taxi yesterday, but he was warding off the affair by pointing out the ludicrousness of it in view of the disparity of their ages. Coward! Her passion was truly terrifying. Jamesey is so engaging that maddened as I am by him at times, I forgive him all his trespasses.

Saturday, 29th May

Poor Professor Richardson created an adverse impression at the Georgian Group meeting—I learned later that he was feeling ill and taking M & B—by implying that the Group's primary objective was to encourage the design of modern architecture on Georgian lines. John Summerson strongly dissented, and so did I. I scribbled a note, which I passed to the professor in the chair, begging that the committee should be given the opportunity to discuss this contentious question of policy before a pronouncement was made at the annual meeting. Dame Una complained that he was irresponsible.

I went as Dame Una's guest to Harold's lecture on Byron at the Alliance Hall. In looking for the Hall I met Harold and accompanied him to a pub for a drink. The pub had nothing but beer, so we left. I was immensely impressed by Harold's fluency and attractive fireside manner of delivery. As a rule I cannot listen to lectures. My attention wanders. But listening to this one was just like reading a book of Harold's. I was not distracted once, and was riveted by the case he made for Byron's poetry. When he read stanzas from *Childe Harold* I was almost moved to tears. Desmond MacCarthy in the chair was mealy and mouthy. Emerald Cunard was there. When the lecture was over Harold ran after me down the street, asking me to find a cab for her. I put her and Dame Una into one. As it left Emerald called out, 'Tomorrow at 8.30. What *do* you think? Wavell is coming.'

Off I went to Herstmonceux to stay with Paul Latham. This was an act of charity because I have never known him well. To my surprise Eddy had told me he would be glad to see me, whereas he declined to see most of his closer friends. I got muddled with my trains and was $1\frac{1}{2}$

hours late. Paul was sitting at the window of the bothy where he lives. He left prison in January having been there 1½ years. He was very thin but healthier and handsomer than I remember him. He still has a frightening look of craziness in the crimped gold hair, anthropoidal head, albino eyebrows and cold blue eyes. He talked incessantly of himself and prison. He is touched that everyone on the estate is nice to him. Indeed the lady taxi driver went out of her way to extol his popularity because of his open-handedness and generosity to all his tenants. Paul has become incredibly sentimental, yet his conversation is more depraved than anyone's I have ever heard. He kept reading aloud poems from the *Spirit of Man* and extracts from the letters written in a garbled fashion from the friends he has left behind in prison. He is obsessed by sex and already haunts the most dangerous places, he told me. He also enjoys repeating disobliging things said about one. How much is true, and how much invented it is hard to say. He is a sadistic man.

He had the grace to acknowledge Eddy's great kindness in helping him. He won't move from the estate or see any close friends from his old world, except Eddy; yet he is irritated by Eddy's devotion. We walked round the grounds and the outside of this fairy-tale castle. The Hearts of Oak Benefit Society have done great damage to the contents, which Paul foolishly left in the building. By the end of the visit I was worn out by listening to so much about Paul by Paul, although some of his experiences were interesting. I am terribly sorry for him but would pity him far more if he were less wayward and less egocentric.

I got back only just in time to dine with Emerald Cunard. Even so I was still wearing my brown country suit. Jamesey took me to task about it next morning. Dinner was at 8.30 yet the blinds were all drawn, the windows firmly shut, and the room was stifling. I was in a muck sweat. There were Field-Marshal Wavell, Sir D'Arcy Osborne, our Minister at the Vatican, a nineteen-year-old Paget girl, Bridget Parsons, Chips Channon, Jamesey and myself. I sat next to Jamesey and Chips, who is bear-leading Wavell, and indeed treating him as a considerate owner would a performing bear before an audience, sitting in the background with a proud expression on his face and flipping the whip gently from time to time. Wavell is stocky, with a smiling rugged face and a wall eye. He is slow, distracted and shy. Emerald's prattle, sometimes very funny nonsense, flowed like a river. I think this embarrassed him at times, as it did the other guests. It was too much of an exhibition contrived by her and Chips in advance. D'Arcy Osborne did not speak once throughout the evening, and looked cross. Lord Queensberry came in at 10.30 and recited Shakespeare sonnets in a torrent of venom. Wavell was coaxed by Chips into reciting Browning and Ernest Dowson, which he did in a muffled, inarticulate voice, incredibly badly. Much too much applause from Emerald and his prompter. It seems extraordinary that a man in his position should be staying with a flibbertigibbet like Chips. I found him cosy and cultivated. The other guests were disappointed with him. He is certainly an old man who seems finished. I had not realized this before I met him, and was inclined to wonder why the Government was not making more use of so eminent a soldier.

Tuesday, 1st June

Feeling singularly unwell today I went to Holt Court near Lacock [Wiltshire] for the night. This house belongs to the Goffs. The main front is a rich, provincial piece of stage scenery in Bath stone. Major Goff is the great-grandson of William IV and Mrs. Jordan. Lady Cecilie told me he had been brought up by his grandmother, Lady Augustus Fitz-Clarence, a great favourite of Queen Adelaide. This accounts for the Goffs having so many portraits and so much furniture from Windsor Castle, in spite of Lord Augustus being the youngest of the King's sons.

Wednesday, 2nd June

On my return I was very ill, and crawled to see my doctor, Pierre Lansel. A recurrence of the old trouble and change of drugs, leading to shingles, retention of urine, catheters, germs in the bladder, high temperatures, agonies, despair, and bed for over four weeks. The worst affliction of the lot was a nurse who positively revelled in philistinism. One day she gleefully smashed the lid of my Worcester sugar bowl. When I remonstrated she got cross, and said it was ugly. 'Ugly?' I screamed at her. 'Ugly! Even if it were, it is old and precious. But it's beautiful. Surely you can see that.' 'I can't,' was the reply. And she added with a shrug, 'Oh, well!' 'It isn't well,' I said. 'It's bad, very bad.'

Next morning she remarked through pursed lips, 'Any-wan mate sue-pose [this is how she spoke] yew pre-furred old ob-jects tew persons,' as though this were the most heinous charge she could bring against my morals. 'Anyone would be supposing perfectly correctly,' I snapped back. She was so flabbergasted by the barefaced admission that she left almost immediately. I got better.

Thursday, 1st July

I went to Wickhamford and was restored to health by Mama, who was angelic to me. Only Mrs. Haines helps her in the mornings. Otherwise Mama does everything – housework, cooking, washing up, to which, because she is hopelessly disorganized, there is absolutely no end. She spends as much time in either complaining or congratulating herself as in actually working. And what she does, she does indifferently. I am reminded of Dr. Johnson's remark to Boswell. 'Sir, a woman's preaching is like a dog's walking on his hind legs. It is not done well; but you are surprised to find it done at all.'

Tuesday, 6th July

Papa drove me to Hidcote to tea with Laurie Johnston who took us round his famous garden. No reference was made by him to the National Trust. The garden is not only beautiful but remarkable in that it is full of surprises. You are constantly led from one scene to another, into long vistas and little enclosures, which seem infinite. Moreover the total area of this garden does not cover many acres. Surely the twentieth century has produced some remarkable gardens on a small scale. This one is also full of rare plants brought from the most outlandish places in India and Asia. When my father and Laurie Johnston were absorbed in talk I was tremendously impressed by their profound knowledge of a subject which is closed to me. It was like hearing two people speaking fluently a language of which I am totally ignorant.

Wednesday, 7th July

From Evesham to Shrewsbury by train, changing at Hartlebury on to the Severn Valley line. What a beautiful valley it is, with gently sloping wooded banks and miniature scenery, even on a grey day with occasional rain. I stayed two nights with the Berwicks at Attingham [Park]. They inhabit a fraction of the east wing. The W.A.A.F.s occupy the rest of the house. The Ministry of Works has at my instigation protected the principal rooms by boarding up fireplaces and even dadoes. The uniform Pompeian red of the walls is I presume contem-

205

porary, that is to say late eighteenth-century. In my bathroom the walls were papered with Captain Cook scenery just like the upstairs bedroom at Laxton [Hall, Northants]. The first night we had champagne to celebrate our and Attingham's survival up to date. After dinner I read through the 1827 Sale Catalogue of contents, many of which the 3rd Lord Berwick, then Minister to the Court at Naples, bought in from his elder brother the 2nd Lord.

Thursday, 8th July

Lady Berwick and I went to tea at Cronkhill, one of the houses on the estate. It was built by John Nash about 1810 and is interesting on that account. It was designed in the romantic style of an Italian villa, with one round tower, a colonnade and overhanging eaves, and is the precursor of many similar Victorian villas. Lady Berwick behaves towards her neighbours with a studied affability, a queenly graciousness which must be a trifle intimidating to those upon whom it is dispensed.

After tea I walked with Lord Berwick in the deer park, having been enjoined by her to talk seriously about Attingham's future, and press him for a decision on various points. I did not make much progress in this respect. On the other hand he expanded in a strangely endearing way. When alone he loosens up and is quite communicative. All the seeming silliness and nervousness vanish. He talked to me earnestly, in his shy, diffident manner it is true, of the ghosts that have been seen at Attingham by the W.A.A.F.s. Lady Berwick would not, I know (and he also knew full well), have tolerated this nonsense, if she had been present. He kept stopping and anxiously looking over his shoulder lest she might be overhearing him, but he did not stand stock still and revolve, which he does in the drawing-room whenever she starts talking business. He told me that Lady Sybil Grant, his neighbour at Pitchford, constantly writes to him on the forbidden subject, passing on advice as to his health which she has been given by her spiritual guides. She no longer dares telephone this information for fear, so Lord Berwick asserted, of the spirits overhearing and taking offence, but I suspect it is more likely for fear of Lady Berwick overhearing and strongly disapproving. He is not the least boring about his psychical beliefs but is perplexed by the strange habits of ghosts. He asked me, did I think it possible that one could have been locked in the housemaid's cupboard? And why should another want to disguise itself as a vacuum cleaner? Really he is a delicious man.

On my way back to Evesham I stopped at Bewdley. I walked to Wynterdine just outside the town and was given luncheon by Kathleen Sturt, with whom I was in love at the age of six. She was then a sprightly spinster in her thirties. She gave me a little box with an onyx lid which I treasured as my most precious possession for several weeks. I then lost it and never gave it or the donor another thought. She is now a jovial, good-natured, grey-haired, tub with a veined face. She could not have been kinder or nicer. After luncheon I was taken upstairs to see Mrs. Sturt, aged ninety-three, in bed. A toothless, clean-looking, smiling old dame, she was an intimate friend of my grandmother in Ribbesford days. Kathleen walked me round the Wynterdine fields and through the shrubberies to the red cliffs with the grottoes above the Severn. I remember these romantic Germanic walks so well. She and her mother are anxious to do what Mrs. Lloyd has done at Areley Kings down the river, namely give covenants.[1] It would be splendid because the Wynterdine land goes right into the heart of Bewdley.

Tuesday, 13th July

I went by myself to Ibsen's *Master Builder*, with Donald Wolfit in the chief rôle. This play is a little too melodramatic and of course damned depressing. I returned to Cheyne Walk thoroughly out of sorts and unhappy.

Thursday, 15th July

Went to see the Picasso of *La Hollandaise*, naked and wearing a Dutch cap, painted about 1903. It was exhibited at the gallery of a character called Bilbo, a German Jew of enormous girth and paunch. He was in corduroy trousers and short shirt sleeves, and was smoking a pipe through meshes of black, wiry beard. Bilbo is asking £6,000 for the Picasso and the Tate is appealing for funds for its purchase. Stuart dined with me at Brooks's very exhausted after a night out yesterday. He left early in order to get to bed at Alice Harding's, where he is staying, before she should come in. Oh the subterfuges and tergiversations of this sublunary life!

---

[1] These unfortunately came to nothing.

My luncheon with Eddy at Brooks's was not altogether a success for we had little to say. This is often the case after absences. The more one sees of intimate friends the more one has to say to them, and the less one sees them the less one has to say. I went to Dr. Simpson this morning and endured every sort of indignity, too squalid to relate. He considers me well which is nice of him; and is recommending to Lansel yet another drug.

I went to the Ritz at 3 to take Emerald Cunard to Keats's House, Hampstead. Everything went wrong. I should have had a cab waiting for her, and not one could be found. It took me half an hour running up and down Piccadilly in the sun. Diane Abdy who was to have accompanied us, failed to turn up, so we were alone. This put Emerald out. When we got there I thought the little white villa looked fresh and pretty through the nightingale mulberry tree branches. Emerald thought it undistinguished. I suppose she imagined that because Keats was a great poet he ought to have lived in a great baroque palace. She thought the inside lacking in character and associative interest. It is in a sense, for there is hardly a stick of furniture or even an internal feature which Keats knew. Emerald was very silly in her remarks about Shelley's immorality in front of the custodian. On the return journey she had an altercation with the nice cab driver about the route. And she was in the wrong. We reached the Dorchester at 4 and although she had bidden me to tea, it was too early, so I took my leave. Her last words were to remind me of the Rutland ball tonight.

Now all today I have been in a maddening, filthy mood. When I told Q. that I could not face tagging on to Emerald's party after dinner and going to the Rutland ball with them, she asked me to 'dine with us', meaning herself and spouse. This infuriated me. I said I would think about it. When she said on the telephone this morning, 'I am not pressing you. I don't want to hear one word from you now, but if you want to come, there is a place for you, and dinner is at 8,' I still said nothing. She rang me up again at 7.15. I said I would not go. And I didn't. Miserably I dined by myself, and gratuitously chucked the only privately given ball since the war began. In fact I deliberately cut off my nose to spite my face, and derived only the tiniest bit of satisfaction thereby.

208

Sunday, 18th July

Today I felt happy because I was alone, and working like a black at Polesden Lacey. I had a sandwich luncheon in the garden, did not lie in the sun, and checked various inventories. Having collected the pictures for K. Clark's exhibition I motored to Clandon to dine with Giana Blakiston. Noel was away. She is so easy that I can chatter with her unreservedly, a thing I can do with very few. The Blakistons seem perfectly content to live in this vast, dust-filmed house, in a makeshift manner. They are not the least deterred by lack of domestic comforts and what are termed the minimal amenities. Giana walked with me down to the lake and back before dinner. I was depressed by the soullessness of this house and the hideousness of the surrounding grounds, for there is no garden. The Onslows can have no taste whatever. Trees have been allowed to grow right up to the front door so that the main elevation (which faces the wrong way and gets no sun) cannot be seen from a distance. A screen of revolting conifers has been planted as a windbreak against the only elevation that could otherwise have been seen.

Monday, 19th July

In the afternoon I took the Polesden pictures to the National Gallery. Kenneth Clark met me in the vestibule to discuss their arrangement. Before I left he showed me a Rothschild collection of French pictures which he is housing. I urged him to exhibit them, but he said he couldn't.

On returning in the bus I was put into a paroxysm of rage by reading in the evening paper that Rome had been bombed. I was to have seen Harold tonight. I did not dare go for I should have been hysterical and abused the Government. Instead I drank three Pimm's No. 1 with Jamesey at the Carlton Hotel. Together we vented our rage over the bombing. He said Churchill had sanctioned it, with 'I don't care a damn what buildings they destroy.' Then I dined with Johnny Dashwood at the Travellers' and drank a whisky and soda, a bottle of Burgundy and a glass of port—and came home sober.

Tuesday, 20th July

John Pope-Hennessy, the Dame and Anthony Blunt are, according to

209

Jamesey, working up a protest against the Rome bombing. And Lord FitzAlan has put down a question in the House of Lords.

In the afternoon I went to see Lord Astor in St. James's Square. Matheson said he wished to see me. But when I was ushered into his room he asked very politely, 'What can I do for you?' So at random I said I hoped he would give me some particulars of Cliveden history for the guide-book I was preparing. I couldn't very well have asked him what he wanted of me. As it happened he seemed pleased and began to rattle off facts and dates, but I had nothing to write them down in. He did not strike me as delicate and tubercular. He is tall and florid, and what the eighteenth century called a black man. Indeed there is a touch of the coal black mammie in his appearance. Lady Astor swept in and began rather offensively with, 'Whatever you people do, I cannot have the public near the place,' and before I had time to expostulate, corrected herself to the extent of adding, 'At any rate their hours will have to be clearly defined.' There is an insolence and silliness about her. But how young and handsome and well dressed she is.

Wednesday, 21st July

I looked at a portrait of Violet Hunt in red crayon that Geoffrey Mander wants the Trust to buy for the Wightwick collection. A pretty thing but I consider the Pre-Raphaelite association too remote. Then to the Steer exhibition at the National Gallery. K. Clark said he had been severely criticized for holding so large an exhibition of a *pasticheur*. It certainly is remarkable how Steer never seemed to develop a recognizable style of his own. But how good he can be. His landscape oils can be like Gainsborough, Constable, even Turner. His early water-colours of Boulogne beaches are as charming as Tissots.

Thursday, 22nd July

I went to Slough in the afternoon to see Sir Wyndham Dunstan.[1] He is a nice old man who is Secretary of the Sudeley Committee.[2] He said no one holding a paid official post could be a member, not even K. Clark. He took me in his car round the confines of Burnham Beeches, for he wants the Trust to induce the L.C.C. to expostulate with the

[1] Sir Wyndham Dunstan (1861–1949), chemist and director of the Imperial Institute, F.R.S. 1893.
[2] Advisory body on museums.

210

army for the mess of it they are making. A difficult thing for us to do, I tried to explain. He showed me his collection of water-colours. He told me he used frequently to stay with Rossetti at the Queen's House, in Cheyne Walk, acting as a kind of secretary to him for a time. His grandfather received the Rossetti family when they first came to England.

On my return to London I called on Harold in King's Bench Walk. A young man was painting his portrait, which was atrocious, and made him look like Gerald Berners. Harold said people were gossiping about Stuart's relations with Alice Harding, and asked, 'What are his conjugal chances there?' Then Victor Cunard[1] walked in. We talked of the Rome bombing, and I was pleased that Victor condemned it strongly. To my surprise Harold deplored it, admitting that so long as it was not repeated he would be satisfied with this one gesture. Anthony Eden had however given him no assurance that it would not happen a second time. Victor said Eden always makes a mess of our relations with Italy. This bombing will have stiffened Italian resistance and will make the Italians hate us for a long time. Harold rushed off to dine with Sibyl and meet Wavell.

I dined with the Princess de Polignac. Clarissa, John Pope-Hennessy and David Horner were present. The last was invited because apparently the princess thought he was E. M. Forster. He is a slightly epicene, elderly young man who lives with Osbert Sitwell. He has a soothing, low voice, but his manner is embarrassingly affected. After dinner we talked of the Rome bombing. John, who is cautious and sensible, advised that we must collate our facts before launching into protests. Then we talked about English novelists. This led to Proust. Our hostess evidently disliked him. She had known him since he was a handsome young man with melting brown eyes, until his death. It was impossible to endure his company for long at a time. He was touchy and took umbrage at every supposed slight. In fact he detected slights where they never were intended—in a tone of voice or a look. As a result he would fire off thirty letters to you in rapid succession. In France before the first war none but the Saint-Germain set recognized his gifts. When the princess found that there was already a Proust Society in England, only *Chez Swann* having been published, she was amazed. Proust was either in the depths or the heights, when he would toss money to servants as though it were chicken food. His life was

[1] Victor Cunard (1898–1960), *The Times* correspondent, diplomat and connoisseur.

studded with unfulfilled romantic attachments. He never ceased to correspond with the princess, although their periods of intimacy were fitful. She supposes he enjoyed quarrelling with his friends. She dispelled the rumour I had heard that she was the origin of Madame Verdurin by telling us that when she entertained Proust lovers in her King's Road house before 1914 they called themselves for fun by the names of characters in *Chez Swann*. One was Cottard, another Brichot, and she was Madame Verdurin.

Friday, 23rd July

Nancy and I lunched at Sibyl's canteen. Nancy said, 'If Henry Yorke had called his novel *Court* instead of *Caught* and written about dukes instead of firemen we would all have acclaimed it.' A woman has written asking her which are the better dinner parties, Emerald's or Sibyl's. Nancy has replied, Emerald's without a doubt, because they are smaller, the food is better, and they are free. Stuart, who had joined us by this time, was shocked by the pleasantry, and began to explain that poor Sibyl could not afford to pay for her parties. 'Yes, I know that, Sarge,' Nancy interrupted him with her mischievous laugh. Stuart, who loves Nancy, criticized her hardness of heart, which only made her laugh more.

This evening I walked home – about three miles – across Hyde Park and down Exhibition Road, listening to the voices of Czech, Polish and French soldiers. I love the present cosmopolitanism of London. Summer nights in London are soft and velvety even if the previous day has been grey. At nights the colourlessness disappears, and the savage emptiness of the black-out is filled with pools of violet, blue and yellow light. I am at last feeling well again and have a zest for living. Harold said yesterday from the bath tub, 'How nice to hear Jim laughing again.' I asked Stuart if I had been gloomy lately. He said, 'Yes, even before you were ill you had become very depressing.' 'Or depressed?' I asked. 'You had become very glum. Certainly you *never* laughed,' he said, as though I must have been aware of the fact.

Saturday, 24th July

I had tea with Logan Pearsall Smith at 5 and left at 7. I enjoyed my visit. The old man coughs and spits incessantly. He is vastly entertaining. I certainly should have visited him before. He has a splendid capacity for mockery and fun. And of course he has literary refinement; perhaps no other sort. Stuart seems to be his present preoccupation. He admitted that at first he thought Stuart too good to be true, endeavoured to catch him out, and failed. Having checked him up through mutual friends he pronounced him to be aristocratic (according to American social rules), rich and popular. He queried whether his success had been achieved through art or nature. At all events it was success. And at all events Logan has succumbed, for Stuart has flattered him by not merely congratulating him on his books (which is easy), but by quoting long passages from them (which is clever). He read me his poem to be published in next month's *Horizon*. But he slushed so that I could not hear a word of it. He knew Henry James intimately, but could only guess at James's sex proclivities. He certainly did not dare discuss them with him. He thought Shane Leslie's disclosures in *Horizon* horrifying. James's letters were written to a young soldier in World War I and were unmistakable love letters. Shane was given 300 of them by the man's widow early this year. Cyril Connolly had evidently not cottoned on to the indiscretion of publishing them. Logan P. S. said there was much that was lovable in Cyril. He instanced the dinner Cyril gave for Ethel Sand's seventieth birthday. We discussed whether one should tell one's friends their faults. He was once told by Ethel Sands that he nearly drove his friends to distraction by criticizing their friends who were not his. At the same time she made him promise he would point out to her any fault she had. He now longs to tell her that she spoils his stories by her own interpretations of them. But he dares not do so because she is bound to take offence. Jean Hamilton was a 'dove'. No one spoke ill of her, but she lacked discrimination, and was taken in by frauds. Some frauds he mentioned were: Sir Ronald Storrs, Professor Joad and Humbert Wolfe. He was pleased when I said I was merely on the fringe of the Mayfair Jezebel world. He feared it might be Stuart's undoing for he too lacked discrimination.

We talked about many things, rapidly, disjointedly, leaping from one topic to another. He recounted one 'awway'[1] after another. Finally he expressed the hope that Stuart was not a 'marrano', i.e. a Jew in Spain who adopts Christian methods, and later relapses into what he was originally.

[1] One of many words and phrases invented by Logan Pearsall Smith and in current use by his circle. He described 'awways' as stories that in one's dotage one tells more than once.

When I told James and Stuart all Pearsall Smith had said, they laughed. They knew all the topics, all the 'awways' by heart. I was disconcerted. In fact Jamesey says he is a poor, senile old man, who repeats himself over and over again.

Sunday, 25th July

Motored to Polesden in a hired car to fetch the two remaining pictures, the Ter Borch *Introduction* and the lovely Jacob Ruysdael. I went early and spent the day there till 8.30, working very hard, going through every cupboard, turning out and throwing away rubbish. A wonderful day. Smith told me that Hilda, the housemaid, who professes to be so fond of me, cursed like a trooper when I insisted on coming down last Sunday; that she bites and bullies everyone, abuses her trust and has her friends to stay all the week. He advised me to watch her carefully. I never expect gratitude, loyalty, affection, etc. from servants. They don't know the meaning of these qualities. From the uneducated one must expect self-interest, meanness, mendacity and guile. Of such is the kingdom of the proletariat.

Monday, 26th July

Today was the Trust's annual meeting; so dull and turgid that I cannot dwell upon it. Stuart dined with me in Soho, and was tired and hot. We are now in the depths of summer. It is like being at the bottom of a well, enclosed on all sides with only a glimmer of relief somewhere miles above one's head. Nevertheless I was in a jolly, carefree mood. I angered Stuart again by repeating, with absolutely no malice prepense, James's complaint made half in jest, of Stuart's approbation of the bombing of Cologne. He denied it, took the charge seriously and was deeply worried. Oh why do people take anything seriously these days? He is too sensitive; and says that my tongue wounds, and I repeat inaccurate gossip; that I am alarmingly bitter about people; and that at times he is genuinely worried about my—sanity! I admitted my insanity, and said he should remember that fundamentally I disliked the human race; that if I were happily married to some retiring woman I would never, never go near society. This was the truth. He was shocked. So I thought I would shock him further. I said I not only hated people, I sought to do them down on every possible occasion by whatever devious means came to hand. He was sorry to learn this. I

214

said I knew my character was a great disillusion to him, who had once thought it fairly commendable. He said this was true. I said I was really a fiend incarnate. I said it, not in anger, not in bitterness, but softly, dulcetly. He was perplexed, and saddened.

Tuesday, 27th July

I dined with Dame Una. Only Rose Macaulay there. She was dry and twitchy. Stuart cannot bear her. She said some silly things about the Germans having been highly civilized in the past when they formed the core of the Holy Roman Empire. Dame Una and I both disputed this fallacy. She talked of her book on the English in Portugal. She has got as far as John of Gaunt.

Dame Una complained that a miller, called Rank, has bought up all the cinemas so that every one shows the same film at the same time. A good plan, I think, for it makes fewer to see. Dame Una can be a little sour.

Wednesday, 28th July

At 10 a.m. to the Travellers' to talk to Major Algar Howard about the chance of the National Trust acquiring the College of Heralds – this will come to nothing – and of his own house, Thornbury Castle [Gloucestershire].

I asked Mrs. Belloc Lowndes and John Pope-Hennessy to lunch at Wilton's to meet Joan Moore. Joan looked as pretty and cool as a porcelain shepherdess on this hot day. The luncheon was, I think, a success. Mrs. Belloc Lowndes fell for Joan, who was sweet and attentive to her. Marie B. L. had two glasses of port wine. Talk was of Violet Hunt and Marie Corelli. Marie B. L. is pessimistic about the outcome of the Italian affair. She says there will be revolution, the Germans will occupy the peninsula and we will make of it a battleground.

I had tea with Stuart – he is no longer to be called the Sergeant and gets fretful when addressed by that term of endearment – at the Travellers'. I can't understand why, since he has so low an opinion of my character, he bothers to see so much of me. Talk was too much of personalities. His social activities make me acid. They arouse the worst instincts in me. While we walked afterwards across the Green Park in the sun he said he had asked Lady Islington why her husband had chosen that particular title. I laughed, and remarked in a bantering way that only an American would ask that question. He was hurt. I should not say such things. I was constantly saying such things, whereas he refrained from saying similar things to me that would be intensely wounding. Now this retort distressed me as much as my remark had distressed him. Neither of us has half a grain of humour between us.

Thursday, 29th July

I took a morning train to Bath. The platform at Paddington was crowded when the train sidled in. Before it stopped I leapt into a first-class compartment and took a corner seat. We took precisely two hours to reach Bath. I was met at the station by Mr. [Robert] Henshaw, an estate agent, and taken to Forts where Major Strutt gave us luncheon. Strutt is a very decent fellow, in the Home Guard. He made me feel too sophisticated, and shallow. We motored to his house, St. Catherine's Court, five miles from Bath. I was sent to see this house in 1936 but Major Strutt had forgotten the occasion. I cannot be a very memorable person. The situation on the western slope of a narrow valley is picturesque. The peace was disturbed by fleets of noisy aeroplanes, a reminder to the poor Strutts that their younger son in the R.A.F. was killed three weeks ago. It was a sunny, boiling afternoon and the dry earth crackled with heat and the valley crinkled with haze. The gabled house with old church in the garden is typically English. The best things about it are the half-octagonal porch with balustraded sides, and the terraced garden, also balustraded. There is a good stone chimneypiece in the hall and a Jacobean screen. Otherwise not much. Strutt's father added to the house not too badly. It is strange how little owners know about their own houses. This family have owned St. Catherine's Court for over 100 years.

Friday, 30th July

One of the hottest days in England that I have lived through. I took Anne Rosse, back from Ireland, to lunch at the Turkish restaurant. We both strove not to break into a sweat. Anne kept stopping in the street, standing immobile and saying, 'Keep quite still. Don't laugh. Don't speak. I may be all right.'

At 5.30 I went to tea with Emerald. She was charming and solicitous about my health. I sat next to Lady Lamington, who is beautiful,

216

stately, stiff and a little prim. She said how much it horrified her to see girls drink. I was far too hot to argue, so hypocritically I agreed by a slight inclination of the head. The Princesse de Polignac came in and said to Emerald, 'This charming young man came to dinner with me, and wrote me a beautiful letter. Then, if you please, he sent me *Tom Jones*—but in a rare edition of two volumes of priceless value.' This frightened me stiff, for I asked myself how much that villainous Nancy would charge me for this book. Anne [Rosse] came in. We talked of 'the situation'. I was much impressed by Anne's intelligence and use of words. She was totally unaffected. Emerald said she was sure great movements were on foot for the Cabinet met last night at 11. She said that the Russians were proposing peace terms to Germany.

I joined Jamesey at Rule's restaurant. We drank quantities of Pimm's and enjoyed ourselves hugely. There is no one with whom I can be happier. We can be as one. I say 'can be'. We were tonight. Unlike Stuart he is far from being seduced by society. He told me Lady Lamington was charming and very intelligent, although she was a little precious. As we talked and laughed in an animated way two very tough-looking men at a neighbouring table were staring at us critically and discussing us. I then realized how we must have struck them, both youngish and out of uniform, both enjoying ourselves, which in their eyes we had no right to do. In truth they had no right to judge us, for James is in the army, and I was.

We walked out of the restaurant into the heat, and down the embankment. We crossed London Bridge to the south side of the river, and ambled along Cardinal's Wharf. Jamesey was extolling in the most candid and engaging manner his age—he is twenty-six—his good looks and his successes, saying he did not believe he could ever die. He said, 'Our relationship is such a one that can never have existed in the past. I don't think anything marks the progress of civilization so vividly as improved personal relations.' I said, yes, I felt certain that before our time personal relations could never have been so intimate, though of course we could never tell what, for instance, Byron and Hobhouse talked about at nights in a tent during their travels in the Morea. I said that more people ought to keep diaries, but the trouble was that the most unscrupulous diarists were too scrupulous when it came to putting personal truths on paper. James said that Cecil [Beaton's] diary would be the chronicle of our age, that we would only live through it. I said Eddy Sackville West kept one. James said, 'We could not be hoisted to posterity on two spikier spikes.' We looked at bombed churches and sat in churchyards, and drank shandies in City pubs.

Saturday, 31st July

At Boodle's I ran into Professor Richardson and together we did a tour of the club. He took a print of Brooks's façade to the window opposite Brooks's, and demonstrated how he hoped after the war to take down the roof balustrade, which should never have been added. He would put back the first floor balcony and the projecting piers on which it rested, as indicated in the print.

I had tea at Windsor with Mrs. Betty who looked older and frailer. She was very stiff with rheumatism. I learned several of her expressions: 'carp' and 'carping' for scandalizing about friends; 'carpet atmosphere' to describe bores, a mild bore being an 'Aubusson', a real bore a 'Kidderminster', and a cracking bore a 'velvet pile'. She said that Stuart, whom she does not like and refers to as 'that Mr. Stuart', forced his way into 'dear Etty's' room when she was at her worst, lying on her front with her face on the pillow, and read poetry to her. Her comment was, 'Have you ever heard of such a cruel thing? It is like the worst Polish atrocity.' I feared that this might mean Lady Desborough had taken against Stuart, but was glad when Mrs. Betty admitted that she still liked him. Mrs. Betty is very penetrating for her years. She alarms me at times by ranking me with her as someone of impeccable taste, culture and judgment.

I walked from her house leisurely down the Long Walk, to Cumberland Lodge. How regal and serene the view is from the Copper Horse. At the end of the drive I sat on a bench to cool and watch the thunder clouds gather. I was surprised to see a stocky figure with stick in hand and coatless in braces, approach me rapidly. It was Lord FitzAlan, very sprightly and fit, come to meet me. Boydie and Magdalen and Alathea were there. I enjoyed this short visit. I pretend to see in this household a Compton-Burnett family. Lord F. is 88, Boydie 58, Magdalen 60, and Alathea 20. It is a pity Alathea is not older and there are no great-grandchildren. Lord F. gave me iced cider to drink. I had a long talk with him about the Italian news. He knows nothing whatever of [Marshal] Badoglio, and could not even pronounce his name. I asked about the new Archbishop [of Westminster]. He said the procedure was for the Westminster canons to elect three names. These were submitted to the hierarchy. The bishops usually reduced them to one name, or else added a fourth of their own choice to be submitted to the Vatican. It was customary for the Pope to consult ecclesiastical and lay opinion in England before deciding upon the candidate. It was apparent that Lord FitzAlan had been consulted. I stayed to supper and talked to Magdalen after Lord FitzAlan went to bed. I left by cab for Egham at 9.20. Lord F. was quite of my mind about the bombing of Rome.

Sunday, 1st August

In spite of the thunder and rain it has been an insufferably stuffy day. I lunched with Clarissa [Churchill] at her flat in the Rossmore Court block. I found her extremely white and pale, wearing a brocade dress down to her ankles, and lying on a Récamier sofa under a long window, the blind partially down but not so as to obscure the views over Regent's Park to Highgate and St. Paul's. She gave me an excellent luncheon. Yet it was not a very vital meal, for Clarissa is languid. She is certainly clever, and might be exasperating. I am bewildered by her present Elizabeth Barrett invalidism. I had invited her to lunch with me but she preferred not to stir in the heat.

Lady Lamington had asked me to dine with her tonight to meet Mrs. [Gilbert] Russell. Was rather annoyed when at 7.30 she rang up to say we were to go to a party instead. So I met her at Mrs. Russell's flat and we walked down South Audley Street to Lady Queensberry's[1] studio at 9. We had no dinner; only a few dry sausages and bits of cheese on sticks. There was dancing and much noise. I knew no one and we left at 10.30. I excused myself from returning to the flat on the plea of fire-watching, which was untrue. Instead I telephoned Stuart and arranged to call on him. I walked across Hyde Park, and there he was on the pavement waiting. We walked down a pitch dark passage, I clinging to his coat tails. He lay on his bed. I sat on a chair. He talked about his week-end at Faringdon in a sort of ecstasy which blinded me with its fatuity. I felt overwhelmed with depression and buttoning up my coat, rose to go. Is this all life has to offer, I asked myself? In a moment the onslaught of truth dissolved. I was back in the happier world of total unreality, as it were under the influence of the opiate of our being. I sat down again on the end of the bed. I stayed. It was cool and wonderful, but unreal. It took me nearly an hour to walk home after midnight.

[1] Cathleen Mann (1896–1959), official war artist. Daughter of Harrington Mann, portrait painter.

219

The 'Brown girls' and Janet Leeper came to tea with me. Ivy Compton-Burnett ate half a pot of raspberry jam, and I was shocked to see her surreptitiously wipe her sticky fingers upon the cover of my sofa. Both she and Margaret ate like horses. This time Miss C.-B. talked a great deal more than Margaret. Her description of the Poetry Reading and Lady Gerald Wellesley's antics was very funny. They are a wicked pair.

Wednesday, 4th August

I took an early train to Birmingham and was met by Lord Doverdale's agent. He gave me luncheon at the Grand Hotel and the low-down about his client's situation. I have known this man for some time. He will take my arm and gaze retriever-like into my eyes. I remember once before thinking this odd, but now I believe it is his idea of being pally. It goes with his constant interrogation, 'Pardon me?' – which I don't want to do – and his ingratiating approval of whatever I say as 'topping'.

We drove to Westwood Park, outside Droitwich. Lord Doverdale met us at the door. For an instant I thought he was an ostler out of livery, for he wore a dark blue double-breasted jacket, striped tie with a thin gold chain to keep it in place, stained lavender flannel trousers, and mole-coloured suede shoes. A suspicion of straw in the hair too. He was also slightly deformed about the shoulders. Delicate undoubtedly, and from what he said about his lungs, consumptive I guess.

He took us round the boundaries of the whole estate of some 5,000 acres. It covers unexciting Worcestershire landscape. The park is not of outstanding beauty, but spread and spacious with a sixty-acre lake. The house however, planned like a star-fish, is eccentric, interesting and splendid. Years ago Desmond Parsons and I trespassed and photographed it from the gatehouse, which with two out of several original garden houses remains. Sir Reginald Blomfield[1] restored the four towers to their present ogee shape to match the authentic caps of the gatehouse and garden houses. In nineteenth-century illustrations the dunce caps of the towers on the house looked more stately. The interior

[1] Sir Reginald Blomfield (1856–1942), architect of the new Regent Street. Author of *Renaissance Architecture in England*, etc.

is very fine indeed. The entrance hall has a mock Jacobean ceiling and beautiful Jacobean panelling brought from a house in Newent. The curious ball-topped finials of the great staircase are most unusual. The best rooms are the splendid saloon, white drawing-room and the Japanese room. The last has a flowered paper on a buff ground. The cornice and ceiling of the saloon are in stucco, dated 1660; and the Flemish tapestries were bought when the room was built. Doverdale has put a Rembrandt self-portrait in the rich oak overmantel. The carpet of the room is Axminster, *circa* 1740, and many of the Chippendale chairs have always been here. In fact the 1st Lord Doverdale, a paper manufacturer with the name of Partington, bought most of the contents of the Pakington family who previously owned the place. Uncharitable people say he bought several Pakington ancestors and dexterously altered the 'k' on the picture labels into 'rt'. The house is well furnished and in excellent condition. It is a weird house inside and one has difficulty in keeping one's bearings. Lord Doverdale, who speaks with that rather common Prince of Wales accent, is interested in motor-racing. He was very friendly and frank, easy and agreeable to discuss business with. I liked him.

Thursday, 5th August

The agent came back at 9.30 and we finished our discussions. Lord Doverdale intends to leave Westwood at the end of the war. Under his father's will the house and park, with an endowment of £1,500 p.a. comes to the National Trust on his death. He wants to hand over now with capital to yield this income. It should be a most satisfactory arrangement. I think this visit has been a success. Doverdale is very lavish with his drinks, and the establishment is un-warlike. All but the staterooms and principal bedrooms are in use, and there is a grand butler waiting.

Friday, 6th August

My birthday. I am thirty-five! The horror of it! Except for my incipient baldness, fortunately on the crown of my head and on account of my height not always noticeable, I do not think I have changed much. My figure is the same as it was fifteen years ago.

At 7 o'clock I went to Jamesey's flat. The gay little creature was splashing about in the bath. He gave me two stiff whiskies to keep up my spirits, which were actually quite high. He made me change out of my nice blue shirt and put on a white shirt of his and a blue tie with large, white round spots, which he said looked more festive. He admired the transformation, explaining that it was like seeing part of himself in me. He gave me as a birthday present a little water-colour sketch of the interior of a church by Pugin. Thus fortified and encouraged I set out with him for Boulestin, where at luncheon time I had ordered a table and food for eight guests. We drank again in the bar where Harold and Stuart joined us. Then Dig and Henry Yorke came. I had not seen Henry since the war. He was absolutely charming and rather reserved; Dig her usual sweet self. Harold gave me a book of Freya Stark's (and later a tooth-brush!). Then Joan Moore came but without Emerald, whom she had said she would bring. Emerald arrived at 8.40 just as we were about to begin dinner. Harold said in front of everybody, 'What worries me about this party is how Jim will afford to pay for it.'

I had Joan on my left and Emerald on my right. The dinner passed with perfect ease. Never was there less need for anxiety. Excellent food—fish in shells, partridge and plenty of Algerian wine; brandy afterwards. Joan was divine. I was so absorbed with her and James with Emerald that I hardly spoke to Emerald. As it happens I prefer listening to her than talking with her; just as I prefer watching a canary flit from perch to perch and scattering feathers and shrill cries, to trying to pick up its song. I enjoyed my party immensely. As we sat on, and the waiters longed for us to leave, Emerald arranged marriages for James, Stuart and myself.

When at last the party ended I walked away with Harold to stay the night at King's Bench Walk because I could not have got home so late. Harold began by saying, 'The worst of women is their selfishness. They must make slaves of men.' He extolled the advantages of homosexuality and relationships between men, who allowed individual independence. Then he praised Vita as an exceptional wife. He said that he and Vita had pledged to tell each other the moment one of them fell in love, but not to confess to casual affairs because that was rather squalid. Their marriage began badly because Vita immediately fell in love with a married woman—Violet Trefusis I presume. He said that in his whole life he had only been in love three times, and these times were before his marriage, with two subsequent ambassadors, and a 'bedint' young man of no consequence, called Eric Upton, whose only recommendation was extreme beauty. 'Oh, I may have once fallen a

222

fourth time, with R.' He told Vita about this fall, and she was wonderful. But then Vita truly *is* exceptional.

Saturday, 7th August

I bought a life of Harriet Martineau from Nancy in Heywood's shop, and there saw Stuart. He said he refused to discuss the war with me any further, my views were too silly.

I went to tea with Ivy Compton-Burnett and Margaret Jourdain. Anne Hill was there; also Dame Una and Rose Macaulay. Again I was the only man among blue-stockings. Rose Macaulay said the Portuguese were having bread riots. Ivy C.-B., I noticed, when she did condescend to speak, shouted everyone else down. The tea was a sit-down spread of breads of different hue, jam, potted meat, biscuits, shortbread and cake, delightful but curiously middle-class and such a contrast to Emerald Cunard's weak China and a thumb-nail of chocolate cake. Ivy, who now addresses me by my christian name, said it took Harriet Martineau[1] forty years to discover what it had taken her eighteen, namely that there was no God.

I joined Rick at 7.30 and we dined together at 97 [Cheyne Walk]. He said I was moving in a set to which I did not properly belong, that since I was far from gregarious by nature, I was behaving foolishly. I admitted that in a sense he was right, but protested that instead of acting foolishly I was acting out of curiosity, if by 'set' he was referring to those people who congregated round the Dorchester. Then we drank coffee with the Robin Darwins.[2] Robin refuted my opinion that Wilson Steer forfeited greatness because he worked in too many styles. He said that because he assimilated so many styles, he *was* great.

Sunday, 8th August

Today London was peaceful and happy. I sat on my window seat in the sun reading. Nancy telephoned and asked me to lunch with her alone in her little house in Blomfield Road. She was in high spirits and full of stories about Eddy's anxieties – 'Chalky water is so binding,' and so forth. She told me she had begun her autobiography but would not be able to publish it until her parents were dead, for it would wound them.

[1] Harriet Martineau (1802–76), miscellaneous writer.
[2] Sir Robin Darwin (1910–73) artist. Rector and Vice-Provost. Royal College of Art 1967–71.

She said the mistake the Redesdales had made was to refuse to educate a clutch of intelligent daughters. I walked home, and continued reading until the late evening. I packed my haversack for firewatching in the office. Stuart, having returned from the weekend, telephoned and asked me to call on him. So I walked to Lancaster Terrace. He had left the front door unlatched. I entered and saw the light through his open door at the end of the long passage. He was in blue pyjamas applying lotion to his hair about which he is very particular. He got into bed and read to me today's parable of the unjust steward which I had failed to understand at Mass this morning. His interpretation of the story did nothing to disabuse me of the belief that it is unfortunate and wicked doctrine. I walked away through Hyde Park to Buckingham Palace Gardens for night duty. It was so dark that I lost my way and ran into a barbed wire entanglement. I was challenged by a sentry, 'Who goes there?' I could not remember the proper reply, and answered after a pause rather feebly, 'Jim Lees-Milne.'

Monday, 9th August

The Astronomer Royal came to see me this morning to ask if the Trust could provide a country house for him. After 300 years the Observatory is leaving Greenwich because of the smoky atmosphere and the glare from the lights at night. I suggested Herstmonceux Castle but he did not seem taken with the idea.

Tuesday, 10th August

I lunched with Emerald Cunard at the Dorchester. It was a match-making party. I sat next to the girl I am to marry. She had a brown, greasy face with a down-covered, slip-away chin. I was not at all attracted. 'But she is very, very rich,' Emerald expostulated. On my other side was an amiable girl who laughed a great deal, and was plain as a pike staff. She is a contemporary of Anne, who tells me she once had great allure and for years was the mistress of Lord somebody or other. Other guests were the Greek Ambassador, Nancy, Louis Goulding and Alastair Forbes.[1] The last is a deb's delight of classic beauty, with fair, unblemished skin. Very young and a little portentous. He is diplomatic correspondent of the *Sunday Times*, ambitious for a parliamentary career, witty, mischievous, censorious and bright. Emerald began abusing the waiters, calling them Bolsheviks and Nazis,

[1] Freelance journalist.

and telling them they deserved to be killed in Sicily. I was deeply shocked. When the waiters left the room conversation began. The Greek Minister spoke of the 'rottenness' of the French. Nancy, who is Francophile, retorted that their government could have done no good by retiring to Africa in 1940. I told the story of George Lloyd flying to Bordeaux in a desperate attempt to persuade Weygand not to give in. The Greek Ambassador confirmed it. He had been Secretary-General at Geneva at the time and remembered the incident. Conversation turned to Spain and Franco. I shocked everyone by saying I had been pro-Franco during the Civil War. Nancy called me a fascist. Such rot, for one does not have to be a Fascist, Nazi or Falangist to fight the world's common enemy, Marxism.

Wednesday, 11th August

Bruce Thompson is in a great state because he left behind at Temple Sowerby [Manor] during our visit his file containing letters and copies of letters between him and me, criticizing Mrs. McGrigor-Philips. Some of mine were strongly worded and I remember saying she was an impossible woman to do business with. Mrs. McGrigor-Philips read all the correspondence and has written to the secretary and the chairman complaining about our misconduct. She said to Bruce on the telephone, 'I thought you were both gentlemen,' which much upset Bruce who is 100 per cent a gentleman to my 25 per cent. I told him he ought to have retorted, 'And I thought you were a lady.' For ladies do not read other people's letters.

Matheson and I lunched with the Eshers at Watlington to discuss West Wycombe Park negotiations. Both Esher and Matheson were ready to reject the offer altogether. I dare to think I saved the situation by suggesting that as a compromise we ask Johnny Dashwood to allow us to hold thirty acres of the far end of the park as endowment land for us to sell for building, if at some future date after the Dashwoods' time the Trust is obliged to raise funds for maintenance of the house and garden.

Got back just in time to join Janet Leeper's party at the Playhouse for *Blow your own Trumpet*, the second play by Peter Ustinov. Janet's nephew Michael Warre had a prominent part in it and acted well. The play was too ambitious and lacked movement and action; and not as good as the first, *House of Regrets*, but the characterization very brilliant.

Johnny Dashwood rang me up first thing and I lunched with him. He agreed to our proposal about the thirty acres. Today I have felt curiously unwell and tired.

Rick, who is on a week's leave, insisted on taking me to lunch at Claridge's with two of his Brigade friends from the Octu. They were both absolute boys just left Eton, aged eighteen and nineteen, in fact almost a generation younger than me, who could actually be their father. They were touchingly naive in trying to appear grown-up.

At 5.15 I went to 33 Portman Square to hear Jamesey deliver a paper on Monckton-Milnes[1] to the Poetry Society. The front row was packed with his friends. I sat between Clarissa and M.A.B. who in the daylight and at close quarters looked raddled and whose breath was distinctly unpleasant. I was nervous at first on James's account, but quite needlessly. He started off with self-confidence and throughout was in absolute control. Even so I refrained from looking at him for fear he might want to giggle. Our front row must have appeared comical to him, composed as it was almost exclusively of old women, such as Lady Crewe, Dame Una and Rose Macaulay. He read from his typed pages and quoted extracts of Lord Houghton's poems very beautifully indeed. The lecture was a great success, the only pity being the smallness of the audience.

Some of us went to James's flat where we drank gin. Cecil [Beaton] had the previous night been at a bomber command station from which the raiders over Germany and Italy set forth. In the control room he followed the full course of the raids. The planes were absent eight hours and all returned safely. Cecil heard the orders given to each crew before they flew off. In talking to him many of the men expressed sympathy with the 'poor I-ties' because their ack-ack defences were so very inadequate. Cecil said it was useless to appeal to their sentiment where historical monuments were concerned. Such things meant nothing to them at all. On the other hand their distaste for taking life unnecessarily was genuine. He said that unlike soldiers and sailors the airmen harboured no feelings of hatred or revenge against the Germans.

[1] In 1950 he published *Monckton Milnes, The Years of Promise*; and in 1952 *Monckton Milnes, The Flight of Youth*.

They were totally objective in their work. He said, 'You simply have to be tough in speaking with them,' referring, I suppose, to the orders and the manner in which their officers issued them. Dame Una said that Badoglio was doing excellently by gradually replacing key posts in Italy with non-fascists, but gradually in order to prevent economic collapse. She maintained that the present economic stability in Italy was entirely due to the fascist efficiency, and the Bank of England recognized this. In fact a banker told her that the Bank of England had full control of British-Italian relations and was even 'running' Sicily, whatever that may mean.

Lady Victor Paget, Jamesey and I drove to Argyll House where Lady Crewe gave us iced cocktails. We took her to dine at the Speranza restaurant. I cannot say that I find her very fascinating. She is devious without being clever, and vain. For her age she is remarkably well preserved. Stuart calls her a great lady, and admires the manner in which she, like Lady Desborough and other great ladies, walks up steps and enters a room or a cab in that confident, blind, unseeing way. Lady Victor is an eccentric. She sat hunched up, her face in her hands, saying how miserable she was and always had been. She told me she had had shingles, once across the forehead, and once round the middle, which was 'like nurturing a hedgehog'.

Tuesday, 17th August

It is half past six. I have been sitting for an hour on my window seat looking at the cheerful river, with the evening sunlight dancing upon the wavelets, and at the gay motor boats, painted black and yellow, dashing down the river and growling busily. There are water boys on them. There are old men with sticks and pipes just below my window and across the road. They are squatting on the embankment wall, smoking and gossiping. 'Are these young men,' I ask myself, 'and these old men wracked by hopeless love, a prey to their miserable natures, slaves to their emotions, and irredeemably wretched?' I think not. They may wish the war was over. They don't want to lose their lives or the lives of their sons. But this is negative wishing. On the other hand they are positively living, with a zest for being alive which they do not stop to question or understand. How sensible they are. Whereas I seldom live carelessly, with abandon. Most of the year I mope, moan, resent other people's happiness, lament my own unhappiness, and waste this precious living. And what is it all about now? Neither last night nor the night before has the voice spoken to me. In the office today I hardly dared leave the room in case the telephone should ring. Whenever it did my heart jumped. And when the voice at the other end was not the right voice I was in despair. I became edgy, bad-tempered. I could hardly bear it when my colleagues were using the line in case my voice was trying to get through to me. And what am I doing now? Waiting again for the telephone to ring. This is preposterous, infantile and reprehensible. I must snap out of it.

Audrey[1] came. I watched her tittuping along the pavement in the highest of high-heeled shoes, like some funny little bird. She looked pretty but her hair was brushed off her nuque into a bob on the crown of her head. She is too small and featureless for this to suit her. Now she really has troubles enough to daunt the stoutest soul, and yet she rides above them; and she never, never mopes or moans. We drank tea. She was enraptured with the view.

Wednesday, 18th August

I went to Dinton, the other side of Salisbury, for the day and met the *Country Life* photographer at Dinton station. We pushed his heavy plates, camera and paraphernalia in a handcart uphill to the village.

Thursday, 19th August

I went to the laboratory in the morning, and until luncheon time had blood tests taken every forty minutes. They bled me and gave me sugared water to drink in pintfuls. By the end I felt faint.

Friday, 20th August

This morning a man came here at 9.30 with a great bag. A clip was put on my nose, a mask over my face and for five minutes on end I breathed into the bag. I was then made to eat three eggs. Mrs. Beckwith my little charwoman did not know how to cook powdered eggs, neither did I, so to my distress I was obliged to take out three crock eggs. These she fried for she had never scrambled in her life.

This evening after dinner I went to Jamesey's flat. He had a bad attack of hiccoughs. We strolled into Kensington Gardens where he

[1] The diarist's sister, then Hon. Mrs. Matthew Arthur, now Mrs. Tony Stevens.

left me to walk home. James said that that ridiculous Lady Crewe thought I was in love with him. She told Bridget Paget it was obvious I suffered tortures when James left the room the other night, and I was longing to go after him. Lady Victor replied, 'He suffered tortures because he has shingles.' James also surprised me a little by repeating a conversation he had had this evening with his mother. He explained to her that the nettle rash on his behind was diagnosed by his doctor as the effect of nervous disorder. This was brought about by his being semi-in love with M.A.B. and Enid Paget and yet physically desiring boys. Dame Una expressed disapproval of his going to a psychoanalyst. 'What, darling,' said James, 'would you rather that I never learnt to get an erection with women?' 'No,' said Dame Una.

Saturday, 21st August

Caught a morning train to High Wycombe and walked up the drive at West Wycombe just as the Eshers arrived for luncheon with Johnny and Helen. Esher was in splendid form, teasing the Dashwoods about their progeny. After luncheon we drove to the far end of the park and inspected the temples, follies and cottages on the property to be transferred; also all that distant part of the park to be held alienably. Esher has a genius for persuading people to act sensibly against their deep-rooted inclinations by his jocular manner and sheer fun. I really believe we may acquire this beautiful house and park in the end. After tea I caught a train which was so slow and late that I missed my train from Waterloo to Woking. I did not reach Send Grove till nearly 9.

Spent the weekend at Loelia Westminster's. Only Emerald and a dull but affable young man called Sharman, staying. Send is an enchanting small Jane Austen house, symmetrical, stuccoed and washed pink. The front is covered by an enormous wisteria. It dates from the end of the eighteenth century. The prospect from the house covers a long expanse of grass, with curving boundary to the left, and to the right open views across a river bordered with pollarded willows in the direction of Clandon. Stuart calls this neighbourhood the New Dukeries, for in addition to Loelia Westminster, the Dukes of Sutherland, Northumberland and Alba live within a few miles.

My hostess has impeccable taste. She bought this house a year after the war when it was not too late to buy French wall papers. As you enter there is a charming little stairwell with a balustered staircase corkscrewing steeply upwards towards a domed ceiling. To the right and left are projecting bays forming a small dining-room and boudoir. Beyond the boudoir is a library with coffered ceiling. The bookcases in this room appear to be late eighteenth century. I arrived late and rather flummoxed. The duchess greeted me at the dining-room door, napkin in hand. I washed and joined the party straight away. A delicious dinner at a small round table. After dinner we talked in the library about Keats and Shelley. Emerald said Shelley had had a child by Claire Clairmont and that Mary Shelley had adopted it as her own. We then talked of eccentric people living in country houses. I told them of my experience with the Dymokes of Scrivelsby.

In 1938 the committee of the Society for the Protection of Ancient Buildings was very concerned about the fate of a cruck cottage in Lincolnshire called Teapot Hall. It was shaped like a tent and the two end walls were of half-timber construction. This unique, textbook house was falling into disrepair and all letters written by the Society to the owner, Mr. Dymoke[1] of Scrivelsby were unanswered. So Rick Stewart-Jones and I, who were on the committee, volunteered to call on the owner. We motored to Lincolnshire, and arrived at the lodge of Scrivelsby Court on the main road. The lodge-keeper was friendly but said that Mr. Dymoke (who was the King's hereditary Champion and Standard Bearer of England) was living in the Court but had not been seen for years. It was not even known whether Mrs. Dymoke[2] were still alive. He, the lodge-keeper, delivered parcels and food to the man who lived in the gatehouse, and he in turn put them into a basket which was let down from a first floor window of the big house. He said the man in the gatehouse over the moat would certainly not let us through. However we walked to the gatehouse. We were denied entry. Not to be outdone we walked away from the gatehouse round the moat, and clambered over a part of it that was dry. The garden up to the house was waist high in grass and weeds. All the ground floor windows of the melancholy house were either boarded up or sandbagged. The place seemed dead. We walked round the house. I happened to look up, and there at a window above us was an ashen face with a snow-white beard, completely expressionless, pressed against the glass pane. As we continued round the outside of the house the same face appeared at every window, gazing down upon us vacuously. Not a word was spoken; not a gesture of annoyance was

[1] F. S. Dymoke (1862–1946), 32nd of Scrivelsby, the Honourable the King's Champion and Standard Bearer for England.
[2] His second wife (m. 1907).

230

made. It was an eerie experience. We came away, and both of us have been haunted by that face ever since.

Emerald told us how when she was first married and lived in the English country, she went to call on the Mexboroughs. She was shown into the drawing-room, and waited. Presently Lord Mexborough[1] was wheeled into the room. He had a long white beard down to his knees and was wearing a top hat. As soon as he saw Emerald he let out a piercing scream, 'Take her away! Take her away!'

Sunday, 22nd August

Emerald did not appear till 1.35 for luncheon. In the afternoon we sat in the garden. The others depressed me by dwelling upon the bad state of affairs at present. It appears from what Sir Paul Dukes told Loelia last weekend, that our relations with Russia are strained, and she may make a separate peace. If she does, I at least shall not be astonished. My view also is that we have badly bungled the Italian situation, which at the time of Mussolini's downfall was favourable to us, by insisting upon unconditional surrender, and so forth. All we have done is to stiffen Italian resistance. Had we been conciliatory but firm, we would have had Italy out by now, and with us. Mr. Churchill is a disastrous man. I hate him more and more.

Tuesday, 24th August

The M.P. for Northampton, one Summers, came to talk about Thenford, the house he has rented for several years and contemplates buying. At 6 I joined Lord Spencer at Brooks's and he took me to Spencer House overlooking the Green Park. He brought torches because it is quite dark inside. All the windows have of course been blown out. The house suffered most severely from the bad raid in April 1941 when I watched the corner house, which also belonged to Lord Spencer, burn to the ground. Incendiary bombs have destroyed parts of the top floor, and blast has torn away the stucco from many ceilings. It is a wonderful house. Lord Spencer lived in it during the 1920s, then let it to a women's club till two years ago. He removed the best mahogany doors and marble chimneypieces to Althorp, where I saw them last year. The rooms facing the park on the ground and first floors are very fine, notably the rooms at the south-west corner, one over the other.

[1] Presumably 4th Earl of Mexborough (1810–99).

The lower room has spreading palm tree leaves from the capitals of the columns—a trick of Vardy the architect, Lord Spencer told me—and the upper room, now alas badly damaged, was painted by Athenian Stuart. The ceiling of this room is almost totally down. The staircase balusters are of tawdry beaten metal work, painted red and gold to resemble drapery and tassels. There are seventy bedrooms, some very small and poky.

Jamesey, with whom I dined, is so disgusted by the attitude of the press that he thinks this country deserves reverses.

Wednesday, 25th August

I went to Knole for luncheon. Just Lord Sackville and me. We ate in the large oak-panelled dining-room. He has a butler, a cook and one housemaid who has 250 bedrooms to keep clean. He was as courteous and charming as ever. We had venison liver from deer killed in the park. In the afternoon we and the agent toured the house very rapidly in order for me to get some idea of the parts which the Trust would lease back to him. Most large houses upon acquaintance look smaller than at first they appeared. Not so Knole. It is a veritable rabbit warren. It turned out today that in our recent discussions we had all three overlooked the north wing, which consists of fifteen bedrooms as well as reception rooms.

On my return to the office I felt a little squeamish about the stomach. Nevertheless I dined late with Cecil Beaton, and like a fool ate lobster and pigeon.

I parted from James at South Kensington station and proceeded to walk home. In the street I was seized with violent attacks of diarrhoea. I was in agony and thought I should never get home. Did so with difficulty and had a terrible night.

Thursday, 26th August

I attribute it to the Knole venison liver. I stayed in bed, reading, all day and ate nothing.

Friday, 27th August

Better again. Drs. Simpson and Lansel's diagnosis of the tests is that I lack sugar content, and do not retain sugar in the system, and am anaemic. Lansel injected me with a needle the size of a dagger, pumping some ghastly mixture into my behind.

After Malcolm Sargent's concert in the Churchill Club I dined with Emerald and Joan Moore. Diana Sandys mistook me for Garrett. We have not met for years. She is very pop-eyed and her figure has lost its shape. Malcolm Sargent told me that the other day old Mrs. Astley Cooper sent for her amorous butler, Fred. She asked him if he knew his Bible and the parable why you cannot serve two masters. Fred all this while was standing stiffly at attention, answering, 'Yes, m'm. Yes, m'm.' 'Then how on earth, Fred,' she went on, 'do you suppose you can serve three mistresses?' Although Malcolm Sargent's figure is still young, and he is brimful of vitality, his little monkey face is sallow.

Emerald grumbled a good deal about war-time conditions when I called for her this evening. She said that she was wretched at the Dorchester; she had no real friends left; was tired, and too old to cope with life. Yet she does and will cope until she drops. I thought she was going to faint in climbing the steep stairs in the Central Hall.

Sunday, 29th August

Having stayed last night with Miss O'Sullivan in her wing at Blickling I spent the morning going round the house with her. We decided to remove a number of good eighteenth-century bedroom pieces of furniture which [11th] Lord Lothian had lent to the R.A.F. Many of them had been badly spoilt. Miss O'Sullivan agrees that Blickling, though melancholy, has a very strong hold upon one. It is a sad, lonely, unloved house with a reproachful air. I dare say it will be burnt down before long.

Tuesday, 31st August

I got up at 7 and went to Polesden Lacey so as to be there when Druce's vans arrived. At last they are moving out the secondary furniture. I got back at 1 and went straight to the Ritz where I met Loelia Westminster. She was dressed in red, and limping from a sprained ankle. We went to the Dorchester in a taxi. She said that Lord Rothermere, with whom she had been staying, told her this morning that the troops had just invaded the mainland of Italy. Churchill would announce the fact in his broadcast tonight. As it happened Churchill made no men-

233

tion of it, and his broadcast was empty verbiage and kowtowing to the Russians.

At Emerald's luncheon were Billy McCann, Mrs. Reggie Fellowes and Duff Cooper, who sloped in late. It was not a sparkling meal. Duff Cooper hardly spoke. He was probably thinking of more important things. He did say that Brendan Bracken had made a mistake in revealing the story of Hess's flight at all, and particularly in giving it to the American press. I said it seemed so innocuous I wondered why we could not have been told as soon as it had happened. He said there was much more that Bracken had not revealed. He has a slightly foxy face. Emerald addresses him as 'Duffy darling.' She said to Mrs. Fellowes, 'Oh dear, no. He has no temper. I ought to know since I have lived with him intimately for so many months now.' Today Mrs. Fellowes was wearing a wide-brimmed black hat and did look handsome. She was very friendly, and said she too had been quite ill after Cecil's dinner. Was this meant to please? For it was Lord Sackville's venison liver, not Cecil's lobster and pigeon which made me ill.

I thought what a contrast my luncheon with Emerald at the Dorchester to my elevenses three hours previously with Hilda and Doris, the two maids, round the kitchen table at Polesden. I enjoyed the elevenses as much as the luncheon party.

Wednesday, 1st September

At an S.P.A.B. meeting I found a small attendance considering a matter of the first importance, whether or not to protest in the press against the night bombing of historic German cities. Maresco Pearse and Marshall Sisson were uncompromisingly in favour of protesting. Esher took the view that to do so would have no effect whatever; that the Government would not be the least deterred and many members of the public would be antagonized. I dare say he is right in saying that protest would be fruitless, nevertheless I am in favour of our making some gesture of disapproval of the indiscriminate bombing. I had come unprepared for such a discussion and thought the committee should have been warned in advance. After much talk it was decided that no letter of protest should be sent by the Society to the press, but that Esher should submit to the Secretary for Air a list to be prepared by Sisson of historic German towns with the recommendation that the Air Ministry might spare them as far as possible.

Had a talk with Blaise Gillie and Anthony Wagner[1] at the Ministry of Planning. They warned me that the Trust must soon inform the Ministry before accepting restrictive covenants over land.

I met Eddy to discuss the Knole developments up to date. Eddy very defeatist and suspicious of his father's motives. He left to dine with Sibyl Colefax.

Eddy told me that at Sibyl's dinner there were T. S. Eliot, Prof. Joad, Arthur Waley, Edith Sitwell, and Cyril Connolly. The pack of lions were so disconcerted by each other's presence that none of them spoke at all.

Tancred Borenius told me that Lydiard Tregoze, the Bolingbroke house, had been bought by the town of Swindon, which proposed to gut it, after removing all the contents; and that the Ministry of Works was unaware of what was afoot. Such things can still happen in England. Gerry Wellesley went many years ago to see this house, which was built by Colen Campbell. Getting no reply from the front door he went to the back. There at a large kitchen table presided over by the Dowager Lady Bolingbroke sat several strapping farm labourers. Amongst them was a youth, the present peer. The others were his elder brothers, born before his mother married their very old father, and so out of wedlock. They were all happily working on the estate in the employment of their youngest brother.

Bridget Parsons lunched with me. She was very sweet and disarming. She talked about the war, her hopes in 1939, her disillusionment today. She believed the Germans were happier under their régime than the British were under theirs. I agreed, because whereas the Germans were fighting to establish a creed, we were merely fighting to preserve the status quo.

I went to tea with old Logan Pearsall Smith whom I found in a black overcoat and black hat, sitting on a bench in the public garden opposite

[1] Now Sir Anthony Wagner, Principal Garter King of Arms.

11 St. Leonard's Terrace. As usual he talked a lot about Stuart, but said he could do without the brother, and next time he would tell Stuart frankly he would prefer him to come alone. He said 'doves' were beautiful, gentle and guileless people, inclined perhaps just a little to silliness. Lady Berwick was one. The last time she was in London he made a mistake in asking her to meet Raymond and Cyril, 'serpents' he called them, corrected himself and asked me what they were. 'Rattlesnakes,' I suggested, 'which are quite harmless creatures.'

He read me a letter from Shane Leslie describing Lady Leslie's death and funeral. We agreed there was something distasteful in Shane's account of the thousands of telegrams he had received from crowned heads, etc., of his placing his brother's grave cross from France in her coffin with a poem of his own addressed to her on her deathbed, and of his carrying his brother's sword instead of the crucifix at the head of the bier. There was something distasteful not so much in the actions as in the satisfaction he so evidently derived from dramatizing the funeral. Logan repeated the story of his practical joke played on Virginia Woolf, adding the sequel that he pretended to demand money from her. And he told how he wrote amorous letters to Lady Leslie in Lord Beaverbrook's name. He calls Stuart's social success a 'swimgloat', and a bore who comes to stay and won't leave, a 'gluebottom'. His last word of advice was, 'You may quote any of the scandalous things I have told you, but do not quote me as the author of them.'

Monday, 6th September

Went to Highfield, near Otford, Kent, at midday. This property of 250 acres belongs to Sir Herbert and Lady Cohen,[1] rich and very gentle Jews. They were very pathetic, for they have lost their two sons in the war and have no one to leave the property to. Unfortunately the house is an ugly villa built in 1885. I do not know how to help them.

After dinner I walked in the twilight to have a drink and chat with Geoffrey Houghton Brown. An armada of our bombers, bound on a Continental raid, passed overhead. It took three-quarters of an hour for them to pass. The roar they made was terrifying. People came out of their houses on to the pavement to gaze skywards. They were pleased and jubilant. As I watched the green lights in the sky twinkling the V signal I felt sad for the thousands of innocent lives the bombers were

[1] Sir Herbert Cohen, 2nd Bart. (1874–1968) married 1907 Hannah Mildred, daughter of Henry Behrens.

236

about to destroy. In Geoffrey's drawing-room the windows rattled with the vibration.

Eardley and I went to the George, Southwark,[1] meaning to lunch, but the inn was so full and dirty that we came away after walking round it. Its general condition is poor indeed. It has suffered from raids and badly needs painting. Forsyth wants to paint it yellow, but I favour the dull chocolate which the Dickensian galleries always have been painted.

I went to Enfield to see Mr. Leggatt, the last of five brothers of the St. James's Street Leggatts. He was a courteous old gentleman of the old school. The object of my visit was to look at the room bought by him from Enfield Palace when the rest of the building was destroyed in the 1920s, and re-erected by him at his villa. The panelling is very rich and intricate. There is a large Elizabethan chimneypiece in one piece of stone. The ceiling is not the original one, for I compared it with the print of the room in C. J. Richardson's book.[2] I returned in the train with the nephew, a charming man. The Leggatts belong to a definable caste of Englishman: the highly respectable, highly respected gentleman dealer.

At 5.20 Raymond rang up Eardley in the office to report that Italy had surrendered unconditionally. At Brooks's it was on the tape and members were talking about it with great excitement. My first reaction was one of relief; my second one of anxiety lest worse fighting than ever against the Germans might take place in Italy. When I spoke to Harold Nicolson on the telephone he said what a relief it was that henceforth we, Britain, would no longer be under the sad necessity of destroying further Italian towns, whereas whatever future destruction there might be we could comfortably attribute to the Germans. I said this reflection was no comfort to me. I should feel no happier if the world's greatest architecture was wiped out by Germans, and not by Englishmen.

Took the 9.10 from Liverpool Street to Cambridge, stopping at every station on the way. Was met at Cambridge and driven by the agent to

[1] Acquired by the National Trust 1937, it is the only galleried inn remaining in London.

[2] *Studies from Old English Mansions*, 4 vols., 1841.

Anglesey Abbey. On our arrival Lord Fairhaven was strutting in front of his porch, in too immaculate a blue suit, and watch in hand. He is a slightly absurd, vain man, egocentric, pontifical, and too much blessed with this world's goods. He is an enthusiastic amateur, yet ignorant of the arts he patronizes. Without waiting we drove straight off to Kirtling Tower, the far side of Newmarket. Lord Fairhaven and I were teed up in the back seat, he looking at his fair, plump hands, picking at his fingernails and flicking invisible specks of fluff off his suit—on to mine. Having begun by adopting the grand manner, he gradually thawed, and by the end of the visit was friendly and communicative. But he speaks as one accustomed to exercising authority and receiving flattery, which I am constitutionally incapable of delivering.

Kirtling is beautiful and English. A wide moat encloses a large terraced layout, part of a larger garden now disappeared. A Perpendicular church like a cosy old hen peacefully nestles under trees, having hatched a clutch of grey tombstones. The North Chapel contains one particularly rich monument to an Elizabethan North: a heavy elaborate canopy carried by six columns entwined with vine leaves. We walked along the moat through an attractive wilderness under trees to the tower. It is a 1530 tall, red brick gatehouse with four angle turrets. The great house to which it led was destroyed in 1801 and a lump of a house was tacked on to the gatehouse in 1872. It is of the wrong brick and has plate-glass windows. There is a vast copper beech just in front of the tower which should never have been planted there. Lord Fairhaven offers covenants over the tower and some 400 acres of surrounding land.

We returned to Anglesey for a late luncheon, I ravenous by then, having breakfasted at 7.30. Even so I did not eat as much as my host, who at forty-seven has a large paunch, a heavy jowl, pugnacious chin and a mottled complexion. He lives too well and smokes endless cigars. The nice agent, a gentleman from these parts (Lord Fairhaven is not from these parts) only spoke when spoken to. Relations between the two are very much those of gracious employer and subservient employee. After luncheon the agent was dismissed and we strolled down the Lode bank into the garden. The day was sweltering with sticky heat as though a storm were imminent. Lord Fairhaven kept wiping his brow surreptitiously as though greatly afraid to be seen sweating. I mopped unashamedly. The garden is well kept up in spite of the war. It has been laid out on eighteenth-century lines. Just before

238

the war Fairhaven planted a long, straight avenue of limes, chestnuts and planes in four rows with caryatid statues by Coade of Lambeth at the far end. Unfortunately the vista does not begin from and so cannot be enjoyed from the house. In the garden are several urns signed by Scheemakers and L. Delvaux.

Anglesey Abbey is, like Packwood [House, Warwickshire], more a fake than not. The only genuine remains are the calefactorium, or crypt (used as the dining-room) dating from 1236, with thick, quadripartite ceiling of clunch, some medieval buttressed walls and the greatly restored 1600 south front. Lord Fairhaven put back the pointed gables and added the cresting to the porch. The interior is entirely his, opulent and pile-carpeted. But his new library with high coved ceiling, lined with books (first editions and un-cut) is fine. He has a desultory collection of good things that do not amount to a great collection. There is a corridor of Etty nudes in his private bedroom wing.

Exhausted, I had a bath and changed into a dark suit. Lord Fairhaven wore a dinner jacket. We had a four-course dinner of soup, lobster, chicken and savoury, and were waited upon by a butler. Lord Fairhaven is served first, before his guests, in the feudal manner which only the son of an oil magnate would adopt. Presumably the idea is that in the event of the food being poisoned the host will gallantly succumb, and his instant death will be a warning to the rest of the table to abstain. Port and brandy followed.

Saturday, 11th September

We motored after breakfast to the north of the county to see Thorney. Lord Fairhaven is driven everywhere in a high-powered khaki Buick by a soldier, for he has something to do with the Red Cross. Thorney Abbey House is a sort of miniature Coleshill, but without a parapet. It is enchanting but now reduced to the status of a farmhouse. The magnificent staircase and most of the panelled rooms survive. At present the wainscot is all painted a uniform mustard. Lord Fairhaven offers covenants over this superb little house which stands opposite the two towers of the Abbey church.

Monday, 13th September

Last night, returning from Ashtead by train, there were, counting two babies, twenty-one souls (would indeed there had only been souls and no bodies) in my compartment.

I lunched with poor Lady Cohen at the Greek restaurant run by the British Council at the corner of Grosvenor Square. She talked of Dr. Weizmann whom she admired, although she said neither she and her husband, nor the d'Avigdor-Goldsmids, nor the Rothschilds were Zionists. They regarded Zionism as quite impracticable. Tonight I went to Nancy Rodd's party at Boulestin's. All the old gang — Raymond Mortimer, Clarissa Churchill, Alice Harding, Gerald Berners, Stuart. I piloted Nancy to the tube station and left her, as it were, at the jaws of hell. I watched her slim, brisk figure descend into the bowels of darkness, and walked home to Chelsea. It took me well over an hour.

Wednesday, 15th September

Clare Sheridan dined with me at La Belle Meunière. Clare is older, but still beautiful in her big, rumbustious way. She is affectionate and sympathetic. But she has become very spooky and talks a great deal about her psychic experiences. She says she lives more in the 'other world' now than in this. She told me that the whole of her youth had been in pursuit of adventure, or rather pursuit of love. She had had affairs with [1st] Lord Birkenhead, who notwithstanding his intellect and beauty was fundamentally coarse, with Lenin, with Mustapha Kemal and with Mussolini. Throughout the last affair Mussolini behaved like a musical comedy joke figure. He was so portentous and self-opinionated that she could not prevent herself laughing at him out loud. Mussolini was a bounder as well as a cad. Clare said she had come to realize that breeding was what mattered ultimately in men and women. Yet she is still red at heart. She disapproves of her cousin Winston in spite of her admiration for him. Earlier this year she spent fifteen hours sculpturing his head while he lay in bed in the mornings, as he does till midday, surrounded by telephones. She was surprised how off-hand Anthony Eden appeared to be with the Premier, in making lame excuses not to lunch or dine with him. One day an admiral was bidden to lunch with Mr. and Mrs. Churchill and [Sir] Stafford Cripps. The admiral sent a message that he had forgotten, when accepting the invitation, that he had an official luncheon elsewhere which he could not get out of. Churchill sent him back a message that unless his engagement was with the King, no other took precedence over his invitation. The admiral came to luncheon. Clare

heard Churchill refer to Aneurin Bevan over the telephone to Eden as
'that son of a bitch'.

Friday, 17th September

Geoffrey Houghton Brown and I went to Glasgow by the day train.
Only by jumping on to the in-coming train before it stopped on the
platform was I able to get two seats in a first-class compartment.
During the journey I read this month's *Horizon*, Elizabeth Bowen's
Dublin Childhood and finished Turgenev's *House of Gentlefolk*. For
luncheon Geoffrey provided a bottle of Algerian wine. Opposite us
was a most beautiful woman with whom we made friends. She had a
peach and white complexion, liquid grey-blue eyes, corn ripe hair and
a Grecian nose. Geoffrey said it was a Roman nose, and then advised me
to stop staring. We stayed the night at the Station Hotel.

Saturday, 18th September

We caught the 8.45 bus to Inverary. In Glasgow the weather was
appropriately grey and misty with that familiar peaty smell wafted
down from the hills. Loch Lomond was glassy calm and the water
blue-grey like my lady's eyes of yesterday. This is my great-grandmother McFarlane's country and the beginning of the Highlands.
When we reached the Pass the sun came out fitfully and spread a gold
and purple patchwork on the hills. At Loch Fyne sun and sky and water
were Mediterranean. As the bus turned a corner I had my first view of
Inverary, a wide bay in the loch with little boats and large ships in the
harbour, and a minute classical town in the background. Then I saw
the gaunt, grey block of the castle, the two classical bridges and the
romantic peaked hill with watch tower upon it. A man from the castle
met us on the quay and wheeled our luggage on a trolley. We followed
him through a gate, and to avoid the soldiery whose huts are in the
park, along the drive and among the shrubs, we took a path through
the desolate garden, and crossed a bridge over the moat straight into
the great saloon.

The castle is built of an ugly stone, which turns grey in the sunlight
and black in the rain. This is a pity, for all the old houses in the town
are of a lighter, kindlier stone. The castle has been greatly spoilt by
peaked dormer windows added in 1880, and unsightly chimneys stuck
on turrets and steeples. Outside it is grim and forbidding like some

hydropathic hotel. The bridge to the front door had a sloping shelter erected over it for the benefit of Queen Victoria. Geoffrey led me through the saloon into a library where the Duke of Argyll was writing. He was seated at a large table in the middle of the room, with a bronze replica of a Celtic cross and one lighted candle on it. He rose and was very welcoming. He is obviously fond of Geoffrey.

He is a short old man with white hair and a smooth white face, for he seldom if ever has to shave. He has handsome blue eyes. He has a woman's voice, very eunuchy. Lady Victor Paget described him to Jamesey as an elderly hermaphrodite. He was wearing an old Harris tweed, deer-red jacket, with wide buttoned revers up the sleeves, an immensely old tartan kilt, old blue woollen stockings (revealing white knobbly knees), dirk, sporran, and most surprising of all, shoes à l'espadrille. He conducted us up a long, stone staircase with plain iron balusters curved for crinolines, and threadbare carpet. The central hall, exceedingly high, reaches to the roof of the central tower. High though it is, it always retains a strong smell of lodging-house cooking. Windows are never opened, and no wonder, for the castle is bitterly cold in September without fires. My small bedroom is just over the front door. It has double doors, with a moth-eaten, red rep curtain over the inner one. On the blue and white wallpaper hang a large framed photograph of the widowed Queen Victoria (looking like Robert Byron) at the time of the first Jubilee, a large oil of an eighteenth-century duke in a beautiful rococo frame, and a foxed print of the Porteous Riots. The Victorian iron bedstead has a red plush covered canopy. The washstand, dressing-table and clothes cupboard are solid Victorian mahogany pieces. A fire is actually burning in the grate—rather feebly. There is a lovely view from my window (which has not been cleaned for years) of the watch tower hill and a corner of the loch.

We had a delicious luncheon of mackerel, and grouse, helping ourselves from the sideboard. The duke is very voluble and has an insatiable appetite for gossip, as well as food. Conversation revolves round people and their relationships. After luncheon he put on a Glengarry green with age, and set off to the hospital in the park with some French newspapers for wounded French Canadian troops. A soldier on guard stopped us going up the long ride. 'What's this? I can go where I like. I am the duke,' came from a high-pitched, slightly hysterical voice. From the hospital Geoffrey and I went on to the little eighteenth-century fishing lodge by the first fall, looking for salmon. I saw one leaping, but the wrong way, not upstream but down. We continued up the burn, the Aray I presume, crossed over a bridge where I pointed out a rock in midstream, like a surrealist sculpture of a torso with one buttock incomplete, and bitten away. We tested each other on the trees we passed. I failed over a sycamore and a rowan. We found the eighteenth-century pigeon house which is at the end of the vista.

Meals here are excellent in that solid Scotch way I love — porridge, bannocks, scones, plum cakes and game. The duke prattles as ceaselessly as the Aray flows over the stones. Sometimes he is very entertaining; sometimes he is boring, and one does not listen. It makes no difference to him. He is a recognized authority on all church ritual, and a scholar of medieval liturgy, hagiology and Saxon coins. He is eccentric. He will rush without warning out of the room to play a bar or two of a Gregorian chant on a harmonium, or to play on a gong, or a French horn. He also has a cuckoo whistle which he likes to blow in the woods in order to bewilder the soldiers. He takes the keenest interest in the soldiers, both officers and men, learns their names and where they come from, and the names of their diocese and bishop. The great advantage of this place is that after meals the duke disappears, and we are left to read, write, walk out of doors, or roam round the house.

After tea we looked at the rooms on the ground floor. Great bushes of laurel and ungainly spruce trees have been allowed to grow close to the house, with the result that the magnificent views from all sides are shut out. Geoffrey once suggested their being felled, but the duke would not hear of it. It is true that today they serve as screens against the myriad Nissen huts. In the lower part of the hall are two ugly fireplaces. Over them and indeed all the way up the walls practically to the roof are ranged archaic weapons, guns, rifles, pistols, spears and daggers, in giant Catherine wheel patterns. Elks' horns are interspersed. In the blank spaces are numerous family portraits. On one chimneypiece stands a bronze equestrian effigy of Richard Coeur de Lion by Princess Louise, 'my aunt'.[1] The staterooms on this floor contain some splendid eighteenth-century furniture and on the rose damask walls of the saloon portraits by Gainsborough, Cotes and Batoni, hung higgledy-piggledy. Amongst these things is the most astonishing bric-à-brac, including a forest of framed photographs collected by 'my aunt'.

[1] H.R.H. Princess Louise, 4th daughter of Queen Victoria, married 1871 9th Duke of Argyll.

The duke trotted off to the Anglo-Catholic church which he has built at enormous expense in the town. We were left with a fine choice of breakfast food, porridge, boiled eggs, sausages, oatcakes and honey. I ate everything. Then spent the morning looking through the books in the library in which we eat. The library is very pretty, and the iron-work gallery was designed by Uncle Lorne, the princess's husband. The design incorporates a galleon, the chequer arms of the Campbells and ducal coronet over all. Among the innumerable books in the library and throughout the house, even piled up in heaps on chairs, I have found none that I want to read. There are books on Celtic brasses and crosses, on lepidoptera, on ecclesiology, on Campbells, on numismatism, but nothing on art, and nothing on literature.

Geoffrey and I walked down the road after luncheon, along the Loch and back through the woods. It was a grey day. He does not think much of the scenery. I think Inverary one of the loveliest places in the United Kingdom.

Monday, 20th September

The first thing I was aware of this morning was the sound of bagpipes. At first I thought they were being played out of doors. But no, the sound came closer and soon reached my bedroom door. It was the duke's piper in the gallery. He does this every morning except Sunday at 8.30 to wake the duke up. I went down the passage and talked to him. He said it was a dirty day. At 9.15 there was a different sound: this time the duke playing a French horn very badly. After breakfast I worked at an article and Geoffrey at the prophecies of Nostradamus. We were interrupted by the duke skipping in and out of the room to fetch and show us Victorian photograph albums of the royal families of Europe, including several of the Queen and her children in deep mourning clustered round a white pedestalled bust of the Prince Consort, whose neck was garlanded with a wreath.

After luncheon—I am eating far too much here—Geoffrey and I walked to the top of the watch tower hill. It was a desperately showery day with deep blue skies between the clouds. There is a cold east wind which makes sitting indoors without a fire uncomfortable. We set forth with sticks, crossing the bridge over the Aray. This is Frew's bridge. The duke told us that when he stayed here as a boy the strangest

244

procession used to take place from the house to the bridge every morning after breakfast. There might be twenty male guests. Over each a footman carried an umbrella. They marched to a spacious privy under the bridge, where they sat facing each other ten in a row. When the last man had finished the platoon marched back two by two to the house, each with his footman and umbrella.

We tried to follow the track which the Queen took in her pony carriage, but lost it. The view from the watch tower is very fine. The great castle thrusts shadows like bulwarks towards us. Boats are dotting the loch for miles, invasion barges, and gondola-shaped vessels with odd prows. The town is tiny from here and I wondered how any enemy aeroplanes could possibly aim at so pin-head a target.

Conversation about people is endless, and at times exhausting. 'Who was his mother? Let me see. He married one of those Rutland women. She capered about with that apish fellow—you know quite well who I mean—that fellow Taplow. That's it. She was quite mad, Beatrice Taplow. She used to climb trees like a baboon, and one day she dropped a coconut on Peter Coats.' 'Peter Coats?' I asked incredulously. 'Yes, he was the brother of old Podgy Glentanar. I'm talking of an earlier generation,' he said snappishly, and on he went. Intelligent conversation is consequently quite impossible. Geoffrey says it is worse than he ever remembers; and besides, the duke gets everything wrong.

Tuesday, 21st September

A beautiful blue and purple day. This afternoon Geoffrey and I walked up the loch, along the road we came by in the bus, to Dundarave Castle, four miles away. There was much army traffic on the road which was a disturbance. It was otherwise a tranquil walk through the chequered shade of trees. Having reached the castle we sat on a rock over a smelly beach looking towards Inverary. Dundarave Castle is compact, medieval and very faithfully restored, so faithfully that the old window openings have been retained; and they are minute and must be disagreeable to live behind. The granite of which it is built is brown, unlike the horrid black stone of our castle. Here the grass grows right up to the walls and there are no flower beds. There is no isolation of dwelling from the wild country, no timid, artificial barrier. The castle is rented by Lord Weir.[1]

[1] 1st Viscount Weir (1877–1959), industrialist and civil servant. Descended from Robert Burns.

At tea the duke talked of fairies, in whom he implicitly believes, as do all the people here. He described them as the spirits of a race of men who ages ago lived in earth mounds, which are what they frequent. They are usually little green things that peer at you from behind trees, as squirrels do, and disappear into the earth. The duke has visited numerous fairy haunts in Argyll. So has his sister, Lady Elspeth [Campbell], who at dinner one night announced with solemnity, 'The fairies are out in their sieves tonight.' 'Crossing over to Ireland no doubt,' her brother replied. 'We are not good enough for them in Scotland. Why! last year at Tipperary there were so many of them that they caused a traffic block.' In the middle of tea a young man, son of one of the duke's crofters on Iona, and now a lieutenant in the navy, called, uninvited. The duke gave him tea and with the greatest friendliness and interest asked after him, his family and relations, remembering each one by name and occupation. There is no doubt the old feudal, clan feeling is still very strong.

Wednesday, 22nd September

It is impossible to judge how many servants there are in this house. Certainly the moment one leaves one's room, the ashtrays have been emptied and one's things straightened. Yet the house is a shambles, and extremely dusty. Although one's shoes are taken away they are never cleaned properly. It is far colder here than in the south, although less raw. I am always sleepy. Breakfast is not till 9.30, yet by 9.30 p.m. I am so tired and yawning that I can barely keep awake till 10.30 when punctually we go to bed.

I was so exhausted by my walk yesterday that today the fronts of my legs ached. Geoffrey and I ambled painfully to the town to post letters. There have been grand military exercises and just as we had settled in the saloon the duke announced that Sir Bernard Paget, Commander-in-Chief, General MacNaughton, the Canadian G.O.C., and his cousin Sir Ralph Glyn, were about to call. Presently they did so, and Geoffrey and I fled upstairs. At 5 we thought they had gone, and slipped into the library for some tea. The duke came in to find us eating, disappeared to look for more cups and saucers, so Geoffrey and I fled again. Afterwards I was sorry not to have seen MacNaughton, who told the duke that his grandfather came from Argyllshire in the 1850s and had been a crofter of his.

Geoffrey and I looked through two heavy volumes of plans and elevations midway on the staircase, hoping to find the name of the original architect of the castle. We discovered plans dated 1746 signed by Roger Morris, and another of the 1770s signed by William Mylne.

Geoffrey and I walked along the Lochgilphead road, sat on a bridge and talked. On our return the sun burst upon a field of golden stooks right in front of us, swept across the indigo loch, and ran up a gentle mountain the other side, leaving wide footsteps of light and shade.

Reading *The Times* today I told the duke that a Nicolaes Maes portrait of the 9th Earl of Argyll was on exhibition at the Guildhall among the late Lord Wakefield's collection. He expressed surprise because, he said, he had got it. He told me to go into the turret room next to the library we were then in, and look at it. What I saw was a Dirk Maes of the 1st Duke over the fireplace. It is a small picture with glowing colours in the drapery, and the face very clearly drawn. There are two other Dirk Maeses here, both of early dukes I think, one in the saloon, the other in the great hall. This duke knows absolutely nothing about his pictures or indeed what he has got. He has a superb collection of family portraits. The full-length Cotes of the Gunning Duchess in a green dress is stupendous; the beauty of her Irish complexion and white bosom was renowned. The Gainsborough of Marshal Wade has at some time been enlarged to make it fit the huge frame.

Geoffrey and I left Inverary by the 10.15 bus for Glasgow. After luncheon we walked from the station to the Art Gallery through several delightful early nineteenth-century squares and crescents in the one-time residential area. What are now offices and lodgings were once the town houses of the rich merchants, like my forebears the White-Thomsons. Perhaps I passed their town house. There are a number of fine churches in the neo-Greek, and neo-Egyptian styles. The 'gloomth' of the blackened freestone is not without its charm. In fact I learnt for the first time that architecturally Glasgow is by no means to be despised. There is a distinctive character in the uniformity of the streets which has not been tampered with. The art gallery is early twentieth century. I find it hideous. All the pictures are now put away.

I left Glasgow this morning for Euston, parting with Geoffrey who went through to Edinburgh. He is a kind, patient and humorous travelling companion, easy-going and always good tempered. Just what one, who lacks all these qualities, most needs.

Wednesday, 29th September

The solicitor to the Wingfield-Digby family came to see Matheson and me about the future of Sherborne Castle in Dorset. Matheson suggested that I should visit Sherborne. He warned me that Colonel Wingfield-Digby detested the arts and despised everyone who did not kill foxes and pheasants to the exclusion of all other recreations. His advice that I should have to control my enthusiasms was not lost on me.

I went to tea with Emerald Cunard before she left for Victor Cazalet's[1] memorial concert. She had a bad cold, and was wearing a black velvet dress which swathed her throat. It was very becoming. Emerald said Mrs. Wellington Koo had complained to her that she did not like London because the English men were all so ugly. I asked, 'What did you reply to that?' 'I said, "Well, that is strange, Mrs. Koo, for to me all Chinamen look exactly the same. They all have flat faces, no noses, and wear round horn-rimmed spectacles."' Emerald complained that Lady Wavell never speaks at meals to anyone. She says not one word. Emerald asked me where on earth I had been all these past weeks. When I told her I had been staying at Inverary, she said she had no idea I was a relation of the duke. I said I wasn't. She said there could be no other possible reason for staying with him.

Friday, 1st October

On stepping out of the train on Dorking platform I saw a couple descend from the next compartment. He was an officer, rather round-shouldered, his face covered with hard pustules. She was wearing an untidy black coat and skirt, covered with hairs and dandruff, her sharp face badly rouged. I passed by them, and the man said, 'Hullo,

---

[1] Victor Cazalet (1896–1943), M.P. Killed with General Sikorsky, Prime Minister of Polish Government and Commander-in-Chief of Polish Army, in a mysterious aeroplane crash.

Jim!' He was Basil Dufferin.[1] I was appalled by the change in his appearance. After two minutes conversation the endearing gentleness of his character was again apparent to me.

A taxi motored me to Wotton House where I lunched and spent the afternoon. Today it belongs to a John Evelyn just as it belonged to the diarist John Evelyn in the seventeenth century. It is a long, rambling, untidy house. The nucleus of it is Jacobean, and a few rich doorways of that period survive upstairs. But the present Evelyn's grandfather spoilt the house in every conceivable way in the 1870s. In the hideous, Ruskin-style library are many rare books, including some 200 of Evelyn's own; also royal seals, miniatures and nineteenth-century busts. There are innumerable family portraits, including three of John Evelyn, of which the Kneller is the most remarkable. There is a table carved by Grinling Gibbons, whom Evelyn discovered, and an Italian ebony cabinet in which Evelyn's manuscript diaries were found. The army have occupied most of the house during the war. They allowed a fire to blacken the classical doorcases, walls and ceiling of the dining-room. Could Evelyn have called in Wren to design this room? The garden, now a wilderness, has a mound cut into terraces by Evelyn, and below it a temple on Doric columns, which he built. All the trees are magnificent, and the beeches are said to have been planted by him.

The present Evelyn is an odd fish. He is only a little older than me, stoops and is quite bald. He seems permanently distracted, does not look you in the face, but looks at nothing in particular over his shoulder. He is an eccentric, shy, clever and presumably unhappy man.

Saturday, 2nd October

Geoffrey and I went to the Guildhall to see Lord Wakefield's pictures, and in particular the Nicolaes Maes of the 9th Earl of Argyll. It closely resembled the three Dirk Maeses at Inverary, being of the same size. The face is carefully drawn and the clothes are painted in the same gorgeous crimsons and greens. We agreed that the Guildhall is vastly improved by having lost its roof. The fakery that remains looks more convincing, blackened as it is with smoke. We agreed too that the setting for the statues was totally wrong, for they need sharp lighting which they don't get here. We walked to St. Mary Lothbury. Why

[1] 4th Marquess of Dufferin and Ava (1909–45), a contemporary at preparatory school, Eton and Oxford. Killed on active service in Burma.

did Wren not bother to make the inside east end wall straight? A disappointing church. We tried to enter St. Stephen Walbrook, and could not. St. Augustine Watling Street is burnt out but the pretty tower is left. I hope the ugly building to the west of it will disappear with the remains of the church. The Perpendicular ceiling and pendentives of St. Mary Aldermary are of plaster. It has a crooked east end wall likewise. We gave first prize for spires to St. Mary-le-Bow, second to St. Stephen, and third to St. Vedast Foster Lane.

In St. Paul's Geoffrey pointed out what I had not noticed before, that the heavy iron railings on the nave cornice over-accentuate the depth of the cornice out of all proportion to the nave it serves. It thus seemingly narrows the nave to the detriment of the whole interior. From below the rails look well wrought, but I suppose Wren never intended them to be there. Whereas the Thornhill dome is delightful, the spandrel paintings are atrocious. Who on earth allowed them to be done, and when?

Sunday, 3rd October

I lunched with Dame Una. She said Jamesey was over-sensitive about his new book, *West Indian Summer*. He dreaded lest the reviews might not be favourable enough. He has just sent me an inscribed copy. Rose Macaulay thinks it brilliant. I hope it is. The Pope-Hennessy family are very self-protective, and each exalts the work of the other. The Dame read me extracts from a Penguin book, just out, by H. G. Wells, in which he says this war is waged between democrats and the Catholic Church; that no Englishman who is a true Papist can be in favour of the Allies, but must be a quisling in disguise; and that the Pope, who is an ignoramus and other pejorative things besides, is in league with the Nazis. The man must be a lunatic.

I met Geoffrey at the gate of Chiswick House. To our surprise we found the place in better shape than we had expected. The garden, though overrun with children, is quite well kept up. True, the roof of the temple, 'the first essay of his lordship's happy invention', is in a bad state. The house requires repointing, replastering and repainting. A great temporary garage for the firemen's engine has been erected in front of the main portico which is supported by iron girders. We could not get inside. I think the chimneys on the Palladian core spoil the house and must have looked worse before the Wyatt wings were added.

I dined at Emerald's. I appreciate her more and more. Bridget [Lady Victor] Paget was sitting next to me. She kept smiling in her gracious, disarming, sphinx-like way, and remaining silent. She drank tumblers of neat whisky when the red wine gave out, and relapsed into a controlled stupor. Emerald complained how the Duchess of Portland has been left a mere £2,500 a year to spend after being accustomed to £150,000 a year. She said it was scandalous of the late duke, and appealed to Bridget, who mumbled that she found it very difficult and tiring to express her feelings on the subject. Lady Juliet Duff told a story about her grandmother Lady Herbert of Lea, whose impassioned correspondence with Cardinal Vaughan has been published by Shane Leslie. Lady Herbert went to confess to her favourite priest. There was a queue waiting on its knees at the confessional. She spied a friend at the head of the queue, went up to her and said, 'I can't wait. Just tell Father X that it was the same as last time.' When the party broke up, Jamesey and I stayed behind to talk to Emerald. She spoke of love and read a passage on the non-reciprocity of it by E. M. Forster. She expressed horror at the soldiers having girls against walls in the dark streets. 'I am told they do these things. Whatever for?' she asked.

Monday, 4th October

At luncheon at the Churchill Club canteen I sat with Nancy, Sibyl Colefax and Mrs. Gladwyn Jebb. They were all full of the news of Gerry Wellesley having succeeded to the dukedom of Wellington. Sibyl asked should she congratulate him. 'Gracious no,' Nancy shrieked, 'you should condole.' 'What! for becoming a duke?' 'For the death of his nephew,' we suggested.

Tuesday, 5th October

At Liverpool I booked a room at the Adelphi, a mammoth, modern hotel entirely lit by artificial light. An old gentleman, Mr. George Leather, one of the Speke Hall trustees, gave me luncheon. He spoke in glowing terms of Lord Woolton, whose business is in Liverpool. From the town hall we were motored by the City Engineer's representative and several other gentlemen of that ilk to Speke.

The object of this visit was for me to see the heirlooms which the trustees offer to make over to us with the house. I made a note of every piece; and a gruesome lot they were, mostly consisting of made-up

251

Charles II chairs with cut velvet stuffed seats and backs, and four-poster beds made out of chests and any bit of oak, ancient or mid-nineteenth century. As for the great embattled chimneypiece in the great hall, I am inclined, in spite of *Country Life*, to date it from the early 1800s, since it is made of plaster. I cannot believe it to be Jacobean.

A neighbouring aerodrome has made the trustees fell the trees on the garden side. The result is a magnificent open view of the Mersey and the Welsh mountains beyond.

Before dark I walked to the Protestant cathedral. It was shut. The outline of the great tower is from a distance impressive. On close inspection the detail of the carving is unconvincing, and repetitive. It is too much a reproduction of the medieval. The nave has yet to be built. The site is very well chosen. The Woolton stone of the tower, being still clean, has a fresh butter surface, whereas on older buildings this stone has become blackened and harsh.

Wednesday, 6th October

I had a great shock at breakfast in reading that poor Diana Worthington, having walked out of Weston [Underwood, Olney] early yesterday morning, is assumed to have drowned herself in the Ouse. She left letters to the effect that she was going on a long journey. Her coat was found on the river bank, and her handkerchief in the river. They have dragged the river, so far without success. She wrote so sweetly asking me to stay with her and recuperate after my illness, and I nearly went. Now I wish I had. When she last came here in May she struck me as almost manic, and not quite rational. How I wish I had talked to her then about what I knew was on her mind, namely Greville having left her. But I thought I did not know her well enough, and refrained. One should never refrain from anything. How this sort of thing hurts!

I came back from Liverpool particularly early to dine with the Princesse de Polignac. But she had rung up, putting off the dinner because Clarissa Churchill was ill.

Friday, 8th October

I went to see Anne in the evening. When I arrived at her flat she was alone, running about in her chemise, pretending as she skipped about to be coy and hiding herself behind an old towel. She can be funnier than anybody I know, and she made me laugh so much that I nearly 'did myself a mischief', as my Aunt Dorothy puts it.

Stuart dined with me at Brooks's. It was a disastrous evening. The moral of it is that there are no limits beyond which the idiocy of adults will not go. At dinner we argued, I cannot even remember over what. I was certainly difficult and disagreeable about some friends of his. He contradicted me. I contradicted him. He said I always snubbed him, and was ruder to him than anyone he knew; and I said outrageous and insulting things to him, just for fun. I said, 'If they are funny, why don't you laugh?' He said, 'They're not funny. They make me want to cry they're so un-funny.' 'But you never do cry,' I said, 'so they must be funny.' 'They're *not* funny,' he almost shouted. 'Remember where you are,' I said. 'We are in the coffee-room.' 'There you go again – correcting, finding fault, patronising.' There was a seething silence of several minutes duration. He looked very put out, and ate nothing. Then he said, 'I am too tired to argue any more.' (How often have I not heard my parents say this?) And he added, 'You had better go.' '*I* had better go?' I asked. 'But it's my club we're in.' 'Oh, so it is,' he said, rising from his chair. 'No, no,' I said, 'I will go all the same.' I paid the bill and went to fetch my coat and umbrella. I said, 'I am off now, and I do not intend that we shall meet again. We have nothing in common'. He said, 'Good night!' I said, 'It's goodbye,' and left. I walked home.

I lunched with Clifford Smith at the Athenaeum. I guessed the poor old man really wanted to find out whether, as the result of the announcement in the press of Knole coming to the Trust, there would be any inventory-making for him. He kept nosing around the subject without getting to the point. So to put him out of his misery I had to tell him – no. I was sorry, and felt I had had no right to take a meal off him, without any return. Anyway I gave him a lift in the National Trust car on my way to a job. Coping with the traffic I paid little attention to what he was saying in his hesitant, halting speech. When we were approaching Hyde Park Corner I heard him mumble, 'Jim, will you, um, 'er, drop the Smith.' So I drew up along the pavement, leant across and opened the far side door for him. But instead of getting out he said, 'What, um, 'er, has happened?' I said, 'I thought you wanted to get out here, Mr. Clifford Smith.' He said rather sadly, 'I wanted you to drop the Mr. and to call me Clifford.' We proceeded to Kensington High Street.

This evening I received a most grateful and charming letter from Vita, thanking me for having warned her in advance of the impending Knole announcement. I know how miserable she must be feeling about it. I also had a letter from Eddy, who clearly does not mind.

Q. and I sat on her sofa. She began: 'Now you are unhappy. What is it? You have quarrelled with Stuart, and it is your fault, I know.' How did she know? She has never met him. Really the intuition of women is uncanny. She gave me much advice, telling me quite severely that I must make it up with him. 'You simply can't lose a good friend for an idiotic reason,' and so forth. We found a cab and she insisted on coming with me to Cheyne Walk. In the cab she took my hands and kissed me over and over again. I lit a fire in my room. We turned the lights out, and sat on the window seat looking at the moon on the river.

Tuesday, 12th October

At 8.20 I telephoned Q., who I knew would still be in bed. She answered the telephone. I said, 'It's me, Q.' 'Is it you, Terry?' she said in a voice of unconcealed excitement. 'No,' I answered, and put the receiver down gently.

I dined with Patrick Kinross at his house, the first time for over three years, since I used to come up from Hobbs Barracks in the summer evenings of 1940. Lady Kinross [his mother] was with him, looking silvery and radiantly good. Yes, Patrick has changed a little, and not only physically. He is bigger than heretofore, and he speaks with a sort of new found inner conviction. He is philosophic about life, holds definite views, is confident and sure of himself. We argued long about war and peace, he disagreeing with my pacific views, and adopting the realistic and conservative attitude on post-war policy and the ultimate treatment of Germany, the squeeze-her-till-the-pips-squeak attitude.

Thursday, 14th October

Went to Koestner's to look at the Nicolaes Maes there of a young prince—of Orange I think. Wrote and told the Duke of Argyll that his Dirk Maeses were probably Nicolaes Maeses.

In the afternoon to Ashford, Middlesex. I was met at the station by a
254

young man in corduroys, with a flaming shock of hair and a red beard. He told me he was an artist and chief of the Echelford Society for protecting amenities in this rather dank part of the world. He took me to Ashford Lodge, over which he wants the Trust to hold a covenant. I had to tell him it was no good. The house has a late Georgian aspect but is of very little merit. He took it so well and was not at all hurt. 'Righty-ho!' he said bravely. We parted friends.

Friday, 15th October

The wretched National Trust car would not start again. The battery was dead. So I took a train to Tunbridge Wells, and a bus to Wadhurst. I was not feeling very grand because last night Pierre gave me my last whopping injection. Hot and cold by turns I walked, wearing my black overcoat down the long, straggly, dull village street to The Gatehouse. For some reason I expected the owner to be a man, having addressed it as such. It was on the contrary an old woman in a mackintosh. I have never been more astonished by such squalid living. The house is a genuine early Tudor—say late fifteenth-century—yeoman's dwelling, typical of this region. It is of half-timber, with sloping roof, overhanging eaves and a central brick chimney stack. There is nothing fake about it. But the condition! It has no services, no water, no drains, no light. The old creature has no domestic help, and obviously no money. For these deprivations I am indeed sorry for her. But the dust, dirt and junk littering every square inch of space inside were indescribable. Filthy saucepans, opened and half-emptied tins of sardines, jam and baked beans, and worse still, piles of snotty grey handkerchiefs and other unmentionable rags littered the tables and chairs of the living-room. The garden shrubs have got so out of control that they obliterate the little light which lattice panes allow at the best of times. None of the windows open. The stench was asphyxiating. The old dame gave me a cold luncheon of salmon, lettuce and cheese, not off plates, but out of tins. I hardly dared swallow a mouthful, and when her back was turned, shoved what I could out of my tin into a handkerchief, which I stuffed into my trouser pocket. Had I seen the kitchen before luncheon I would not even have eaten one mouthful. After this terrible meal she insisted upon my looking at the kingpost upstairs. Now if there is one thing which bores me it is a kingpost. However, obediently I trudged up the creaking staircase. But when I reached the top landing I dared not proceed for fear of putting a foot through the crazy floor boards

I*

and the ceiling of the downstairs sitting-room. When I turned back she knew that I hadn't seen the damned kingpost, and was very hoity-toity. She then told me that she wished the Trust after her death to allow the Women Farmers and Gardeners Association to have the use of the house as their rest home. By which time the whole rickety old dump will have collapsed in a heap. I could not be encouraging, and I suppose I showed my boredom with her ceaseless rattle about the importance and antiquity and rarity of the house. I was not well, and I did not respond as dutifully and enthusiastically as is my wont to offers which I know from the first glance are unacceptable.

When I left her on the high road, she said, 'I don't think much of the National Trust.' 'You mean', I replied, 'that you don't think much of me, I'm afraid.' 'You have done nothing but sniff and crab the place,' she said, giving me a stiff handshake, holding her arm high up in that injured manner peculiar to the very sensitive poor. I felt a little abashed, a little ashamed and sorry that I had not been more forthcoming. But I did not feel guilty of her accusation. It was just not true that I had crabbed. I may have sniffed, for I am beginning a cold. I had merely tried, possibly a little too forcefully, to check her extravagant enthusiasms with which she relentlessly bombarded me. With the exception of that odious old gentleman, Colonel Pemberton of Pyrland Hall, she is, I think, the first owner with whom I have failed to make friends.

Saturday, 16th October

A Georgian Group committee meeting this morning. I sat next to Dame Una and Trystan Edwards,[1] who fascinated me with the number of objects tied to his person by black strings; fountain-pens, spectacles, magnifying glasses, etc. It was a good meeting and the professor in the chair dealt well with the items. I brought up several: Claremont—the park advertised for building plots: Chiswick—Lord Burlington's little temple in poor condition: 37 Portland Place—the beautiful central façade of the last intact terrace being demolished now: Dropmore—the estate bought by speculative builders. When I got home for tea Jamesey telephoned proposing a night of adventure. I was thrilled and for once our enthusiasms coincided. We drank first at the Ritz, then the Gargoyle, dined at the White Tower and visited disreputable pubs in that area. The only person we met was Guy Burgess, drunk and

[1] Trystan Edwards (1884–1973), architect, planner and writer.

truculent, and we soon shook him off. We both agreed that depravity was a bore, and that on this account alone the evening would have been worth while as a gentle reminder—in the hideous sweaty faces, the human stench, the risk of beer being spilt upon one's best suit, of one's pocket being picked, and ten to one the likelihood of meeting no one rewarding. We returned to the Gargoyle and joined a table of Brian Howard,[1] that affected, paradoxical figure of the twenties, and two other dreary queens. As I walked home about midnight from South Kensington station I ruminated upon the loneliness of my lot.

Sunday, 17th October

I walked to the Ladies' Carlton Club, met Puss Milnes-Gaskell and taxied to the Ritz with her. We were joined by Douglas Woodruff and Blanche Lloyd. While we were ordering luncheon Stuart and Lady Islington sat down at the table next to ours, Stuart with his back to mine, our chairs practically touching. Electric sparks of indignation must have been visible to others in the space of inches between us. Neither of us made the slightest sign of recognition. Blanche Lloyd is no longer handsome, is thinner and older. Today she had an un-scrubbed look. She was affectionate but distrait. She wanted me to go to Clouds Hill for a weekend. But without George Lloyd I don't think I could face it. Douglas Woodruff was far more genial than last time, but still wore that expression of intellectual complacency. He was cross with the Vatican for not giving us an archbishop; and said the usual policy was to hold a successor up the sleeve when the actual holder of that dignity was an old man. There should not be a long interregnum. We went on to the Coliseum for a variety show in aid of the Lord Lloyd Memorial Prize for the Navy League. Anything less suitable for this particular purpose could hardly be conceived. The jokes were bawdy beyond words. Sandwiched as I was between the two po-faced ladies-in-waiting I did not dare laugh when a joke was funny, which was seldom.

To my surprise Stuart telephoned, proffering an olive branch. So we dined at Brooks's. He made absolutely no reference to our last meeting and behaved as though there had been no row. In fact we behaved like two old club members finding themselves next to each other at the same table. We were both bored. He said he might soon be going abroad. I said what a good idea that was. I said I might be going

[1] Well-known aesthete at Eton and Oxford in the twenties.

to Italy (there is little likelihood, worst luck). He said what a good idea that was. By 9.15 we could bear the cold and gloom of the club no longer. Outside it was pouring with rain. We put scarves and handkerchiefs on our heads and ran to the Green Park tube station. There I said, 'Would you like to come home for a drink?' He said, 'How can I in this rain?' So I said not a word and dived into my train.

Monday, 18th October

All today I walked about with a hollow in my chest where my heart once was. I kept singing sadly to myself, 'I cares for nobody, not I, and nobody cares for me.'

But I had a busy, not unsuccessful day. I had asked Paul Methuen and Colin Agnew to lunch. Both accepted but only Paul came. He was very charming and we talked about Corsham's future. We have done this for years now ever since I first worked for the Trust. He says his brother is at last coming round to the idea. Talking of Lydiard Tregoze, he said none of us must upset the hyper-socially sensitive Mayor of Swindon, who is an excellent fellow and an engine driver. Professor Richardson and Sir Charles Peers[1] joined us over coffee. Paul was vastly entertained by the professor. Peers told me that the neo-Greek, unlike the neo-Roman style, was not suited to this climate for it depended essentially upon a clear atmosphere, sharp light and shadow. He said Nash would always hold his own in the hierarchy of British architects, although he borrowed designs for façades from other architects, stuck the façades up anyhow and used the shoddiest lath and plaster and patent cements.

Eardley and I went to Mr. Lloyd-Johnes (who gave us Dolaucothi) at his flat in Holland Park, to see his pictures and furniture. They include much fine stuff, notably interesting family portraits, and some Chippendale chairs with original tapestried seats. I made a list of what he stipulates shall return to Dolaucothi after his time. He is a wicked old fox determined to diddle his family at all costs, and is a de-frocked clergyman on what account I do not know.

Saturday, 23rd October

Patrick Kinross lunched. He was much more like his old self. He

[1] Sir Charles Peers (1868–1952), antiquary and editor of *Victoria County Histories 1903* and Inspector of Ancient Monuments.

admitted that at first he found it difficult to reconcile himself to the un-war minded lives of his friends in London. They seemed unaware of and unconcerned with what was happening overseas. Furthermore, having accustomed himself to leading a picnic sort of life for so long he slightly disapproved of the conventional, pre-war way of living here. But he is already getting over these inhibitions. They are quite under-standable. He still misses the mixture of seriousness and fun of his friends in the desert. He says that in spite of their deprivations they are happier than people here who have their comforts; and that in the 8th Army there is much wholesome buggery.

I slipped away from a tea party at the Kennets when charades started, and went to Mérode Guevara's flat in Athenaeum Court. She talked a lot about Russia and communism. She shouts one down like everyone else these days. She said she was trying to like England and Englishmen again without succeeding. Stuart says she is stupid and dull. James says, 'Let's face it, she's a moron.' Emerald says she is brilliant. I don't know what to think.

I called for Emerald and escorted her to dinner at the Argentine Embassy. I like the tall, dark and cultivated ambassador. There were only four of us, the fourth being his younger daughter, who has fair hair scooped up in a friz on top as they all have it now, and a pretty pouting mouth. Emerald talked of the Duke of Alba's love affairs that last long and always come to nought. I said but all love affairs come to nought, and not all last long. She then described her recent visit to 10 Downing Street. Mr. Churchill candidly admitted that he was enjoying the conduct of the war, and so did Randolph. Mrs. Churchill has become so pious about the war that she will not even allow her daughter Mary to go to a dance. Odious family! By 10.30 the ambassa-dor was longing for us to leave. Whereupon Emerald, who hates leaving, began her maddening telephoning for cars. Eventually one came at midnight and I accompanied her to the Dorchester. As the car would not take me to Chelsea and it was too late for a bus I was obliged to walk.

Monday, 25th October

Passing St. James's Palace on my way to the London Museum I came upon Blanche Lloyd, a stick-like figure in black, scuttling along and carrying bags. She looked pathetically humble and poor (I hope she is neither of these things). How unlike the high and mighty ex-Governor's

259

lady of Portman Square days, only a decade ago. She said she was off to wait upon the Princess Royal. I longed but did not like to tell her that she had a preposterous black smudge on her nose.

Drown gave me back the little David from Polesden most beautifully cleaned and restored.

Tuesday, 26th October

I motored Lord Ilchester and Professor Richardson to Polesden and back within the morning. We just had time to study Richardson's design for Mrs. Greville's monument *in situ*. I am pleased with the result. I had my way in persuading both that the yew hedge which the professor proposed should be done away with altogether. We got back to Brooks's just too late for Anthony Blunt whom I had asked to luncheon. He came in however for coffee, and I asked him how best I could get sent to Italy under Amgot. He said he would see what he could do, but advised that the right plan was to approach Lord Rennell[1] direct. Nancy also advised this, and I have now approached him.

The fog was so bad tonight that no buses were running. Consequently I missed the 9.50 train I was to have taken for Truro. However I caught the 11.30. There was no sleeper and I had to sit up all night. A terrible train for stopping. It did not reach Truro until 11 a.m. Having had no breakfast I was famished.

Wednesday, 27th October

The [Trevor] Holmans met me at Truro. Unfortunately no time to see the cathedral. They motored me to Chyverton and gave me coffee, toast and marmalade. This is an attractive 1730 brick house with a pair of wings oddly enough in stone. They were originally connected to the main block by retaining walls. All the interior decoration dates from the early nineteenth century. The grounds are especially beautiful. There is a wooded valley filled with rhododendrons and maples. I left Chyverton in the afternoon, and took a train to Ivybridge where Eardley met me. We motored to Salcombe, having lost our way down lanes—all the signposts having been removed so that the German parachutists shall not know where they are—in the dark.

[1] Major-Gen. Lord Rennell of Rodd, Nancy Mitford's brother-in-law, then Civil Affairs Administrator in the Middle East, East Africa and Italy.

Woke to find the sun shining upon the sea. Salcombe is as mild as the Mediterranean. At ten we went to Lady Clementine Waring's[1] house, a cheerful, Gothic villa in which Froude wrote his history, and to which he added a wing. Lawns slope down to the sea. Lady Clementine looks at one with the intensity of a psychoanalyst. And the expression on her face says, 'I have seen the inmost recesses of your squalid little mind. You are a worm only fit to be trampled underfoot.' She is a handsome and forbidding woman, who is chairman of the small local committee which runs the Sharpitor property. This contains a perfectly hideous villa called after its donor, the late Mr. Overbeck, a mysterious German quack doctor whose interests embraced stuffed birds, oriental brass, Wedgwood cameos, every conceivable form of bric-à-brac, and small boys. The garden is famed for its rare shrubs, and is as unappetizing as the house. It has no layout. It is crisscrossed with serpentine paths of yellow flags and tarmac, and is adorned with pergolas fashioned out of drainpipes, handrails made of tube pipes, terracotta urns on concrete piers, and the soppiest sculpture of simpering little children. The eucalyptus trees, which really must have been attractive features, were all killed by the frosts of recent winters.

Having inspected this unprepossessing property we lunched under the eagle eye of Lady Clementine and motored to Dartmouth. After crossing the ferry we continued to Brixham. I don't like Devon in spite of the beautiful coastline and cliffs. There is a littleness about its valleys and lanes, a meanness in the cramped views, an oppression in the claustrophobic, dinky little towns. Besides it is being overbuilt, spoilt by rashes of Tudor bungalows with miniature drives of grey granite pebbles and white-washed boulders at the gates. And, oh the gates! Either made of old wagon wheels, painted orange, or the rising (or is it setting?) sun in cheap metalwork. Devon is too much beloved by too many of the wrong people.

Brixham is like a foreign fishing village; and is indeed filled with Flemish fisherfolk, who escaped here with their craft from the Netherlands. We watched the fishing smacks sail in and unload, while we had tea. We reached Torquay in the dark and stayed in tremendous luxury in the most expensive hotel in England, the Imperial. It has been decorated and furnished by Betty Joel.

[1] Lady Clementine Hay, married 1901 Captain Walter Waring, M.P.

The bay reminds me of Nice. And the sea this morning was as blue as it is at Nice. Sitting on the terrace after breakfast, it being 9 o'clock by Greenwich, but not by Mr. Churchill, we got quite hot in the sun. After browsing in antique shops we proceeded to a property which must be nameless. I had warned Eardley that the owner might be just a little bit smelly. But I did not expect that she would on this occasion, when she was expecting us, stink worse than a badger. Indoors the stench was fit to kill. Indeed I nearly died of it, in spite of the fact that the leads of most of the windows have been torn out by bomb blast. We made every excuse to walk in the garden. Even so, when sitting on a bench Eardley in leaning backwards was practically supine. I was obliged to light a cigarette.

Saturday, 30th October

Professor Richardson button-holed me in Brooks's and asked if I would consider the post of secretary to the Fine Art Commission. I said I was only an architectural amateur, and suggested Anthony Blunt. He thought Blunt was too much of a dilettante. I said he was a scholar, and besides had a good manner. He does not think Summerson would be interested.

After tea I took a train to Woking. There I waited an hour for a taxi which never came. Eventually I took a bus to Send, and walked to Send Grove, carrying my bags. I arrived just in time to change for dinner at 8.30. A house party staying. Conversation at dinner was of rape and unnatural vice, the women, Loelia Westminster, Georgia Sitwell[1] and Joan Duff having some odd notions of both. After dinner we played until midnight a paper game of Loelia's invention – of the 'Truth' variety. It was great fun, and very scandalous. The party was divided into two schools of thought over one question: 'Would you sooner steal the affections of your best friend's husband or wife, *or* commit a fraudulent act, involving the penury of widows and children?' I said that of course I would have less compunction in doing the latter – so did Georgia and Loelia. The others said the opposite, and were as shocked by us as we were by them. Another question – 'Who do you consider the most sexually desirable woman?' I answered, 'Bridget Parsons or Evelyn Laye.'

[1] Wife of Sir Sacheverell Sitwell, present Baronet.

A drizzly, muggy, drab day. I had breakfast downstairs with Charles Ritchie and Philippe de Rothschild, the latter in his dressing-gown. He looks like Johnny Churchill and is 'galant'. Takes the women's arms and paws them. He escaped from unoccupied France only this year and said that the English here have no idea of conditions on the Continent. He was pained by the bland way in which the English criticize the behaviour of various French men and women in France. They do not realize the pressures put upon them, or the motives behind their behaviour. They may be perfectly honourable ones. We discussed our different ideas for the preservation of peace in the post-war world. The two men favoured the creation of a federal block in Western Europe for practical purposes. By this means future war might be averted for longer than the interval between Wars I and II. (So far so good.) By the end of that period the weapons of war would be so devastating that with the growth of armaments in the opposing blocks, the likelihood of an outbreak would surely be nil. I disagreed with this notion, although I felt bound to admit the interesting fact that in this war gas has not so far been used simply because both sides realize the deadliness of a weapon which would rebound on the side which first used it. We all agreed that meanwhile the peoples of the whole world must be indoctrinated against the war spirit, and its futility.

Wednesday, 3rd November

Margaret Jourdain, who lunched with me at the Istanbul restaurant, amazed me by saying that she and Ivy, in order to effect economies when they needed a change in the country, used to stay in convents. Their only embarrassment was caused by meeting the Host carried through the cloisters when they were in their Jaeger dressing-gowns, spongebags in hand, on the way to the bathroom. Should they then kneel, or merely genuflect as a matter of politeness? They are of course avowed agnostics, not to say scoffers. When I told Geoffrey this he said it was no bad thing, for it would convert them in the end.

I dined with the Princesse de Polignac, arriving with David Horner whom I met bound for the same destination on a bus, just as the all-clear went. The princess's flat is in a block next door to the Dorchester. You pass down long passages behind the doors of which similar people are giving similar parties with similar smells of food issuing therefrom.

The princess, being very frightened of air-raids, sits in the passage outside her flat on a milking stool until they end. Tonight there were Mrs. Anthony Chaplin, who cooked a delicious dinner; Sir Paul Dukes, a curious, slim, dandyish man, a great authority on Russia; a Mrs. Peto Benet (?), a Norwegian who had been having tea today with King Haakon. She was expressing fear lest the Russians would after the war seize the top of Norway so as to gain access to the North Sea. The king however feels quite sure Russia has no expansionist ambitions and is confident of her integrity (which strikes me as naive). There were also Mrs. Taffy Rodd, a pretty, jolly girl; the aforementioned David Horner, croaking like a cheap gramophone; and a young Frenchman, the Prince de Beauvau.

I sat on the princess's left. She wore a Juliet cap on the back of her head. She spoke seldom and always to the point, in a deep voice and a trenchant manner, ending each sentence with a French epithet which I often could not understand. The hero of the evening was the young Frenchman just escaped from France. He had been in Paris only in August. He said there were no cars of any kind there, no taxis, no buses, and the métro was running at most three times a day. People have to walk, and the rich hire pedal bicycles with wicker-work side-cars. The opera takes place every night, but only German officers and their wives attend. A meal at Maxime's costs 1,000 francs per person. Today all French people listen-in to the B.B.C. and you hear the British news blaring from every house. This is quite a new development The prince says the French are united in a way they have never been before. The underground movement is organized to the nth degree. We are dropping arms and ammunition all over France where it is instantly collected. The French are living for the day when they can drive the Germans out, and they will not relish anyone else doing it for them. Whereas until lately there were many collaborationists, today the French are as one people revolting against the Germans, who like locusts have fleeced them of everything. At first the Germans were polite and conciliatory. Now the Gestapo is well established and thoroughly organized. But it does not co-operate with the Wehrmacht. Neither knows what the other is doing. Each distrusts the other. German troops in France already talk of Germany having lost the war. Prince Beauvau laughed as he told us that the Germans had cut down the legs of every chair in his *château* for fun. For no apparent reason they move furniture from one *château* to another. He witnessed with his own eyes Germans destroying the Rubenses and Van Dycks of his cousin, simply because he refused to collaborate. As against this Jamesey tells me that at Benghazi the Germans removed an ancient Greek statue out of the danger zone, admittedly with the intention of taking it back to Germany as loot. But when the Australians came in they destroyed the statue as junk.

Thursday, 4th November

At 3 o'clock an appointment with Sir Leonard Woolley,[1] an old gentleman with courtly manners, now a colonel in charge of the monuments section of Amgot. As I entered the room he rose and said, 'Lord Esher told me you would be coming to see me.' Now how could Esher have known, for I had told no one at the National Trust? Woolley burbled in an undertone so that I could barely hear, about the little damage to works of art in Sicily, apart from a few baroque buildings, which, he said, nobody could regret! In fine I gathered that at present no more volunteers for Italy were wanted. Nevertheless he took down my name and asked me to send him particulars of myself. If Amgot should extend to other countries, then they would want more volunteers with experience. Unfortunately this would entail joining the army; it would be difficult for me.

Friday, 5th November

Jamesey telephoned to say that he stayed at Bridget Paget's party last night till 4.30 this morning, and made great friends with Noël Coward.[2] He loved it all. There must be something very much the matter with me, for I hated every moment, and slipped away at 11.

Saturday, 6th November

Emerald lunched with me at the Ritz. I called for her at the Dorchester and walked straight into her sitting-room. Whereupon I heard a very scared, 'Mercy! Shut the door!' shouted at her maid from the bedroom. When our taxi reached the lights by the Green Park station Emerald leapt like a gazelle on to the road regardless of passing traffic. At luncheon she complained about the steak in her pie, the Brussels

[1] Sir Leonard Woolley (1880–1960), archaeologist and author.
[2] Whose biography he was beginning to write just before his own death in 1974.

265

sprouts and the rice pudding. She said there was grave dissatisfaction in high places with the present Government, and there were to be changes, because 'the food situation is so very bad,' which is of course quite untrue. She said that at tea yesterday Jamesey was much impressed by Hore-Belisha's happy flow of words and wit. She has the highest opinion of James's intelligence. The 'Bibelot' she calls him affectionately. Most of our conversation was about the derivation of words, and the exact meaning of 'meiosis', 'litotes' and 'euphemism'. I love her interest in etymology and literature.

I bought in Chelsea for 7/6 a small white marble bust of, I think, the Empress Eugénie. It is very pretty. Elizabeth Stewart-Jones saw me with it, and said, 'What on earth did you buy that thing for?' I washed it under the tap and it is as white as snow.

Monday, 8th November

Meeting day. Esher asked me to lunch with him at the Grosvenor Hotel. It was to tell me that Anthony Martineau was to be appointed to the staff with a view to becoming the National Trust's solicitor exclusively; but that I was to remain assistant-secretary. I said I hoped old Mr. Horne[1] would not be affronted, or upset. Esher agreed that the staff was underpaid, and asked me what I thought I should be receiving. I did not know how to answer because there is no other comparable profession. He intimated that Bruce's, Eardley's and my salaries would be raised next Wednesday. He is so kind, friendly and funny that I love him dearly. He almost begged me not to go to Italy under Amgot, even if I got the chance — 'which you won't get of course,' he added.

On looking through old letters this evening I came across this one from Jamesey, written to me in July 1940: 'Your collapse from pacifism into the class convention of the Guards[2] worries me, but then everyone who began the war with one viewpoint has now got some other. Harold defending Chamberlain is the best example. My own detestation of the war, which I do not much attempt to rationalize, has on the other hand increased; I had a few months of thinking it was a just war, but now I see it as the destruction of everything that could even now be saved, a destruction planned by the Germans but made possible by us, and to which there is no alternative; we have become a

[1] Whose firm, Messrs. Horne & Birkett, had acted as the Trust's solicitors since its foundation in 1895.
[2] J. L.-M. joined the Irish Guards in 1940.

purely *Daily Mirror* nation, and our vulgarity seems to me little better than Nazi injustice. And I have always preferred evil to stupidity—haven't you? My patriotism wanes; it is anyway largely a literary and architectural one, and I have to think very hard of the Brontës and Castle Howard when I want to remember that we represent something I like. How I envy you your age. At least you have enjoyed the twenties, and I was beginning to so much. I wish I felt inspired by something to do with the war—but to be living at the moment of modern history bores me merely, and I feel no interest in a future generation or a better world, because I believe in neither. Christianity is of course still there, but it seems a clear and tranquil stream running parallel to but utterly detached from the turgid river of the war, and as I said the other day too unapropos for words. There is a complacency about Christ that begins to irritate me; nailed on to that cross through all the churches of the world, and making the sort of no-effort Heywood Hill does at Doreen's lunch-parties.[1] And as for that Pope on a board bed . . . The war seems to me to have made idealism impossible and sterile; only Edwardian liberals like Harold, or *New Statesman* fanatics can believe in any future for mankind or in perpetual peace or in democracy. Personally I foresee a general fascism in which one's moral duty will be limited to hacking out a niche for oneself and trying to keep in touch with the few people one does feel attached to. Don't you agree? It annoys me to have seen so little of the old Europe and to realise that I must now rely on reading in lieu of direct experience . . . Your point of view about the war amuses me, it is exactly between mine and Mummy's; but I have before noticed this about your points of view. They form a bridge from the pre-1914 to the pre-1940. Which is natural.'

I don't prefer evil to stupidity, and alas, I did not enjoy my twenties as much as I should have done. As for the rest of Jamesey's letter I am at one with all his sentiments. And some of the things he wrote then are a reproach to me now.

Wednesday, 10th November

As the result presumably of my talk with Lord Esher, my salary has been raised to £600 a year.

I left at 4 for Lincolnshire, arriving at Gunby Hall at 7.45 in time for

[1] Doreen Colston-Baynes (Dormer Creston the biographer), a great mutual friend. Died 1973.

267

dinner. The old Field-Marshal [Montgomery-Massingberd] in his dark velvet jacket and expanse of dazzling evening shirt looked inconceivably white in the face. At first glance he appears the epitome of blimpishness. In fact he is benign, simple-hearted and understanding. Lady Massingberd is vivacious, a little bit arch, and very godly and kind, not to say motherly. After dinner we talked exclusively of Gunby's future. They both adore this place.

Thursday, 11th November

Today was bright, sunny and very cold. Yet after breakfast the field-marshal took me walking to the chalk pits and the northern part of the estate. He moves very slowly, muffled up in a rain coat, and voluminous scarf, and wearing enormous gumboots. Every six yards he stands stock still to emphasize a point, while I freeze. He seems impervious to the cold. Whenever he meets someone he stops again. He is charming to, almost humble with his employees and tenants, and especially the ordinary soldiers. After luncheon we walked over the other part of the estate, across the railway line to Bratoft, where we looked at the square moat of the Massingberds' old castle, destroyed when Gunby was built. Nothing else remains. After dinner he showed me books of letters of Bennet Langton,[1] scrupulously copied and edited by Bennet's son Peregrine, who became a Massingberd by marriage. I exhorted him to have them published, they seemed so full of interest, and Bennet Langton was after all an intimate of Doctor Johnson and Boswell, a delightful sketch of whom by another son still hangs at Gunby. A huge steel structure like the Eiffel Tower with a beacon on the top has been erected on the tennis court, close to the house, as a guide to pilots and a safeguard of the house. I am overjoyed that the Trust has been largely instrumental in preventing this dear old place from being razed to the ground in order to extend the runway.

I was distressed to see in *The Times* today an announcement of George Lennox-Boyd's sudden death from pneumonia in Edinburgh. Poor George, I was distressed, but not rendered inconsolable. I had not seen him for a year or more. The sad truth is that prolonged absence does not make the heart grow fonder.

---

[1] Bennet Langton (1737–1801), Greek scholar and friend of Dr. Johnson.

After a visit to the doctor I dined with Stuart at the Travellers'. When dinner was over he announced that he must go to Michael Duff's to say goodbye. He added that he had already said goodbye to him three times. I said that seemed a pretty generous quota. I returned to Cheyne Walk on foot in the moonlight. There was no raid. The Germans do not seem to favour a full moon without clouds.

Saturday, 13th November

Lord Newton came to see me about Lyme Park (Cheshire). I have seldom met a man more beset by domestic tribulations and worries over what to do with a vast house. He looks and behaves like a dazed, elderly hare watching the pack of beagles close in. We fixed a date for me to go to Lyme.

Monday, 15th November

I had written to Alan Lennox-Boyd[1] condoling with him over George's death. When I got back to London I found that Alan had been telephoning me. He asked me to meet him urgently. This I did today at the Travellers'. He, poor man, has just been made Parliamentary Secretary to the Ministry of Aircraft Production. He looked grey and very tired. He asked me to write a tribute to George for *The Times*, which I did this evening. He told me George was delirious for twenty-four hours before his death, during which time he never ceased talking and begging Alan and their mother to take him out of a lunatic asylum. The irony is that the military hospital they took him to was in fact an asylum, and on arrival he saw the lunatics at large. This preyed on his mind.

Tuesday, 16th November

Joan Moore, Mérode Guevara (whom Clarissa calls the 'black crocus') and Colin Agnew lunched with me at the Ritz. In the afternoon I went to Hampstead to see Grove Lodge where Galsworthy lived. It is a low, rambling, attractive house, Queen Anne-ish but not of architectural distinction. It has a spacious garden at the rear. Mrs. Galsworthy is selling it, and her furniture and his books were still there. Furniture and

[1] Now Viscount Boyd of Merton, 1951-2 Minister of State for Colonial Affairs.

decoration had a greenery-yallery flavour. Galsworthy's study where he wrote was at the top of the house, approached by a separate staircase from the garden.

Thursday, 18th November

I attended Kenneth Clark's lecture at Greek House, the Greek Ambassador in the chair. The subject of the lecture was the influence of Greek art upon British art, in particular architecture. K. must be the most brilliant of lecturers — superhuman learning worn with ease, diction perfect — because he makes me concentrate as though I were immersed in a book. I can say this about no other lecturer, except Harold. He sat beside me for a few moments before the lecture, talking most graciously. Gracious is the word. He makes me feel like a nurserymaid addressed by royalty. He makes me feel a snob because I record that he spoke three words to me. Is he a very great man, and am I a very small one? The answer to both questions must be Yes.

Friday, 19th November

I went to Wisbech and met Alec Penrose[1] on the train. I had not seen him for four years and had forgotten what an extremely nice and intelligent man he is. After a very short time we resumed the intimacy of heretofore. We share the same interests. He has a quiet manner of speaking with little inflexion in the voice, and a whimsical turn of phrase. We went to tea at his old aunt's, the Honourable Alexandrina Peckover — I like the roll of the prefix and names — at Bank House on the North Brink of the Nene. We discussed with the old lady, who is eighty-six, the advantage to her of handing over the property to the National Trust now. I found her rather pathetic, for she is stately and proud, and yet was clearly incapable of understanding what we were driving at. I remarked afterwards to Alec that so often old ladies must be cheated by unscrupulous lawyers and business tricksters. Miss Peckover is a strict Quaker. When her father died she inherited a fabulous cellar of vintage port and wine. Before Alec had time to stop her, she and her maid had poured the contents of every single bottle on to the roots of her vines in the greenhouse.

[1] Alexander Penrose (1896–1950) of Bradenham Hall, Norfolk.

Saturday, 20th November

I had tea at Dame Una's and fetched the tweed James has given me for a new suit. The fog was so dense that on my way home I had to stop at Geoffrey Houghton Brown's and dine with him. On leaving him the fog, which I thought had lifted a little, became worse by the river so that, even with my torch I walked by mistake across Albert Bridge to find myself in Battersea.

Monday, 22nd November

At Brooks's I talked with Simon Harcourt-Smith about Anarchism, for he too believes it may be the only political creed that holds out a hope for peace and justice. He said that his wife, Rosamund who is about to become a Papist, was a confirmed Anarchist. The Farm Street Jesuits told her that far from being incompatible, Catholicism and Anarchism were reconcilable, and she could embrace both. Simon knows no Anarchist except Herbert Read, whom he greatly admires and to whom he will introduce me. I tried to press him for light on the positive side of the creed. I admitted that I shared the dislikes, but was a little bewildered by the negative likes, and apparent lack of constructive policy. Simon was not able to enlighten me. He said Anarchism was a state of mind, presenting a goal to be kept in the mind's eye, however distant and unattainable. When I told Carol Dugdale at luncheon that Simon was the only anarchist I knew, she said: 'Thank you very much. I don't need to know any more to be put off Anarchism for ever.'

Simon Harcourt-Smith also imparted that Tom Jones[1] of the Pilgrim Trust told him if Winston Churchill had been born ten years later he would, in the 1930s, have made England a fascist state, ranged with the other fascist powers; but that he was too old a man with roots too firmly planted in the Victorian aristocratic traditions to adopt so alien a philosophy.

Tuesday, 23rd November

Went to Kenneth Clark's second lecture at the National Gallery, and sat in the front row with Clarissa. As he came in K. Clark said to me, 'You are being sacrificed.' I dumbly said, 'To what?' He said, 'My

[1] Thomas Jones (1870–1955), civil servant, administrator, diarist and private secretary to Lloyd George, Bonar Law and Stanley Baldwin.

lectures.' Again this one was beautiful, scholarly and shaped like a work of art, rather like a Walter Pater essay. The subject was romantic landscape painters related to romantic poets, Girtin and Wordsworth, Turner and Byron. To my disappointment and shame I had to leave before the end to accompany Clarissa to *The Ideal Husband*. Martita Hunt in the principal rôle; décor by Rex Whistler. James and Bridget Paget were of the party. Clarissa had a hired car to take her to and from the theatre, which for a girl of twenty-three struck me as rather nonsense.

Wednesday, 24th November

This afternoon Madame de Polignac rang me up and asked me to dine tonight. At first I said 'no', because I was on fire-watching duty, then succumbed to the temptation when she said I might leave early after dinner.

I arrived at 55 Park Lane earlier than I should have done. Only Alvilde Chaplin there. She told me before my hostess came in how worried she was about the princess's health. She has angina and lately has been having as many as twenty attacks a day, and the drugs she takes seem to have less and less effect. The attacks are worse at nights. Then she came into the room wearing a green dress and nothing on her thick grey hair. She moved slowly and sedately. Her remarkable face, like some mountainous crag, was sunset pink. I talked to her before dinner and, almost exclusively, during dinner. All the other guests were French, including her niece, Madame de Vogüé. The dinner was more delicious than words can express, and ended with a succulent mince pie, followed by an egg savoury flavoured with garlic. Algerian wine to drink. I told my hostess about Kenneth Clark's lecture and she said she would write and ask him to let her read the script, since she supposed the series of lectures would be subsequently published. She too has an immense regard for K.

She recommended me to read all the books by E. M. Forster I could get hold of. She said Proust's limited knowledge of England came through Ruskin; and that one of the first things he wrote was a preface to a French translation of Ruskin. The last time she saw Proust was at a dinner party given for him in Paris. He attended pale and ill, wearing a long seal-skin dressing-gown down to his ankles. The Duke of Marlborough, who was at the dinner party, was indignant at the informality of his clothes. The duke had no idea who Proust was when he was explained to him. The princess again told me she never liked Proust. He was always hopelessly, but platonically in love with someone who did not requite his love. And this was wearisome for his friends.

I left early for firewatching in my office.

Thursday, 25th November

I caught the 10.15 for Stockport, where I was met and driven to Lyme Park. As we climbed the long drive there was snow lying on the ground. This vast seat is 800 feet above sea level. The park gates are at the entrance to the suburbs of Stockport. In other words Lyme forms a bulwark against Manchester and its satellite horrors. The greater part of the 3,000-acre property stretches in the opposite direction, towards the Peak. All morning while I was in the train the sun was shining. At Lyme it was snowing from a leaden sky. A butler met me at the front door and conducted me through the central courtyard, up some stone steps and into the hall on the *piano nobile*. Lord Newton lives and eats in the great library with a huge fire burning, and two equally huge dogs lying at his feet. Lyme is one of England's greatest houses. The exterior is practically all Leoni's work. The south side is a little too severe to be beautiful. Lewis Wyatt's chunky, square tower over the pediment is ponderous, like the central imposition on Buckingham Palace. A corridor runs the whole way round the first floor (from which staterooms open), with windows looking into the courtyard (which is architecturally the most satisfying composition at Lyme). The contents of the staterooms are magnificent, notably the Chippendale chairs, the Charles II beds and the Mortlake tapestries. There is a fascinating Byronic portrait over the staircase of Thomas Legh in Greek costume standing by a horse. My bedroom on the west side of the first floor had two Sargent portraits, one of Lord Newton's mother and the other of his mother-in-law.

Lord Newton is hopeless. The world is too much for him, and no wonder. He does not know what he can do, ought to do or wants to do. He just throws up his hands in despair. The only thing he is sure about is that his descendants will never want to live at Lyme after an unbroken residence of 600 years. I am already sure that he will not see out his ownership.

There were forty evacuated children in the house, but they have now gone. The park is cut to pieces by thousands and thousands of R.A.F. lorries, for it is at present a lorry depot.

A rather dreadful thing happened. I had providentially brought with me my electric pad, for the cold at Lyme was intense. When we went to bed I dived around the skirting to look for a plug hole, attached the electric cord to it and turned on the switch. Instantly there was a loud sizzling sound and a blue flash ran round the cornice of the room. Simultaneously the dressing-table light went out, but not the reading lamp by the bed, or indeed the pad. It remained deliciously hot all night, and after reading peacefully I turned out the lamp. This morning I stumbled down darkened passages to the library for breakfast. No light in the library. The plate warmer not even working. Lord Newton was pacing up and down the room in a frenzy. He said, 'A most extraordinary thing! Every single light in the house went out last night soon after we went to bed. I can't understand it. Such a catastrophe has never happened before. I have had to send to Stockport for an electrician. I had a dreadful night for I was unable to look for candles, and I can't sleep without reading first. How did you manage?' 'Oh, fine!' I said, 'I read all right. My lamp worked perfectly.' I felt a fearful cad.

On my return I dined with Stuart at White's. I was very distressed by his greeting me with the news that the Princesse de Polignac died suddenly last night. She told me on Wednesday that she was dining with Sibyl Colefax the following night. She did so and sat next to Bogey Harris. Jamesey talked to her after dinner. She left at 11, was unwell in the taxi and sat, with Ronald Storrs, downstairs in her block of flats until she felt better, then went upstairs to bed. At 2 a.m. she died of a bad heart attack in the presence of poor Alvilde Chaplin and a doctor. She was a very remarkable woman indeed, and I am glad that at the end of her life I had the privilege of meeting her. I shall revere her memory.

Saturday, 27th November

At 12 o'clock Bogey Harris and I went to 4 Cheyne Walk to see the painted ceiling and staircase walls. They are evidently mid-eighteenth century and possibly Italian. The painting is directly on the walls, not on canvas. It is a beautiful house. George Eliot died in it. Bogey Harris then took me to No. 23 which he has bought. It is a dear little house, but with rather dark flowered wallpapers. Nancy Rodd lunched with me. She was as amazed as I was at Stuart paying a call on Alvilde Chaplin

274

yesterday morning at 10 o'clock, to find her in tears only a few hours after the princess's death in the next room. An extraordinary thing to have done, considering how little he knows either. Oh well, customs differ on the opposite sides of the Atlantic! Nancy told me that Tim Bailey [her cousin] has become a Papist in a German prisoner-of-war camp, and this has distressed and aged his parents more than the death in action of their two other sons, Anthony and Chris. Her mother has told her that Tom Mosley, who was very ill and thought to be dying, is already improved in health since leaving prison; and that Diana is radiantly happy to be out and with her children again. Nancy's aunt at Olney gave her news of Diana Worthington's pathetic behaviour before her death. Diana was practically out of her mind and had taken it into her head that the village people were against her. Of course the very opposite was the case, for everyone loved her.

Keith Miller Jones introduced me to Oswald Normanby,[1] another hero. He is shockingly bald but handsome, with charming manners. He said he would not give his house to the National Trust for anything in the world. May he never have occasion to. He said that in his German prison the inmates were provided with a newspaper in English entitled *Camp*, edited he supposed by some pro-Nazi Englishman, as well as German newspapers. Anthony Beaumont with whom I dined said that Robin Campbell,[2] an exchanged prisoner, enraged Mr. Churchill at Chequers by telling him how well the Germans had treated him, and how nice they were. Churchill replied, 'It is a pity they did not take off your head as well as your leg.'

Tuesday, 30th November

I lunched with Eddy at Brooks's. He has just recovered from influenza. His nose bled continuously throughout luncheon. He complained that his broadcast of the *Odyssey* in conjunction with Benjamin Britten last week had not been well received by the press, and that congratulations from his friends meant nothing to him in consequence.

I went to a shop in Kensington Church Street to look at a small oil painting, a religious subject by Christina Rossetti. The owner of the shop, an eccentric man called Wilson, spoke of his hatred of the

[1] The present Marquis of Normanby, severely wounded, taken prisoner and repatriated. Parliamentary Secretary to Secretary of State for Dominion Affairs 1944–5.
[2] Robin Campbell, D.S.O., Director of Art, Arts Council.

Government. I took him to be a brother Anarchist. When I asked him if he was, he said he had never been so insulted in his life. He said he was an arch conservative. I said I was too. I think he took me for a lunatic.

I dined with Ivy C.-B. and Margaret J. Basil Marsden-Smedley[1] who was there spoke vehemently against the Jews in this country. He told us how his Ministry of Economic Warfare intercepted code messages through the mail between neutral countries. By this means he had Ribbentrop's brother-in-law arrested in America.

Wednesday, 1st December

The Princesse de Polignac's Requiem Mass at Farm Street was a very solemn and dignified affair. Peter Pears sang Bach, Mozart and Fauré most movingly. When the Mass was over James, who had joined me in my pew, and I walked to Heywood Hill's shop. We watched Nancy returning to it ahead of us. She was running down South Audley Street to get warm. She made a strange spectacle, very thin and upright, her arms folded over her chest, and her long legs jerking to left and right of her like a marionette's. I really believe she finds it easier to run than to walk.

I have been wanting to see Harold since his return from Sweden. He asked me to dine tonight. To my disappointment he was not alone. There were Godfrey Nicholson, M.P., Guy Burgess and a Dr. Dietmar. The last is a tall, fair young man now teaching in a secondary school at Raynes Park. Harold got him out of an internment camp a few months ago. He is immensely grateful to Harold, earnest and rather a bore. Guy actually left us before dinner and rejoined us immediately after. Harold gave us champagne. I ought to have been firewatching in my office, and when the siren went during dinner rose to go. Harold quite rightly was shocked, for he has never once shirked firewatching duty in the House. However, the all-clear sounded almost immediately, so I sat down again, chastened. Talk was about lying. Harold said he never lied except over sex matters. Then he and Guy became engrossed in political shop which I found very tedious. I am interested in politics *per se*, but long anecdotes on how Mr. Bevan snubbed Lady Astor, who got her own back by insulting Mr. Attlee strike me as childish and contemptible. I also think that when M.P.s treat politics like a game for

[1] Basil Marsden-Smedley (1901–64), barrister, member of L.C.C. and Mayor of Chelsea 1957–9.

scoring off one another they are behaving dishonestly towards their constituents, who have not voted them into the House of Commons for that purpose. Guy is obsessed with this aspect of the beastly business.

I walked to Victoria and my office with Godfrey Nicholson who I would say is an honourable, conscientious but not a brilliant man, aged about forty. He told me he was passionately in love with his wife, and deplored the fact that Vita was not a more womanly wife to Harold whom he considers deserving the greatest matrimonial happiness. I did not feel inclined to discuss Harold and Vita's relations, merely remarking that I thought they were a blissfully happy couple. Nicholson said the House of Commons held Harold in poor esteem; and his brain counted for little with them. More fools they, is my opinion. I have always supposed Harold's great abilities to be wasted in that ridiculous place.

Thursday, 2nd December

Went by train to Bath for luncheon. Lunched with Major Strutt and Henshaw, and talked about St. Catherine's Court. Strutt is unwilling to make over as much endowment as the Trust asks for. I returned in time to dine with the [Peter] Heskeths, having had a brief talk in Brooks's with Simon Harcourt-Smith and Lord Donegall.[1] Both said Rommel and von Keitel had flown to Cairo with peace terms, which Roosevelt and Stalin were favouring, but Winston Churchill was not.

Friday, 3rd December

A foggy morning. I collected the National Trust car from Moon's garage, picked up Jamesey at his flat, and drove through the East End to Ipswich where we lunched. We browsed in a secondhand bookshop and bought a few books. In pouring rain we drove to Helmingham Hall. We first of all looked at the flint church, which was filled with monuments to the Tollemache family. One should always visit the parish church before the big house in order to learn the history of the land-owning families from the memorials. We walked through the churchyard and across the park. The object of this expedition was to see as much as possible of the outside of the house. The Trust has been left £20,000 in reversion for the Hall's preservation. The present

[1] Present Marquis of Donegall, Hereditary Lord High Admiral of Lough Neagh, journalist and British war correspondent 1939–45.

holder of the barony is disputing the will, and won't allow the Trust to inspect the place or go inside the house. From what we could see without approaching too close, the Hall with its moat and drawbridge was gabled and romantic. On our return we had tea at Colchester and a drink at Ingatestone. The whole long, joyous day we gossiped and rocked with laughter. Our talk was scandalous, unedifying and highly constructive. James said, 'Being with you is like being by myself, only nicer.' I said, 'I am glad it is nicer. Surely when you are by yourself you don't talk and laugh quite so much.' 'Yes, I do,' he said, 'inwardly. And I say to myself things I would not dare say to anyone else, except you.'

Sunday, 5th December

At Mass in Cheyne Row I felt devout again. My devoutness is more readily maintained by having my rosary and telling beads. It is when I am distracted from my devotions—I can't honestly say, prayers—by trying to make sense of the liturgy, or indeed listening to the sermon, that everything goes wrong. The moment reason takes over faith flies out of the door. But concentrating on my rosary to a background of symbolic acts, punctuated and not interrupted by rising for the Gospel, kneeling for the sanctus bell and elevation, and crossing myself on approaching certain well-known and loved landmarks, then I can often be devout. Then I can feel I am making contact. I wonder if other Papists feel as I do. God preserve us from too much illumination. What I need is a twilight atmosphere relieved by myriads of twinkling candles from crystal chandeliers, a plethora of gold, jewels, rich raiment, silver vessels, clouds of incense, and the tinkling and tolling of innumerable bells. Beauty in fact, not austerity, is what I crave in order to be religious.

Bridget Parsons lunched at the Ritz Grill. Afterwards we walked all round Hyde Park in the cold sunshine. Although Bridget was not looking her best in an old teddy bear coat and a Russian hat of frayed astrakhan, her hair as it were suspended from it like leather straps, nevertheless she was mysterious. (Stuart complains how badly she dresses, just as he complains how badly I dress, whereas his clothes hang on him like sacks.) Bridget talked politics. She is terrified of American influence upon our way of life. She despises Americans for being children, as many English people do. She also fears their desire to get out of the war at any price, and is certain that were it not for

Roosevelt, they would kick off. On this account she is in favour of a speedy negotiated peace, not 'at any price' she explained, that not being necessary now we have the upper hand. For the sake of arguing I disagreed. I do honestly believe that the Brits would have every justification in stringing up Churchill and our war-mongering politicians if at the end of the war they discovered nothing had been achieved by the whole ghastly business.

I dined with Emerald. Only Jamesey and Enid Paget, aged 19, whom he is now mad about, were present. Emerald said Sibyl Colefax had telephoned that Cecil [Beaton] was back in England, his plane having burst into flames on rising. He and all the passengers escaped, but his luggage was destroyed. Cecil is badly shocked and in bed. No wonder!

Talk ranged over love and the drama. Emerald explained very succinctly why Oscar Wilde's *Ideal Husband* displayed utter cynicism. For not only does the hero get away with his outrageous fraud, but is rewarded by the fulfilment of his grossly material ambitions; and the audience is made to sympathize with and wholeheartedly approve his behaviour.

Monday, 6th December

Cyril has told Stuart that Cecil's strongest passion is spite. So I have told Stuart to ask Cecil what Cyril's strongest passion is.

I stayed at home this evening and began editing the S.P.A.B.'s memorandum on Bath and new uses for Georgian town houses after the war.

Tuesday, 7th December

Everyone is talking of the imminence of the Germans' rocket shells. The Germans themselves announced over the wireless on Saturday that these shells would shortly rain upon London and totally destroy it. The War Office takes them very seriously, and soldiers are commanded to carry steel helmets again.

Wednesday, 8th December

I went to the Charing Cross Hotel at 1 o'clock. In a private room was a large table to seat some twenty members of the Cocked Hat Club, an inner circle of the Society of Antiquaries. There was an old cocked hat in the middle of the table, and a flag bearing each member's coat of arms in front of his seat. One other person and I were guests. James Mann,[1] my host, introduced me to several distinguished antiquarians whom I knew already, like Lord Ilchester (the Chairman), Sir Charles Peers, Rob Holland-Martin and Professor Richardson, and some I didn't know, like Dr. Mortimer Wheeler, now a brigadier and just back from Italy. I got slightly nervous as we sat down and asked Mann whether there were to be speeches. 'Only rather informal ones,' he said, 'and you will be asked to say a few words.' Now I cannot speak even two words in public, and this news dismayed me just as I was beginning to enjoy myself. I had only sipped a glass of sherry before luncheon, so I ate very little and drank just as much hock as I could get down. Oh God, the dreadful humiliation! I would far rather go over the top into a nest of German commandos, armed with hand grenades and bayonets, any day, than rise and say, 'My lords and gentlemen, it is a great privilege to be received in this august company.' Oh Lord! oh lords, the fatuity too!

I dined with Johnny Dashwood at the Travellers'. The British consul in Lisbon was there. He is what is called a rough diamond, shrewd, self-pushed up, with dozens of amusing stories—a sympathetic man. He told me that Gulbenkian, now living in Lisbon, was being slighted by the British Embassy and society because although a British subject, he was evading income tax. Consequently Gulbenkian had hinted to the consul that he might after all not leave his pictures and collections, now in England, to this country. Did I know Kenneth Clark? And would I do something? I have written to K. Clark about this.

Thursday, 9th December

I went to Sittingbourne to see the Court House, Milton Regis. I found it but could not get in. It was locked, and the owner, a retired postman, had been called upon to resume his duties today, and so was away on his rounds. However, without seeing the inside I estimated that it was not a suitable property for us. It is a fifteenth-century, half-timbered building with overhangs, in a shocking state of decay. I was disappointed not to meet the postman in order to find out why he was the owner.

[1] Sir James Mann (d. 1963), Director of Wallace Collection and Master of the Armouries, Tower of London.

Friday, *10th December*

Lying in the bath this evening, with the hot tap gently running and the water making throaty noises down the waste-pipe—a thing one is strictly enjoined not to allow in war-time—I thought how maddening it is that the worst sins are the most enjoyable. I wondered could it possibly be that these sins would recoil upon me in my old age. For at present they don't seem to do my soul much harm. And the lusts of the flesh, instead of alienating me from God, seem to draw me closer to him in a perverse way. He on the other hand may not be drawn to me. Yet I feel he ought to know how to shake me off if he wants to. Can it be that he is too polite, as I am when Clifford Smith button-holes me at a party, and I am longing to escape? How oddly one's body behaves in the bath as though it did not belong to one. Admiring my slender limbs through the clear water I thought, what a pity they aren't somebody else's.

Saturday, 11th December

I woke at 7 and left the house in pitch dark for Paddington. There I met Paul Methuen on the platform. Having with difficulty engaged two seats in a first-class compartment I went to a telephone box. Rang up K. Kennet just to say good morning and goodbye and Jamesey who, thank God, did not propose to Enid Paget last night, as he had told me he was going to do. When he asked for my advice I warned him not to. He said it was not my advice (I bet it was) but his better judgment which dissuaded him.

Paul Methuen is very difficult to communicate with. I like him immensely and I admire him because he has so many interests besides painting, of which he is a professional. But his mind works in a curious, laborious way. One thinks he does not hear because he may completely ignore what one is saying to him. Ten minutes later, when one has either moved on to another topic of conversation or forgotten the previous one, he will reply, or make an oblique reference to what one was saying. His mind is far away from mundane matters, and he is not the least interested in gossip or the behaviour of his friends; he is only interested in their ideas. If they have no ideas, he is not interested in them at all. We were met at Chippenham by his sister-in-law, Mrs. Anthony Methuen, who motored us to Ivy House where she and her husband live. The brother is a stiff man, and looks years

281

older than Paul. Up to now he has opposed Corsham, which is entailed upon his son, being made over to the National Trust. The cold in the A. Methuen's house was Siberian.

Wednesday, 15th December

I left London early by car for Lacock [Wiltshire]. It is exhilarating to motor long distances again. Driving alone I feel happy and carefree. Every expedition is an adventure. I gave a lift to an R.A.F. sergeant instructor as far as Marlborough. He told me that our new bombers did not need to see their targets, and aimed by mathematical, or navigational precision. I asked if the results could possibly be accurate. He said they bombed from a height of four miles and guaranteed to drop their load within ten yards of the target. He said that girls were much more accurate in plotting than men. He spoke highly of the W.A.A.F.s. He said 'morality' – and this word always makes me smile – was far greater among girls in the forces than girls in the factories; and venereal disease was less rife because every girl in the W.A.A.F.s was examined once a week, whether she wanted to be or not.

I reached Lacock Abbey at 2. Miss Talbot[1] was bustling about the great Sanderson Miller hall as I entered. A large log fire was burning, and the room was filled with smoke which has blackened the walls and ceiling. It was warm and smelled sweet and cosy. Miss Talbot said, 'I hate fresh air. It is the cause of most of our ills in England.' She is a dear, selfless woman, and extremely high-minded. She has the most unbending sense of duty towards her tenants and the estate to the extent that she allows herself only a few hundreds a year on which to live. She spends hardly a farthing on herself, and lives like an anchorite. She wants to hand over Lacock now, abbey and village. I believe we shall acquire this splendid property quite soon. Her old agent, Mr. Foley, took me round the house again. It certainly could well be adapted to institutional purposes.

Thursday, 16th December

In the morning I motored to Sutton Court. Lord Strachie showed me

[1] Miss Matilda Talbot (1871–1958) succeeded her uncle in 1916 and assumed the name Talbot in lieu of Gilchrist-Clark. Lacock was inherited by the Talbots by marriage with the Sharington heiress in the sixteenth century. Miss Talbot gave the abbey, most of the village and 320 acres to the National Trust in 1944.

round. The house, which has historical associations with John Locke, has been in the Strachey family for centuries. It is built of a cold grey stone. The outstanding features are a crenellated curtain wall, and a central square pele tower with circular stair turret, dating from Edward II's reign. Bess of Hardwick, one of whose husbands was a Strachey, added the north wing. But the whole house was horribly restored in 1858, so that I doubt its acceptability. There are many interesting family portraits, and one by Dance of Clive of India to whom the first Strachey baronet was private secretary. The estate of 500 acres covers a pretty but not spectacular landscape.

I lunched in Bath, looked at the Assembly Rooms and was surprised that all the outer walls were intact. Bought two Rockingham china pen trays at Angells shop. Saw Henshaw about St. Catherine's Court and went to Great Chalfield Manor,[1] where a children's Christmas Tree party was in progress. The old Fullers are always friendly. He explained where he intends hanging the tapestries which he is buying for the great hall. I approved.

Saturday, 18th December

Bridget and I went to welcome Hamish Erskine who has returned. His mother [Lady Rosslyn] and brother David were there when we arrived, both jubilant. Hamish is much thinner in the face, but has a good colour. After Tobruk he was in hospital and prison in Italy. He escaped and walked all the way down to our lines. Lady Rosslyn produced from a cardboard box and tissue paper the trousers, old black tail coat and hat he had lived and slept in for nine weeks. You would not clothe a scarecrow in them.

Wednesday, 22nd December

James dined at Brooks's. He was on night duty and I was to firewatch in my office. I gave him for Christmas one of the Rockingham pen trays with which he was delighted. We were both dull this evening, presumably because we had no money even to pay for one glass of wine. He was much distressed by Father Burdett's death. I accompanied him to the War Office. In the Mall we agreed that, no matter how much we might kick against the pricks and no matter how disloyal we were to the Church, Catholic principles were for us the only right and

[1] Given to the Trust in 1943 by Major R. Fuller.

true ones; that we were both temperamentally and fundamentally Catholic; and that we were both bitterly opposed to the prosecution of this war and to the government's uncompromising determination to smash Germany to smithereens.

Thursday, 23rd December

Today the announcement of the National Trust's acquisition of West Wycombe Park appeared in the press: at last, after protracted negotiations since 1938.

I lunched with Lord and Lady Newton at their flat in Park Street. They were pleased with the suggestion that Manchester University might rent Lyme Park from the Trust. Lady Newton must once have been handsome. She is tall; and she is thin like everyone else these days. But she is languid and as hopeless as her husband. Both said they would never be able to reconcile themselves to the new order after the war. They admitted that their day was done, and life as they had known it was gone for ever. How right they are, poor people.

Friday, 24th December

At Brooks's I saw Eddy and a guest lunching the other side of the room. They beckoned me over to their table. The guest was William Plomer, a thick-set man with small moustache, aged about forty. His face was unremarkable until I looked into it. His manner was quiet, but when he spoke he spoke forcibly. Rather a winning smile. They had practically finished eating when I joined them, and soon left.

Then a large man of about sixty with a rough, smiling face and rather coarse features, with a bald top to his head and white hair at the sides, sat down opposite me. He said, 'Good morning' with much geniality. I had no idea who he was. He had a north-country voice. I recommended the treacle tart I was eating. He observed that the club food was very good. I said it had improved lately, but that food generally was pretty indifferent nowadays. I wondered how the poor managed on their limited rations. It was all right for us who could go to restaurants. He said the British Restaurants had been started to help the poor man. I said how good most of them were, and I hoped they might continue when the war was over. He said, 'They will. My name is Woolton.'[1] He told me he visited the British Restaurants all

[1] 1st Earl of Woolton, at the time Minister of Food.

over the country and spoke to the people in them. He always asked for their opinions. He received an average of 200 letters a day from strangers, making recommendations or complaints. We talked of Speke Hall, which at one time he thought of renting; but his wife said it was too inconveniently planned.

Saturday, 25th December

Christmas Day. I met Stuart at the Brompton Oratory for High Mass. Children's beautiful voices singing. We walked to the Hyde Park Hotel, where we sat and talked rather sadly. I left him for Dame Una's Christmas luncheon in Ladbroke Grove. John, Jamesey and Nancy Rodd were there. We exchanged little gifts. I gave them each a piece of soap shaped like a lemon. Dame Una gave me a honeycomb, and Nancy one of her hen's eggs and an ounce of real farm butter, golden yellow. A huge turkey was carved, and we had an excellent plum pudding. The boys soon left for their respective offices. The Dame, Nancy and I talked about Italy, the looting by British troops, and the Italians' dislike of us. The Dame said Montgomery hated the Catholic Church and was determined to destroy Rome. Even Nancy was aghast at this and wished our bombing were not so relentless.

I bussed and walked with Nancy to her house in Blomfield Road. We looked at the terraces round Paddington Station and the Canal basin, and the house Browning lived in at Little Venice.[1] It is now shabby and bombed, but so romantic. I left Nancy in the Harrow Road on her way to deliver a leather tea cosy for her charwoman who is in hospital. She is sweetly kind in this way. I went to tea with Emerald Cunard, who was alone. She gave me a book for Christmas. At first she was absent-minded. Then she warmed up and was enchanting. She talked of Chips Channon and the Stuart row. 'Do you really think, dear, he made up to him?' Of Hore-Belisha, who designed the battledress, she said: 'He is not a man of taste.' She talked of the Knighthood of the Garter, mandragora, Shakespeare, Galsworthy 'who looked a gentleman and may have been one', of a friend of hers who loved a man with £3,000,000, of the lack of culture among Americans and the English middle-classes. 'Do they really not care for the arts? How extraordinary of them!' I stayed till 7 o'clock.

---

[1] Ultimately destroyed, not by Hitler, but by the L.C.C.

Margaret Rénéville, Clare Sheridan's daughter, is not as handsome as her mother. There is little love between them. Margaret says Clare is mad these days and thinks herself the reincarnation of Queen Emma. This may well be so, but Clare is not the least bit boring.

Friday, 31st December

Having dined with Geoffrey I walked home and went early to bed. I read, but the Battersea church bells started pealing across the river, contrary as I thought to the regulations. It was more than I could bear, so I went downstairs to put cotton wool in my ears. Still I heard them. At midnight I stuffed my fingers into my ears in order not to listen to the striking of the little tortoise-shell and silver clock at my bedside. The loneliness of this moment, wholly artificial though it be, harrows me. When it had passed I went on reading. At 12.30 the telephone rang. I threw the sheets back and leapt out of bed. Book, paper and pencil clattered to the floor. It must, I thought, be the voice I longed for. It would be contrite, solicitous, loving. No such thing. It was that bore Dr. Dietmar to wish me a Happy New Year, as though 1944 could augur anything but the direst misery of our lives. Only a German could be so obtuse. I was not very friendly, and pretended that he had woken me up.

Index

INDEX

293

294

L